CASSELL STUDIES IN PASTORAL CARE AND PERSONAL
AND SOCIAL EDUCATION

MANAGING TO LEARN

Books in this series:

CASSELL STUDIES IN PASTORAL CARE AND PERSONAL
AND SOCIAL EDUCATION

MANAGING TO LEARN

Aspects of Reflective and Experiential Learning in Schools

Patrick Whitaker

CASSELL

For Keir

Cassell
Villiers House
41/47 Strand
London WC2N 5JE

387 Park Avenue South
New York
NY 10016-8810

First published 1995

British Library Cataloguing-in-Publication Data
A catalogue record for this book is available from the British Library.

ISBN 0-304-32783-2 (hardback)
    0-304-32782-4 (paperback)

Typeset by Litho Link Ltd, Welshpool, Powys, Wales
Printed and bound in Great Britain by Biddles Ltd, Guildford and King's Lynn

Contents

Series Editors' Foreword

One problem that has long beset the discourse of pastoral care is the implicit assumption that teaching and caring, learning and being cared for, are essentially separate in a child's experience of school. In recent years, the idea that good practice seeks to avoid creating a 'pastoral academic split' between 'teachers' and 'carers' has been vigorously advanced.

Yet the schism remains. The preoccupation of those who designed – and imposed – a 'national curriculum' for the maintained sector has been with an academic curriculum and not with the wider developmental needs of children. The relationship between these needs and the caring ethos of the school has been severely neglected.

Nor have the developments of the past decade been founded upon a sophisticated model of teaching and learning. Rather, they have presumed an archaic model of the curriculum as bodies of knowledge. The National Curriculum is primarily about the content that is to be learned and assessed, and not about the *learner*. It continues to be narrowly conceived because its architects began without a coherent or worked-out theory of the learner. The introduction of cross-curricular elements ('dimensions', 'themes', 'skills') was an afterthought, and these elements remain visibly peripheral to the Programmes of Study. Today's curriculum is primarily about knowledge, objectified, pre-existing and external to the learner, isolated from the social, cultural and physical environment within which it is encountered. In this context, personal and social education appears as a supplement to 'real' knowledge, with pastoral care relegated to its traditional role of clearing away the odd emotional obstacle to learning.

Patrick Whitaker devotes the first five chapters of this book to the articulation of a paradigm of teaching and learning that is in stark contrast to the new orthodoxy of teaching in the age of the National Curriculum. A concern for curriculum content and management structures is supplanted by the recognition of the learner as active, creative, divergent; of learning as reflective, experiential, experimental; of learning experiences as a dynamic of knowledge, knowing, intention, skill and judgement. Within this paradigm, teaching emerges as demanding managerial skill but always in the context of moral agency within an interpersonal landscape. Schools are organizations, but it is human commitment that makes them work (or not, as the case may be).

Patrick Whitaker rejects the fragmentation of experience that comes if we focus for too long upon subject content or bureaucratic systems. His is a holistic model of learning. For purposes of analysis, it may be necessary now to focus upon the learner, now upon the teacher as the facilitator or manager of learning, now upon the social and physical environment of the classroom, school or neighbourhood. But none of these aspects of the whole disappear because we choose to concentrate for a moment upon any one. To borrow a metaphor from an earlier age (Marland 1980), they are like facets of a gemstone, each catching the light for an instant but always but one facet of a complex whole. For Patrick Whitaker, it is the learner who is always and firmly at the centre of the gemstone, giving meaning and purpose to the entire project. Several models of teaching and learning and the context in which they take place are offered in the early chapters, but these (like all models) simplify and generalize. The reality of experiential and reflective learning – and its corresponding pedagogy – is vastly more complex. The facets are certainly more numerous than any two-dimensional representation could portray. The challenge is: how to convey this complexity without losing sight of the whole?

The device that Patrick Whitaker employs to meet this challenge is the alphabet: we are offered an A to Z of learning. Each entry – each facet – is of equal value. Rather than contrive themes to tie these together, he presents them in alphabetical order so they can be contemplated alone or considered in combination with any number of others. In this way they comprise 'an agenda for consideration and practical possibilites for development'.

Patrick Whitaker has performed a valuable service in putting learning and the learner back at the centre of teaching and caring. We commend his agenda for serious consideration by anyone committed to the education of the whole person and who wishes to explore alternatives to the aridity of current official curriculum policy.

Ron Best and Peter Lang

Introduction

When I began life as a classroom teacher in 1966 I had no concept of what my future in education would bring. Now, over twenty-five years later, I look back on a rich catalogue of experiences, opportunities, highlights, disappointments, frustrations and challenges. I have come to experience learning both as a delight and as a struggle – each is important and both are necessary. As I became more involved with pupils and teachers in schools I noticed that it was my own curiosity about learning that was the driving force for my professional work.

My memories of being a pupil in schools are vivid. I remember the smells – acrid coke fumes, wax crayons, sour milk, changing rooms. More vivid still are the feelings – the confusion of not knowing what I was supposed to know, the dread of humiliation, the fear of punishment and retribution. There were joys too – the teachers who noticed me and seemed to like me, the sheer relief of passing the 11+, being picked for a school team. But perhaps more than anything it was a relentless journey of obedience, a pursuit of other people's purposes, a striving to reach their standards and a requirement to get it right first time and in best writing.

Although my professional life has been marked by a preoccupation with the process of learning and with how it might be better managed, it is only recently that I have come to appreciate fully my own skills as a learner. It was, despite my theorizing, amazing to discover that I can do it for myself especially with encouragement and high-quality support. For me the deeper joys of learning have waited for my later life, confirming a belief that learning is a voyage of discovery, a gradual unfolding of powerful forces and innate capacities. My pleasures as an educator have been enriched by discovering neglected and hidden potentials within myself.

What has fascinated me most in my work as a teacher, headteacher, local authority adviser and more recently in my role as an education consultant, is the question of how, in overcrowded classrooms and in the face of overdemanding expectations, we can contrive to release the awesome potential of learners and organize teaching to satisfy both pupils' aspirations and societal requirements. Through my observations of learning in classrooms and countless conversations with pupils about their learning, I have become increasingly convinced that, as well as instruction and practice, learners need the time, skills and opportunities to reflect deliberately on the process of learning itself – on how the mind copes with information, on the techniques of memorizing and recalling data, on the problems of forgetting and not quite understanding, on the solving of tricky problems, on the planning of complex tasks and on the careful preparation and organization needed to get things done. When pupils are encouraged to reflect on and think about these things, and then to talk about them with others faced with similar challenges, they seem to become clearer and more aware of what it means to be a learner, of how learning works in different ways at different times and how sometimes it seems to come easily and at other times not at all. This process, focusing as it does on the experience of being a learner, helps pupils to grapple with complexity and confusion; it encourages them to face the emotional challenges that apparent lack of success can bring and it enables them to build a sturdy appreciation of their birthright – an awesome potential to grow, learn and develop.

So too with teachers. In recent years I have been fortunate to have had many opportunities to work throughout the country with schools and teachers on issues connected with the management of learning. I have found that when teachers engage with other professional colleagues in a deliberate exploration of their professional world, they are more able to bring insight and meaning to the elaborate and complex business of teaching. By reflecting on what they do, how they feel about it and how they would like it to be, and then examining the details through dialogue with professional colleagues, personal and professional learning is achieved, understandings arrived at, dilemmas resolved, decisions made and plans for change created.

What has interested me, both with pupils and their teachers, is that the same basic process – reflection and dialogue – seems to enable significant learning to take place. Carl Rogers (1967) frequently emphasized the difference between casual learning and significant learning. He states:

> significant learning is more than accumulation of facts. It is learning which makes a difference in the individual's behaviour, in the course of action he chooses in the future, in his attitude and in his personality.

It is with significant learning that schools should be concerned. I have come to believe that any improvement in standards of achievement or quality of learning will require as much attention being paid to the process of becoming a learner as has been devoted to the design of the curriculum and the structure of the schooling system. We need to give detailed attention to questions about how pupils manage their own learning potential and channel it in productive and effective ways.

This book is an attempt to offer help with this task. It is an offering to those who, like me, are curious about the complexities and paradoxes of learning and who are keen to cross boundaries and forge new pathways in schools and classrooms. But like the painter who cannot finish the portrait in case it is not quite right, the final stages of writing have been characterized by a dreadful awareness that what I have said is partial, incomplete and somewhat temporary. The ideas expressed are intensely personal, sometimes overstated, often blind to other viewpoints and possibilities, but they have evolved from my own ways of perceiving and experiencing the learning process both as a pupil and as a teacher.

While I am excited about making a contribution to the debate about the learning process, I am saddened that the debate itself is so disputatious and acrimonious. Given the culture of disapproval, blame, recrimination and mistrust that we work in, it is surprising that we manage to learn at all. I hope that within the many assertions, viewpoints and perspectives contained within the book there emerges a recognition that learning is a gentler process than we have assumed, that it works best when we breathe life into learning potential and kindle the embers of curiosity, aspiration, striving and the sense of wonder.

For the past ten years in education obsessive attention has been paid to the curriculum for learning. Never before has so much energy been expended on attempting to define the prescription for what it is that learners should focus on in schools. The National Curriculum reforms build on the assumption that if only we can get the definition of content right then standards of learning will rise. It is important to challenge this assumption and to claim that the practical means by which the learning process is transacted between teachers and learners is also of vital importance. In recent years attention to pedagogy and methodology has been sacrificed in the struggle to rewrite programmes and install new content.

Personal and social education has no explicit place in the National Curriculum and there is a danger that its important contribution to effective learning will be diminished. It is vital that any attention to content is accompanied by healthy attention to the process of learning and the management of classroom life.

The skills of learning are more important than ever before. Fast and accelerating change means that schools are preparing pupils for a world that cannot be anticipated. Business organizations are realizing that it is their ability to learn faster than the rate of change in the external environment that holds the key to survival and success. So too with the individual. Success in the fast changing future will not depend on how much information has been accumulated, but on how new skills and knowledge can be acquired quickly and applied in changed circumstances.

Over recent years new insights and understandings into how individuals learn have been accumulating. Much of this new understanding suggests that we have vastly underestimated the capacity of individuals at any age to manage their own learning, and that when instruction and teaching is too heavily managed it can have a counterproductive effect. The concepts of reflective and experiential learning offer vital insights into the procedures necessary to make learning a more complete process, emphasizing the importance of reflection on experience, analysing and theorizing and then trying out ideas to see what happens. Experiential learning now forms the basis of much management and human relations training for professionals. Its enormous potential needs to be released within schools and classrooms and to form a much more significant part of initial teacher training.

This book offers a practical guide to a wide variety of reflective and experiential classroom approaches. All such approaches are based on the experience of teachers and pupils and are relevant to the whole age range represented in schools and colleges. The experiential approach places a heavy emphasis on the active participation of the learner and the setting of an appropriate psychological climate. It promotes a more person-centred approach to teaching, recognizing and encouraging the enormous learning potential that pupils bring with them to school.

The book has two main purposes. Firstly, to help teachers to reflect on some of the options and choices available to them in developing effective classroom learning; secondly, to offer a range of practical strategies for classroom work. The book is in two parts. The first three chapters explore in turn the key factors in the management of learning – being a learner, being a teacher, and the cultural, psychological and organizational setting in which the learning takes place. These chapters offer a personal view of learning and teaching and how they might be practised within the schooling system. They offer ideas for consideration and possibilities for practice. They focus specifically on:

- the nature of learning and the challenges of being a learner in today's schools;
- the complexities of teaching and how it might be more effectively managed;
- the environment and climate in which learning and teaching are conducted and how it might be developed.

These three chapters contain ideas for consideration, frameworks for development and possibilities for practice. They represent what I believe to be powerful possibilities as we strive to discover more effective educational pathways into the future. They are intended as stimuli to thinking and are offered in the spirit of what is worth trying rather than what is right.

The second part of the book consists of a collection of shorter pieces. The range of these entries defies an easy thematic classification and so they have been arranged in alphabetical order. The entries represent themes and ideas that have featured in my professional work with pupils and teachers in recent years. Each entry has something to say about the process of learning and the challenges of teaching. They raise philosophical as well as practical considerations and are relevant across the whole age range of schooling and to adult and professional learners as well. I have avoided a complicated cross-referencing structure, leaving the reader free to make connections and pursue specific lines of enquiry. A complete list of the A–Z entries is included in the subject index.

I have thought hard and long about the word to describe the children and young people in our schools. I have used *learner* wherever possible and *pupil* from time to time. To call them *students* seems to imply an autonomy and sense of personal direction that, as yet, the system is not ready to bestow.

Effective learning has both individual and collaborative aspects. This book is the product of a long and sometimes lonely process of synthesizing, selecting, drafting and changing. The personal and professional experiences from which the themes and issues of the book are drawn have been for the most part collaborative ones – listening to pupils, working alongside teachers, taking part in curriculum projects, involvement in courses and conferences and countless conversations, arguments, debates and discourses. I wish to acknowledge the contribution to this book and to my own learning of the following friends and colleagues: Barbara Bates, John Bird, John Brookes, Margot Brown, Roger Casemore, Jill Cole, Bob Croson, Chris Day, Robert Dupey, Andy Fookes, Coral Goulding, Carol Hall, Eric Hall, John Hammond, Paul Hanbury, Stephanie Hawksworth, George Henson, Dave Hepworth, Dave Hicks, Judith Holland, Tony Huntington, John Jackson, Nancy James, David Johnston, Bob Kirby, Georgeanne Lamont, Sylvia McNamara, Frank McNeill, Chris Newman, David O'Grady, Diana Prince, Allan Randall, Jane Reed, Robin Richardson, David Selby, Sushma Sehmbi, Saranjit Shetra, Geoff Southworth, Miriam Steiner, Chris Tilley, Ruth Walker, Vi Welbourn and David Wren.

I am particularly grateful to Peter Lang for his patience, forbearance and trust through the somewhat turbulent preparation of the book and to Ron Best for his most helpful comments and suggestions. I extend my special thanks to Claire and Keir, my constant companions in learning.

Patrick Whitaker

1

Learners and Learning

There has been a tendency to perceive learning as something that others do to us rather than as something we do for ourselves. Many definitions of learning point to a process of acquisition – the child as an empty repository dependent on inputs from the adult world, gradually filling up during the processes of socialization and schooling. Success is measured in terms of how quickly and how completely this filling up process is completed. The education system is desperately in need of new definitions and understandings if it is to succeed in liberating learning from the stranglehold of traditional orthodoxies and the limitations of too narrow an understanding of its complex processes.

Plutarch said that a child's mind is not a vessel to be filled but a fire to be kindled. Sylvia Ashton-Warner (1980) notes: 'What a dangerous activity teaching is. All this plastering on of foreign stuff. Why plaster on at all when there is so much inside already.'

In the struggle to improve the quality of our educational system we need to adopt an altogether more life-enhancing and optimistic appreciation of the learning process and of the enormous potential of young children to make their own way in the world.

Alternative and more life-enhancing definitions of learning abound and it is important to note some of the elements that go to make up such a vital but complex process in the development and well-being of people. Diana Whitmore (1986) emphasizes the awakening aspect: 'Learning should be a living process of awakening – a series of creative steps in unfoldment.'

Joseph Zinker (1977) points to the creative contribution of the human spirit and suggests that learning involves: 'releasing oneself, heart and soul into the world'. He also highlights the importance of the individual learner's will and determination: 'developing the courage to push against boundaries and test new behaviours'.

Jack Mezzirow (1983) sees learning as a process of adjusting and acclimatizing to the world. For him, learning is 'the means by which people come to perceive, interpret, criticise and transform the worlds in which they live.'

One of the keys to understanding the learning process, and of being able to contribute to it successfully as an educator, is the appreciation that all the resources for learning are already within us; they are not acquired through teaching. Theodore Roszak (1981) emphasizes the central importance of this potential:

We all bring into school a wholly unexplored, radically unpredictable identity. To educate is to unfold that identity – to unfold it with the utmost delicacy, recognizing that it is the most precious resource of our species, the true wealth of the human nation.

Good teaching can awaken and direct this potential while at the same time encouraging and supporting the unfolding of identity and destiny. We need to appreciate that virtually all of us are born as *going concerns* – with all the resources for successful growth and development available to us at birth. Successful learners are those who are able to activate those resources in relation to circumstance and need.

Violet Oaklander (1978) captures the wealth of these resources and many of the essential qualities of learning that children bring with them to school:

Children are our finest teachers. They already know how to grow, how to develop, how to learn, how to expand and discover, how to feel, laugh and cry and get mad, what is right for them and what is not right for them, what they need. They already know how to love and be joyful and live life to its fullest, to work and to be strong and full of energy. All they need is the space to do it.

Strongly associated with many traditional concepts of education is the assumption that learning demands a dependence on the teacher. Many of us come to believe that to succeed at learning we inevitably require the directing and controlling presence of a teacher or instructor. This obsession with the primacy of teaching and instruction has stolen from the individual the awareness that one of our most significant genetic features is an awesome capacity for self-development, intellectual growth and self-directed learning. Natural learning, as Seymour Papert (1980) has observed, requires neither teacher nor curriculum, and by the time most children start school they have exercised their huge learning potential in myriad ways to become sturdy individuals, with the skills of adaptation, self-management and communication already well established.

In her study of children's thinking Margaret Donaldson (1978) concludes: 'there exists a fundamental human urge to make sense of the world and bring it under deliberate control'. Christian Schiller puts it another way:

To young children the world is one. They are active, they are curious, they want to explore and experience. They run from one part of the field of experience to another, quite regardless of the fences we put round what we call subjects. They do not regard them because they do not see them, and if we insist on recognition we simply impede their progress and retard their learning.

It is this essential urge that humanistic psychologists have referred to as the *actualizing tendency* – that basic directional force within people to strive for understanding and fulfilment. The role of the educator is to stimulate and encourage this awesome potential and provide the conditions and resources for its healthy growth and development.

Perhaps more than anything, learning is a creative process, a bringing into being. Joseph Zinker (1977) expresses something of its enormous complexity and tantalizing intricacy:

> Creativity is a celebration of one's grandeur, one's sense of making anything possible. Creativity is a celebration of life – my celebration of life. It is a bold statement: I am here! I love life! I love me! I can be anything! I can do anything!
>
> Creativity is not merely the conception, but the act itself, the fruition of that which is urgent, which demands to be stated.
>
> Creativity is an act of bravery. It states: I am willing to risk ridicule and failure so that I can experience this day with newness and freshness. The person who dares to create, to break boundaries, not only partakes of a miracle, but also comes to realise that in the process of being . . . is a miracle.

MANAGING TO LEARN

One of the unfortunate aspects of formalized educational systems is the growth of the assumption that education only happens in schools and is delivered through formal instruction. Although the narrow association of learning with schooling is a difficult one to shift, there have been significant developments in recent years which have helped to develop a much wider and more integrated concept of education and learning.

Research and development in the field of adult education and learning has produced a range of exciting new insights and methodologies. The need to look beyond the somewhat restricted notions of *pedagogy* – specifically the art and science of teaching children – has produced *andragogy* – the art and science of helping people to learn. This significant conceptual innovation has helped to move the definition of education from one about teaching to one of encouraging and supporting learning. The principles of adult learning are based on a number of critical assumptions about the characteristics of adult learners and the ways they differ from those of child learners. Knowles (1983) states as follows:

1   An adult's self-concept moves from one of being a dependent personality towards one of being a self-directed human being.
2   Adults accumulate a growing reservoir of experience that becomes an increasing resource for learning.
3   An adult's readiness to learn becomes oriented increasingly to the development tasks of social roles.
4   An adult's time perspective changes from one of postponed application of knowledge to the immediacy of application thus shifting the learning orientation from one of subject centredness to one of problem-centredness.

Twenty years after this important theoretical breakthrough it is interesting to consider to what extent these four assumptions highlight important characteristics of learners irrespective of age. Day and Baskett (1982) have challenged the distinctiveness of these apparent differences, suggesting that many of the principles upon which adult learning is based are also relevant to pupils in schools. What is needed, they argue, is a re-examination of our understanding of the nature of pupil learning in the light of these insights.

Developments in adult learning theory have supported and enabled major innovations in education. Perhaps the most significant of these was the establishment of the Open University which broke totally with tradition, espousing the almost heretical assumptions that degree level learning could be embarked upon without any prior educational qualifications, did not require a face-to-face relationship with a teacher and could be managed through self-directed activity in the home. Building on this highly successful breakthrough the notion of open learning is gradually becoming an established part of educational theory and practice.

Notions of continuing and community education have also challenged many of the traditional assumptions upon which the educational system is built. Firstly, that education has to be age-specific. In community schools and colleges, pupils learn alongside adult members of the community to mutual benefit, creating a different and more liberating classroom culture. Secondly, the inspiration of The University of the Third Age in Toulouse has demonstrated that learning capacity does not diminish with age but can be applied successfully well beyond the assumed retiring age. Thirdly, the spread of self-help groups has demonstrated the enormous learning potential of the group, especially when it is based upon principles of involvement, participation and equal rights and responsibilities.

Within the more pioneering and experimental world of adult education the following set of assumptions has helped to bring about a more comprehensive understanding of the learning process and resulted in a more dynamic relationship between educator and learner. As Day and Baskett suggest, the differences between adults and children may be nowhere near as profound as we have traditionally assumed, and these assumptions form a vital agenda for considering the sort of educational experience we should be providing for both teachers and pupils in schools.

1 Pupils are voluntary participants in learning; they engage in it as a result of personal choice. (The system can insist that children attend school, it cannot insist that they learn. This remains a voluntary act of the learner.)

2 A relationship of mutual respect needs to be established between participants and teachers if the optimum conditions for effective learning are to be established. It is also essential for teachers to recognize that they too are learners, capable of learning from the different experiences of class members.

3 Organized learning is a collective experience and needs to be viewed by teachers as the building of relationships of trust.

4   A vital feature of learning is the process of action and reflection – looking back on past experience in order to make decisions about the future.
5   Teachers need to remember that most formal learning takes place in an organizational setting. This adds complexities and special challenges to the process of change.
6   The process of personal change can be difficult and painful. As a result of previous experience, some learners find it very hard to accept help and guidance. Trying to change their ways of working can involve loss of confidence and self-esteem.
7   Differences in the social, economic and cultural backgrounds of learners need to be respected and taken into account in designing and developing learning activities.
8   The motivation to learn is a key consideration. Pupils bring a wide variety of needs, hopes and aspirations to the learning process.
9   One of the most important contributions a teacher can make to this learning partnership is to promote and facilitate a climate of critical thinking in which learners are encouraged to lay open to examination their thoughts and feelings about their learning.
10 A key aim of those involved in the management of learning is to encourage self-direction. This involves gradually reducing dependence on the teacher and supporting the learner's own aspirations, learning strategies and self-evaluation.

Not all of these assumptions are easily assimilated into the principles of schooling, but they do offer an agenda with which to consider some of the essential ingredients of successful learning and growth and some of the directions we need to take in educational development in the future.

More recently, Boud *et al.* (1993) have identified a set of basic propositions about learning from experience:

1   Experience is the foundation of, and the stimulus for, learning.
2   Learners actively construct their experience.
3   Learning is a holistic process.
4   Learning is socially and culturally constructed.
5   Learning is influenced by the social and emotional context in which it occurs.

These propositions draw from and build on previous work, adding to our growing understanding and appreciation of the intricacies and complexities of the learning process.

TRADITIONAL ORTHODOXY

If the education system is to find its way out of its current dilemmas and difficulties it will need to depart from its traditional reliance on permanency, and the perpetuation of traditional assumptions about learning and learners. Reforms to education have tended to focus on two key areas: the structure of schooling and the content of the curriculum.

The structure of schooling

A catalogue of structural changes – selective secondary education, comprehensive schools, an increased span of compulsory attendance, the expansion of nursery provision and more recently the introduction of City Technology Colleges (CTCs) and grant maintained schools – have all been attempts to create structures designed to improve standards. But attention to structures, without an equal consideration for the social and psychological dynamics they create, is unlikely to achieve the changes that are most necessary if schooling is to satisfy the considerable hopes raised for it.

The content of the curriculum

Compared with modifications to the structure of schooling, those directed at the curriculum have been immense. Over the past thirty years vast resources have been allocated to curriculum research and development. Firstly the Schools Council, and later the School Curriculum Development Committee were formed to co-ordinate development and dissemination of new ideas in the fields of curriculum and examinations. Now with these bodies long gone there is little evidence that the prestigious projects of the early 1970s have radically modified the curriculum in either primary or secondary schools. The plethora of reports by HMI, DES and government committees of inquiry remain largely unread by the majority of those involved in the day-to-day teaching in our schools.

The Education Reform Act 1988 has radically changed the process of curriculum development and reform, imposing on schools a national programme of content based on core and foundation subjects, four key stages of learning, programmes of study and attainment targets. In addition a national system of assessment and testing has been introduced with external examinations being conducted at the ages of 7, 11, 14 and 16.

Among the most significant features of this change have been the difficulty of imposing an untested model on pupils and the challenge of producing a definitive set of targets relevant in a fast changing world. Major changes to the core subjects have had to be made even before the foundation subject curriculum has been agreed. New bureaucracies have been created to devise, implement, monitor and evaluate this new system but it is difficult to make a case that they will succeed in helping the process of schooling to become the liberating and deeply satisfying experience it should be for its participants.

The process of learning

As a result of these preoccupations with structural alterations and curriculum reform, educational development has failed to take sufficient account of a significant third way to progress. While structural change and curriculum development will always be necessary in a fast changing world, it is vital to incorporate into the reforming agenda a proper consideration of this third and neglected dimension. Simply put, this can be described as the process of learning. It is concerned with the ways in which learning is organized and the means by which pupils are helped to apply their potential to educational tasks and experiences. Over the past fifteen years of the great debate, scarce attention has been given to the dynamics of learning, the methodologies of teaching and to the vital relationship between pupils and their teachers in the classrooms of schools. It is essential to give attention to such vital factors as:

personality: how children acquire a self-concept which reflects their successful experience as learners, both in the years before school and throughout their careers in formal education;

aspiration: how pupils are encouraged to define and pursue their own learning ambitions and to incorporate them comfortably with the curriculum framework of the school;

needs: how the emotional and psychological nourishment so vital to supporting the inherent potential to learn can be supplied within schools and classrooms;

relationships: how pupils can work together to develop the skills and qualities necessary to becoming successful learners, and how pupils and teachers can build creative mentoring partnerships to ensure sustained educational growth and development;

interactions: how pupils can be guided to use dialogue with their friends and teachers to explore and examine the challenges of the learning experience and so develop a sharp awareness of their own developing skills and abilities;

values: how pupils can be helped to develop a strong, satisfying and lasting relationship with learning and come to value the place of education in their lives;

behaviour: how pupils can be supported in becoming increasingly able to take responsibility for the choices they make, the actions they pursue and the consequences they encounter;

experience: how pupils can be presented with opportunities to reflect on their experience of learning in order to make sense of it and so as to make considered choices about learning behaviour in the future.

These elements contribute in significant ways to the creation of satisfactory conditions for learning and teaching and to the capacity of pupils to acquire and develop knowledge, skills and qualities in the collective setting of the classroom. It is with these factors that this book is concerned.

It is important to note that as management and organizational theory has developed in recent years, increasing consideration has been given to the concept that workplaces are essentially organizations of people, brought together to pursue specific aims and purposes. Current experience indicates that if the needs and motivation of the workforce are satisfactorily related to the agreed purposes of the organization, then effectiveness and efficiency are likely outcomes. The evidence from a detailed examination of well-run companies is that long-term profitability is best achieved where management processes are built around personal empowerment and the active involvement of all workers.

In recent years theories of management have affected the ways that schools are run. Management training in education is increasingly concerned to present a model of leadership based on participation, and headteachers are encouraged to involve all staff in decision-making and the day-to-day management of the school. It is becoming increasingly important to see leadership as a process of harnessing the potential of individual participants, not controlling and prescribing their behaviour. The process of human endeavour is increasingly recognized as equal in importance to considerations of task and product. Commercial organizations are quickly learning that survival in a fast changing world depends very much on the creativity, flexibility and resilience of staff. Management is adapting from its concern with bureaucracy, maintenance and efficiency to a determination to maximize the abilities of people by attention to the needs and aspirations that each participant brings into the organization. This involves the creation of a management culture in which individuals feel more able to release their energies to shared visions and objectives. In other words, process is concerned with an enhanced view of human potential. It is concerned to create conditions in which the people involved can grow and develop and become more than they currently are.

So too in the process of learning, survival in a fast changing world may well depend upon the ability of pupils to develop skills in adaptation, flexibility, co-operation and imagination. The process of schooling needs to be seen as a key focus in the management of change. It has been largely ignored in the recent concerns to improve the quality of education. Obsession with structure and content has resulted in a dangerous neglect of the learning process, perhaps the most important factor contributing to successful educational change and development.

TOWARDS A NEW PARADIGM FOR LEARNING

Marylin Ferguson (1982) has articulated one of the key paradoxes of the schooling system:

> As the greatest single social influence during the formative years,
> schools have been the instruments of our greatest denial,
> unconsciousness, conformity and broken connections.

She raises the idea of pedagogic illness – the educational equivalent of iatrogenic or doctor-caused illnesses. Learning disabilities, she suggests, are caused by the separatist and often alienating experiences of many students in classrooms.

In her proposal for a new educational paradigm she suggests that the key lies in looking to the nature of learning rather than to the curriculum and methods of instruction. To succeed in satisfying the needs of a fast changing and uncertain future she proposes some elements in the paradigm shift (see Table 1.1). This suggests that educational reform and development need to focus less on structure and curriculum and more on practice and process. It is basically the difference between learning in order to know and learning in order to be.

Table 1.1 The paradigm shift in learning

Old paradigm assumptions	New paradigm assumptions
Emphasis on content, acquiring a body of 'right' information, once and for all.	Emphasis on learning how to learn.
Learning as a product, a destination.	Learning as a process, a journey.
Hierarchical and authoritarian structure. Rewards conformity, discourages dissent.	Students and teachers see each other as people not as roles.
Relatively rigid structure, prescribed curriculum.	Flexible structures, varied starting points, mixed learning experiences.
Age-related learning.	Integration of age groupings. Learning not age-specific.
Priority on performance.	Priority given to the self-concept as the key determinant of successful learning.
Emphasis on external world. Inner experience considered inappropriate in school setting.	Use of the pupil's inner experiences as contexts for learning.
Guessing and divergent thinking discouraged.	Guessing and divergent thinking encouraged as part of the creative process
Emphasis on analytical, left-brain thinking.	More emphasis on right brain, intuitive activity.
Classroom designed for efficiency, convenience.	More concern for learning environment – colour, comfort, personal space and privacy.
Education seen as an age-related social necessity.	Education as a lifelong process and only partially related to schools.
Teacher as instructor and imparter of knowledge.	Teacher as a learner too, learning from the pupils.

A great deal of insight into the fundamental assumptions underwriting the schooling process can be gained by noting the questions posed by those charged with designing the educational process in our society. Right at the heart of the whole debate about the National Curriculum lies the question: what do we want our children to know? The National Curriculum stands as the temporary and incomplete answer to this question. Perhaps a more helpful question for those concerned with the purposes, design, management and evaluation of formalized learning in our society is: how do we want our adult citizens to be? If education in schools is a prerequisite for a successful social community, then the key question in education must focus on what human attributes, characteristics and behaviours are regarded as the hallmarks of such a society.

An interesting angle on this problem has been provided by David Fontana (1987) who, in an article entitled 'Knowing about being', makes the important distinction between these two aspects of personality. This can be summarized diagrammatically (see Table 1.2). Our educational

Table 1.2 Knowing and being

Knowing	Being
Acquisition and application of formal knowledge and skills.	Focus on the ways of experiencing living.
External knowledge.	Personal knowledge.
Convergent thinking.	Divergent thinking.
Thought and action.	Intuition and emotion.
Second-hand experiences.	First-hand experiences.
Behavioural objectives, assessment and attainment.	Emancipation from self-rejection and self-punishment.
Outer behaviour.	Inner health.
Passing examinations, gaining qualifications and getting a good job.	Pursuit of happiness.
Quantity	*Quality*
The measure of our cost or worth.	The determinant of our humanity.

upbringing and training has tended to emphasize the *knowing* dimension at the expense of the *being* so that we come into adult life incomplete and in many ways inadequately equipped to deal with the challenges and demands made upon us. What is required is a balancing of the two, an integrating of what we know and what we have become as a result of experience. Both aspects are vital to the expression of the whole person that an active and responsible citizen undoubtedly needs to be.

We work in a system which is confused, frustrated and polarized. Something we had for so long thought to be simple and straightforward – the education of the young – turns out to be exceedingly complex and confusing, involving a far greater range of factors and considerations than the pioneers of state-managed education had assumed. It is vital for those with responsibility for managing learning to acknowledge this complexity with its concomitant confusions, contradictions, paradoxes, ambiguities and uncertainties. Being an educator means engaging in a struggle of immense proportions, a struggle that is not won by only seeking simple solutions to complex problems.

The essence of this challenge is captured by Robin Richardson (1990) in his exploration of how children learn:

'I wish', says a child in a poem by James Berry, daydreaming at the back of the classroom:

'I wish my teacher's eyes wouldn't
go past me today. I wish he'd know
know it's okay to hug me when I kick
a goal. Wish I myself wouldn't hold back when an
answer comes.'

It is a beautiful statement of what every learner requires first and foremost: to be noticed, to be attended to, to be valued, to be affirmed. Out of that attention and affirmation grow the confidence and, yes, the courage to learn: if the teacher dares to teach, that is, to attend to and care for the learners, then the learners in their turn can dare to learn.

EXPERIENCE AND REFLECTION

For many, difficulties in formalized learning in school are created by a deep-seated fear of *getting it wrong*, of being found deficient. For some, there is still the lingering but powerful association between learning and punishment. Nowhere is this more graphically illustrated than in the child-rearing manuals studied by Alice Miller (1987a). The following is taken from Schmid (1887):

> In school, discipline precedes the actual teaching. There is no sounder pedagogical axiom than the one that children must first be trained before they can be taught. There can be discipline without instruction, but no instruction without discipline.
>
> We insist therefore that learning in and of itself is not discipline, is not moral endeavour, but discipline is an essential part of learning . . .
>
> The perverse will, which to its own and others' detriment is not in command of itself, must be broken.

No wonder we have to struggle so hard in the schools of the late twentieth century to achieve a more liberating and enriching learning process for the students. It is only very recently, and somewhat reluctantly, that corporal punishment has been withdrawn as an agent of control in the learning process of schools.

The major shift, as Ferguson suggests, is to an appreciation of the potential for learning that all pupils have demonstrated in their pre-school development and which John Holt (1971) describes so graphically:

> Almost every child, on the first day he sets foot in a school building, is smarter, more curious, less afraid of what he doesn't know, better at finding and figuring things out, more confident, resourceful, persistent and independent, than he will ever again be in his schooling or, unless he is very unusual and lucky, for the rest of his life.

Describing entry into the classroom, he says:

> In he comes, this curious, patient, determined, energetic, skilful learner. We sit him down at a desk, and what do we teach him? Many things. First, that learning is separate from living. 'You come to school to learn,' we say, as if the child hadn't been learning before, as if living were out there and learning were in here and there were no connection between the two. Secondly he cannot be trusted to learn and is no good at it. Everything we do about reading, a task far

simpler than what the child has already mastered, says to him, 'If we don't make you read, you won't, and if you don't do it exactly the way we tell you, you can't'. In short, the child comes to feel that learning is a passive process, something that someone else does to you, instead of something you do for yourself.

The tradition of domineering and coercive teaching has deep roots in our own experience and in the traditions of parenthood, schooling and the organization of work. The paradigm shift is a movement away from this constraining dynamic towards a more enriching and liberating experience based on a deep respect for human potential and dignity, and a determination to create the best possible conditions for human growth, development and expression.

In a different way, Seymour Papert (1980) has provided insights into our positive experience as learners. He observes that children hold theories of the world that are coherent. These theories, he says, are spontaneously *learned* by all children in the pre-school years through a process which schools should envy:

> It is effective (all children get there), it is inexpensive (it seems to require neither teacher nor curriculum development), and it is humane (the children seem to do it in a carefree spirit without explicit external rewards and punishments).

Ultimate success in the formal learning process, he argues, depends upon our capacity to catch *cultural seeds* – ideas stemming from the cultural environment which capture the imagination, form visions of possibility and motivate courses of action. It also involves a capacity to struggle with *cultural toxins* – those ideas that plant a sense of failure within the self-concept. Using the example of mathematics he says:

> If people believe firmly enough that they cannot do maths, they will usually succeed in preventing themselves from doing whatever they recognise as maths. The consequence of such self sabotage is personal failure, and each failure reinforces the original belief. And such beliefs may be most insidious when held not only by individuals but by an entire culture.

If the balance between cultural seeds and toxins weighs too heavily to the latter then *learning disengagement* results. We begin to give up on learning, believing that it is too hard for us and we cannot do it. Eventually deficiency becomes identity:

> I don't have a head for figures.

> I'm tone deaf.

> I'm not well co-ordinated.

Education, Papert suggests, has little to do with explanation and everything to do with engagement – or *falling in love with the material*. Our capacity for growth and development is inextricably linked to the captivation of our awesome imaginations and to key aspects of our surrounding culture: to the steady growth of a sense of self-belief and possibility and to opportunities for practical exploration and experience. It would seem then that the climate for change has much to do with our capacity for *natural learning* and the extent to which we have optimum control of the learning experience. It also involves deliberate attention to the cultural seeds and cultural toxins.

REFLECTIVE PRACTICE

In order to create the conditions in classrooms in which pupils can play a more active and dynamic part in their own learning, it is necessary to establish a framework upon which classroom practice can be built.

Central to the development of a new paradigm for the management of learning has been the process referred to as *experiential learning*. Developed by David Kolb *et al.* (1971), this approach suggests a cycle of discrete mental processes following concrete experience (see Figure 1.1). In order to make sense of our various experiences it is necessary to reflect on them and to think about them. This enables the experiences to be assimilated into our framework of concepts and constructs. Further thinking may follow in which new learning is used to formulate fresh concepts and develop changed constructs which can be acted upon.

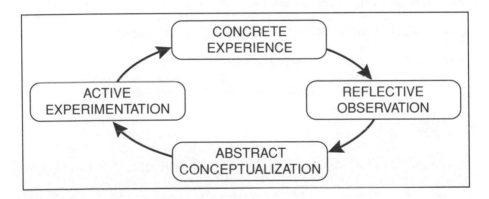

Figure 1.1 The experiential learning cycle.

One of the disadvantages of the cyclic model is that it constantly turns in upon itself, whereas in the reality of classroom life the cycle repeats itself with new material each time a new experience is encountered. A modified version of the model illustrates this (Whitaker 1993a) (see Figure 1.2). This version makes a distinction between experiential learning which is incidental and that which is deliberate. We learn in and through experience all the time, thinking about our experiences and either sustaining or modifying our behaviour in the light of our realizations. This process becomes altogether more powerful when we engage in it through deliberate choice – allocating time to it and seeking the support of others as we talk it through.

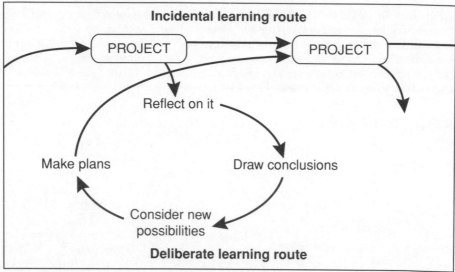

Figure 1.2 The deliberate learning cycle.

It is important to remember that the most precious resource that pupils bring with them to the classroom is their experience of learning. We manage our learning more effectively if we create *time out* opportunities to use the process of critical reflection, both to make sense of past experience and to consider appropriate changes and developments for the future (see Figure 1.3).

Critical reflection is a process whereby we submit to examination incidents and events in our past in order to make sense of them and place them within our framework of developing ideas and values. We also reflect on past experience in order to sort out what we consider to be specific successes and difficulties. With the detailed information that we are able to derive from this process we are in a good position to look ahead to the future incidents and events of our learning programme and to make precise practical plans in the light of what we have learnt. This iterative process of action, reflection and planning is at the heart of all successful learning and needs to occupy a significant place in the schooling process.

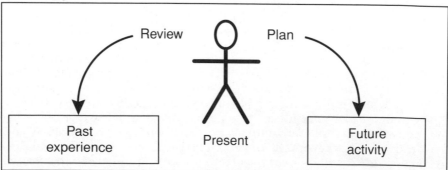

Figure 1.3 The reflective learner.

What this means in practical terms is that structured learning experiences need to be punctuated with deliberate periods of reflection and critical thinking. For learning to be effective and successful it is as important to focus on how the learning is being conducted and managed as it is on what is to be learnt.

The Brazilian educator Paulo Freire (1972) has highlighted three vital elements in the learning process:

1 *Praxis* – the continuous sequence of experience and reflection involving critical thinking and dialogue. If we can work out how and why specific actions succeed or otherwise we are better able to act deliberately next time.
2 *Problematization* – focusing on those parts of learning which require attention and change, which prove difficult and frustrating. If these aspects of learning are ignored or rationalized away, then cognitive dissonance or learned helplessness is the inevitable result. This applies especially to early learning in the basic skills. Lack of success in reading is far more likely to occur because pupils learn to believe that they are unable to learn to read or are no good at it, than for any cognitive reason, as adult literacy programmes have so effectively demonstrated.
3 *Conscientization* – the process through which learners, through a deepening awareness of the social and cultural contexts in which learning takes place, are able to develop a capacity to understand and transform that reality.

Thus pupils need to focus not only on the subject matter of learning – the exercise or the attainment target – but they also need to focus on the means by which they bring their own developing learning capacities to bear upon it. This involves attention to such questions as:

1 What are the problems and challenges of this learning situation?
2 In what ways is this particular learning situation a problem for me?
3 What can be done to overcome the problem?

What so often happens is that instead of being encouraged to pursue their own answers to these vital questions, pupils are told what their problems are and they become ashamed of them, particularly when the solutions suggested by others are not easily understood or applied. As Freire (1972) observes:

> In the banking concept of education, knowledge is a gift bestowed by those who consider themselves knowledgeable upon those they consider to know nothing . . . the students, alienated like the slave in the Hegelian dialectic, accept their ignorance as justifying the teachers' existence.

Freire's pioneering work with disadvantaged learners has demonstrated the supreme importance of attention to process and the need to submit all taken-for-granted assumptions about learning to the most rigorous examination. Managing to learn successfully is a process in which application and reflection need to be in a balanced and dynamic relationship. Traditional practice has insisted on an almost exclusive devotion to application, a seemingly relentless pursuit of the acquisition of knowledge which shows a contempt and disregard for the struggles and confusions of the journey. It is time to bring these two key factors into a more harmonious relationship.

STYLES AND STANCES

Teaching style has long been regarded as one of the keys to successful classroom practice. Less attention has been paid to the styles and stances adopted by pupils in their learning. This is surprising, since questions about how and why we are able to manage to learn are fundamental in attempting to formulate an effective framework for classroom management.

Valuable insights into learning behaviour have been provided by the ORACLE Project (Galton and Simon 1980), which undertook detailed observation of pupils in primary school classrooms. As well as identifying a range of teaching styles, the research describes four distinct types of learner:

1 *Attention-seekers* – pupils who spend considerable amounts of time
    out of their place, moving round the classroom and waiting to gain the
    teacher's attention.
2 *Intermittent workers* – pupils who are frequently distracted from their
    work but do not draw the teacher's attention to themselves, flitting
    from one conversation to another without getting on with their work.
3 *Solitary workers* – pupils who receive less teacher attention than
    others but listen and watch when other pupils receive attention. They
    tend to be reluctant to interact with other pupils and remain
    relatively static.
4 *Quiet collaborators* – pupils who appear busy and co-operative but
    who rely heavily on the support of the teacher for which they are
    prepared to wait.

While all these learner types could be identified in all the classrooms observed, their proportions varied according to the teaching style adopted. Learner behaviour can change according to needs and circumstances – an attention seeker in one teacher's classroom may become an intermittent worker in another's.

Of significance in this research are the insights into the inner needs that learners exercise in classrooms – the need for attention, the yearning for friendship and interaction, the fear of failure, the longing for approval and the dread of embarrassment or humiliation. Many pupils spend much energy gaining and avoiding contact with teachers and other pupils. Sensitive teacher attention and friendly pupil dialogue seem to be prerequisites for comfortable learning in classrooms, and an awareness of the differing degrees of confidence and insecurity children experience in the classroom setting is vital to pupil welfare and progress. What many pupils are struggling for, perhaps instinctively, through dialogue with other pupils and with the teacher are the reflective processes outlined above. They strive in often awkward and sometimes apparently deviant ways to seek understanding and insight into what is expected of them and how they can deliver.

Traditionally, the world of the classroom has honoured the brain and denied the heart. Careful observation of pupil behaviour seems to suggest that learning involves a lot more than a cognitive tussle. It is often an overwhelming struggle to cope with and survive the collection of demands, expectations and pressures that are activated moment by moment in classrooms throughout the land. That most of us survive has become the sole justification for traditional practice – *it didn't do me any harm!* Perhaps unwittingly we have allowed our horizons to be lowered. Learning should be a glorious affair, not a struggle to survive.

Something of the complexity of the learning process is revealed in the work of Honey and Mumford (1986). Building on the pioneering work of David Kolb and associates they have suggested that in the process of learning we incorporate four specific stances:

1 Learning by feeling
2 Learning by watching
3 Learning by thinking
4 Learning by doing.

As we build and develop the skills of learning we draw on all four of those elements, but often, in the light of circumstance and experience, we develop a preference for one or two and a relative disinclination towards the others. Since each of us will incorporate and utilize these elements in different ways and in different combinations we each acquire a distinctive and unique learning style. Our success in formal learning will depend to what extent these four elements are catered for in school and the extent to which individuality of style is supported sensitively and creatively by teachers.

Honey and Mumford acknowledged that all learners incorporate each of the four elements in their learning but found that they also develop a preponderance for one or two. Four distinct styles are defined:

1 *Reflector* – reflecting on concrete experience and drawing conclusions.
2 *Theorist* – reflecting on data and information and developing ideas.
3 *Pragmatist* – thinking about problems and trying out possibilities.
4 *Activist* – trying out ideas, responding to challenges and taking risks.

In a similar vein, Denis Postle (1993) points to the work of John Heron, who has suggested four modes of learning which provide an insight into what is going on in the psyche when we learn:

- *Action*   learning by doing
- *Conceptual*   learning about a subject
- *Imaginal*   the use of the imagination
- *Emotional*   learning by encounter and direct experience.

Heron suggests that while each mode depends upon each of the others, the capacity to learn at an emotional level is the nourishment for the whole learning process, providing a foundation for the involvement of the imagination, which in turn acts as a spring for the conceptual stage which then pushes through into learning action.

Since the traditional assumption is that there is a single proper way to learn and that is how we have to train children, we have not paid attention to the burgeoning skills of learning that pupils have been developing for themselves since birth. Teaching styles need to be designed to acknowledge and support the different styles that learners adopt when faced with learning challenges and, as teachers, we need to build on the preferred elements pupils have evolved while encouraging and nourishing the neglected and avoided ones.

Perhaps one of the most frustrating challenges for educators is that while we can isolate many of the elements that contribute to effective and successful learning and point to some of the problems and difficulties that inhibit and frustrate it, the learning process itself is largely unpredictable, confusing, haphazard and messy. Perhaps what we need to learn more than anything else is to trust the learners to do more of it for themselves. It is worth recalling the observations about good learners made by Postman and Weingartner (1971):

- they enjoy solving problems;
- they know what is relevant for their survival;
- they rely on their own judgement;
- they are not afraid of being wrong and can change their minds when necessary;
- they are not fast answerers – they think first;
- they are flexible and adapt according to situation and challenge;
- they have a high degree of respect for facts;
- they are skilled in enquiry;
- they do not need to have an absolute, final, irrevocable solution to every problem;
- they do not get depressed by the prospect of saying *I don't know*.

As teachers, we need to be guided by the learners themselves. We have to create opportunities for them to talk about themselves as learners – about what excites them, frustrates them, challenges them and inspires them in their learning. We need to recognize that our single most important contribution to their future well-being is to help them to develop into effective and capable learners. Noting the new educational challenges created by fast and accelerating change, Alvin Toffler (1971) notes that pupils will need skills in three crucial areas. Firstly, they will need skills in learning itself. Schools must not only present data and information but help pupils to develop the skills of handling it. Pupils must learn how to discard old ideas and how to replace them. Secondly, they must learn about relating to others. Increasing pressures in society and faster change will increase the difficulties in maintaining human ties. Education must help pupils to accept the absence of deep friendships, to accept loneliness and mistrust, or it must find new ways to accelerate friendship formation. Thirdly, rapid change will multiply the types and complexities of decision-making facing individuals; therefore education must address the issue of over-choice directly.

WHOLENESS AND INTEGRATION

The term *holistic* has entered the language to promote a view that an attention to wholeness is as important as attention to the separate and contributory parts. Deriving from the Greek *holos* – whole – the concept refers to an understanding of reality in terms of integrated wholes whose properties cannot be reduced to those of smaller units. The cognitive tyranny in education has produced a hierarchy of human attributes, placing intellectual rigour and physical prowess over emotion and intuition as the pinnacle of human expression.

There are signs that reductionism is being challenged. New integrative and holistic theories can be seen coming together from work in the sciences, ecology, philosophy, health, therapy, sociology, religion and politics. A concern for connecting principles is emerging. This concern stresses the interdependence of every aspect of our environment. It suggests that descriptions of reality which focus on division and separation do not accurately reflect the way the world is and how we experience it. Rather it extends the notion that we are all part of one interconnected and seamless planetary system. The scientist David Bohm (1980) coined the phrase *the implicate order* to describe a view of the world in which consciousness and physical matter are part of an ever-changing flow. Existence is seen as a dynamic web of relationships – an unbroken wholeness in which every part unfolds and implicates every other. The theoretical scientist Fritjof Capra (1983) has suggested that the mechanistic world view of Newton and Descartes has brought us perilously close to destruction, and advocates a new vision, systems-based and holistic, which is more consistent with the findings of modern physics.

> This theory of integration and wholeness stands in contrast to the traditional theory of reductionism which demonstrates a preoccupation with seeking explanations to phenomena through fragmentation into smaller and smaller constituent parts. Human activity, like traditional scientific theorizing, is characterized by division and distinction. Human endeavour is circumscribed within concepts of nationhood, language, religion, race, gender, class and economic wherewithal. We are labelled and compartmentalized according to such criteria and, in order to protect our interests, we learn to be secretive, devious and manipulative. We frequently come to regard others, especially those who are in different circumstances, as enemies to be feared, resisted, shunned, discriminated against, and in extreme situations, to be fought against and killed. What is worse, we have come to believe that these behaviours are both inevitable and acceptable and so we teach them to our children.

A more holistic approach to education places learning within the context of whole experience rather than as only a part of experience. The traditional orthodoxies of education derive from a reductionist view of learning that emphasizes the processes of thinking and knowing at the expense of other aspects of human endeavour. The National Curriculum has been designed to give the strongest emphasis to knowledge. Attainment targets currently give only grudging recognition to the non-cognitive aspects of learning. Despite the pioneering work of Benjamin Bloom and others in articulating the two domains of learning – cognitive and affective – it is the former which continues to dominate the curriculum and learning processes in schools.

The holistic approach to education strives to restore an appropriate balance to the learning process by giving equal status to experience, imagination, creativity and intuition as it does to knowing, thinking, remembering and reasoning. Holistic education sees the purpose of learning as directed towards capable being in the world, rather than only knowing about the world. This involves a reconsideration of both the curriculum we offer to pupils and the nature of the learning experiences that deliver it.

In attempting to develop a more holistic approach to learning it is important to consider the different dimensions of personhood that we bring to our growth and development. The psychologist Carl Jung has suggested that human completeness consists of four key attributes: the physical, the emotional, the intellectual and the intuitive. It is significant to note how in society and its education system, these attributes have been separated. Figure 1.4 illustrates this. The vertical axis has been the obsession of the English public school over the centuries. The horizontal axis – emotion and intuition – has been acknowledged, but disparagingly. Part of the public school ethic has been to develop character by concealing emotions and feelings and suppress them while at the same time discouraging intuitive thinking and imagination by extolling the virtues of rationality, logic and deductive thinking. It is, of course, no coincidence that the polarization of these attributes has been a central feature of gender socialization.

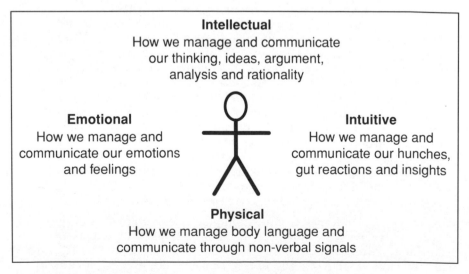

Intellectual
How we manage and communicate
our thinking, ideas, argument,
analysis and rationality

Emotional
How we manage and
communicate our emotions
and feelings

Intuitive
How we manage and
communicate our hunches,
gut reactions and insights

Physical
How we manage body language and
communicate through non-verbal signals

Figure 1.4 Dimensions of personhood and learning.

What is needed in our classrooms are opportunities to redress this harmful polarization. Emotional and intuitive development are vital if creativity is to be cultivated and a more complete potential for growth and development released.

There has been a strong tendency in our society to prize the intellectual dimension above the emotional and intuitive and to denigrate and disparage those who introduce feelings and intuitions into organizational affairs. Bureaucracies are designed to operate according to rational principles, not to be sensitive to human needs and aspirations. Gender perceptions particularly have polarized in this way, creating a dangerous incompleteness in the ways communication is regarded, both in personal relationships and more especially in organizational life.

An effective learner is more likely to be one who brings all dimensions of being into the process of growth and development, thereby increasing the capacity to draw upon a full range of qualities and skills. For too long, the emotional and intuitive elements have been discounted in organizational learning, inhibiting the full expression of human potential. When people are only operating on two of their available cylinders, then serious under-performance is the inevitable result.

John Mulligan (1993) has developed a model of learning which adds to the framework outlined above. He proposes a set of internal processes or skills which help us to learn effectively. At the heart of the four dimensions of personhood, which he refers to as reasoning, intuiting, sensing and feeling, he places *willing – the processor which integrates and harmonizes the use of all the others*. In addition he also incorporates *remembering* and *imagining*, both of which depend upon a synthesizing from each of the four dimensions.

THE INTEGRATED LEARNER

The protracted and disputatious debate about the detail of the National Curriculum has revealed the tendency to see success as lying in making the right choices – whether knowledge is more important than skill, design of the curriculum more important than its delivery or structure more relevant than process. The problem lies in the creating of false dichotomies and the posing of dilemmas. These vital issues affecting the management and development of formal learning in schools cannot be reduced to questions of either/or. What is needed is an acceptance that all are important and that each has an appropriate and significant contribution to make to the whole. What is equally vital is that we learn to appreciate that it is the relationship between these necessary contributory parts that holds the key to change and improvement. Until we realize that the key to understanding human affairs and activities lies more in making connections between the various factors than in struggling to define a pecking order of relative importance, we are unlikely to satisfy our desperate need to raise the quality of learning in schools.

In further attempting to create a more synthesizing definition of learning, it is useful to consider three specific and interdependent elements. These are set out in Figure 1.5.

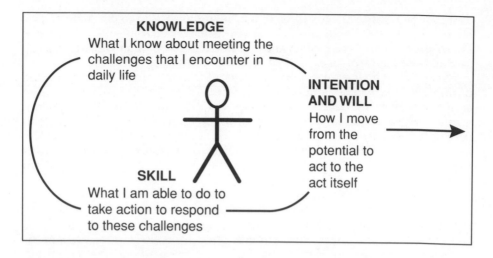

Figure 1.5 The integrated learner.

This interpretation of learning suggests that a preoccupation with determining a single correct balance between knowledge and skill, a key feature in the debate about the National Curriculum, fails to give attention to a missing third element: the will and determination of the learner. It is not enough to be concerned only with the capacity to learn; we have to give more concerted attention to the learner's inclination and determination to learn – to those factors which create learning commitment in pupils. In the race to articulate the smartest target and the most rigorous programme of study we are in danger of avoiding the most vital of factors – the learner's own relationship to these prescriptions. Theodore Roszak (1981) observes:

> Everybody has an interest in education, but what is the child's interest – independent of all adult intervention and influence? Does that seem an impossible question to answer? Very likely it does. As impossible as it once seemed to say what a woman's interest was in life independent of her husband or her father. As impossible as it once seemed to say what the interest of slaves might be in life independent of their masters. There are those who live in such ingrained, seemingly 'natural' conditions of subjugation that we cannot begin to imagine what autonomous interests they have in the world. Children are in that category, more so than any other social dependant. Yet, they have their own interest, it is the interest that each of us discovers, if only in moments of unaccustomed exhilaration or strange absorption, when we become our own person, caught up in our own work, our own salvation. In such moments, we find an autonomy and an adventure that alone deserves to be called life. That is the child's interest, and it needs to be defended from nothing so much as the terrible 'practicalities' that are always foremost in the adult mind.

The art and skill of the educator lies in an ability to relate deeply and powerfully to this dimension of learning. It stems from an unshakeable belief in the awesome learning potential of pupils and their innate capacity to release it. It also requires a persistent curiosity about the conditions needed for learners to release this talent with vigour and determination. Unless pupils bring a desire and commitment to learn with them into the classroom their achievements are likely to be partial and incomplete. Learning is a complex act of creation; it requires a reaching beyond perceived boundaries to something as yet unknowable. It requires courage and it also needs support. Teaching is a process of engaging day by day with these aspects of learners and nourishing them into full expression.

2
Teachers and Teaching

COMPETING ASSUMPTIONS

One of the current difficulties for teachers lies in the disputatious environment in which they work. Reforms to the schooling system have been accompanied by a relentless disparaging of teachers and their professional integrity. Draconian legislation has been produced almost as revenge against teachers who seem to be blamed for social ills and economic difficulties. The contempt for specialists expressed by government ministers has produced a deep depression among those who have chosen to dedicate themselves to the education of the young. At a time when education has needed the most inspiring and sensitive of leadership, the teachers have been served with contempt, disapproval and recrimination.

Instead of recognizing that there is a genuine ideological argument to be pursued about the management of learning and teaching, government policy has been to assert single, correct panaceas for education and enforce them without creative discussion and debate. An over-simplistic construct of *traditional* versus *progressive* has been used to conduct disputes about current difficulties and dilemmas. Policy-making for the education service has become a battleground with casualties that can ill be afforded.

In attempting to create a more comprehensive and synthesizing approach to educational decision-making it is important to note the range of assumptions that exist about the educational process. Four broad traditions have been noted (Walford 1981):

1 The liberal humanitarian tradition which is primarily concerned with passing on the basic cultural heritage from one generation to another.
2 The pupil-centred tradition which values self-development, self-reliance and social harmony for the individual learner.
3 The utilitarian tradition which sees the main job of education as equipping students to go well prepared into an already defined future.
4 The reconstructionalist tradition which sees education as a potential instrument for changing society.

To pursue one of these at the expense of all others is to produce an incomplete and dangerously restrictive model of education. Each of these traditions is important. What is needed is a synthesizing, a bringing together of vital and important elements into a new paradigm for development and change. It is necessary to accept that education is problematic and that there are no simple correct ways of managing it. Within a broad framework of purposes, specific aims and objectives will vary from time to time to reflect particular conditions and situations. It is naive to believe that if we try hard enough we can produce a framework that will last for the foreseeable future. Those with responsibility for the education system need to accept and incorporate into their thinking the inevitable confusions and ambiguities that attend such a complex process, and recognize the essential interdependence between the different parts. In a fast changing world, novel challenges will present themselves with alarming regularity and many solutions will need to be temporary. In such a world, the role of the professional educator takes on new meaning and significance.

TEACHERS AS MANAGERS

Perhaps one of the reasons why teachers have been disparaged so readily lies in a false and dangerously limited perception of the nature of the work they do. Regarded at best as the skilful transmission of subject knowledge, teaching has been reduced to a basic formula by those who have driven the legislation. It has been difficult and stressful for teachers to be dictated to by those who hold such a simplistic and limited model of what teaching in schools comprises. Over the past twenty years the teaching profession has moved away from simple, formulaic approaches to teaching. A great many teachers, aware of the restrictive and dispiriting effects on pupils of simplistic nostrums, have engaged in a search for more life-enhancing and effective processes.

Many of the notions currently put forward by politicians seem to reaffirm those inhibiting and restrictive notions of schooling from which teachers have been trying to move on. These are summarized well by Carl Rogers (1980):

1 Teachers are the sole possessors of knowledge: pupils the expected recipients.
2 Teaching is the means of getting the knowledge into the recipients. Tests and examinations measure how much the pupil has received.
3 Teachers alone possess power, pupils obey.
4 Rule by authority is the accepted policy in the classroom.
5 Pupils are to be distrusted, they cannot be expected to work satisfactorily without the teacher constantly controlling and checking them.
6 Pupils are best controlled by being kept in a constant state of fear.
7 Democracy is taught about but not practised in the classroom. Pupils do not play a part in the formulation of their individual goals, these are determined for them.

8 There is no room for whole persons in the education system, only their intellects. Emotional development is not regarded as a necessary area for learning.

One of the ways we can help to bring about a more informed approach to educational decision-making is to articulate a more comprehensive analysis of the work that teachers actually do. The current perception of teaching is dangerously limiting. Even in some initial training institutions, teaching is still regarded as pedagogy – the science of teaching children. Very little attention seems to be given to the fact that in addition to a wealth of cognitive and curriculum considerations, teaching also encompasses a whole range of organizational issues that are generated when purposeful activity is conducted in a collective setting. Issues of institutional management, organizational psychology, culture, climate and personal welfare are major concerns for classroom teachers, demanding knowledge, skills and qualities beyond those traditionally associated with pedagogy. It is time that teachers in schools were afforded the same understanding and respect as those who occupy positions as managers in other kinds of organization.

If we adopt the frequently used definition of management as getting things done with and through other people, we can see the relevance. Teachers are charged with tasks to do with organizing learning in a pupil community. The complexities of this responsibility are certainly equal to those experienced by senior managers in industrial and commercial organizations. But we still conceive of teaching as a discrete, specialized activity somehow devoid of organizational and management implications. Educational management has tended to focus only on the non-educational elements of organizational life and has concerned itself largely with the roles and responsibilities of senior staff. The essence of management in schools is the transaction of classroom learning. The co-ordination of a subject or department, while challenging and complex, is less significant by comparison. Perhaps the key contribution that management training and development can make to education is to focus on the complexities of classroom life and the challenges to teachers of managing learning in a large group of pupils with differing abilities, needs, behaviour and self-awareness.

One way to create a more complete understanding of teaching as managing is to examine the range of elements which combine to describe and explain it. These can be summarized in three categories:

1 Skills and qualities
2 Personality and experience
3 Operational modes.

1. Skills and qualities
It is useful to distinguish three distinct types of skill:

1 Occupational
2 Personal
3 Managerial.

Occupational skills

These are the skills and qualities that are developed through training and experience. They are of a specialist and technical nature and specific to particular occupations and professions. Teachers have different occupational skills from nurses, lawyers or engineers, for example. In the teaching profession these may include:

- subject specialization;
- teaching methods and techniques;
- child development and psychology;
- history of education;
- curriculum design.

They are often the key focus of job-related training within organizations.

Personal skills

These are the skills and qualities acquired and developed through the process of socialization. Their purpose is to develop and sustain relationships and enable social living. They determine our capacity to get on well with other people in both professional and social settings. A complete list of personal skills and qualities would be very long indeed, but would include:

- being courteous and considerate;
- conveying a sense of warmth;
- listening to what others say;
- speaking clearly and appropriately;
- being assertive;
- responding to the needs of others.

Until fairly recently, these skills rarely featured in the formal educational process, although they are constantly referred to by adults in the socializing of the young. Whilst they are crucially important in teaching, they have rarely been the subject of training and development. It is often our relationships with others that cause our most difficult and emotionally painful moments. It is not surprising then that the additional pressures of work can increase the challenge and stress in our own relationships.

Success in teaching requires us not only to be aware of this, but to improve our own skills in order to manage our relationships effectively and sensitively.

Managerial skills

These are the skills and qualities needed to work with and through other people. Teaching has not traditionally been associated with that professional activity known as *management*, but even a cursory glance at the following analysis will demonstrate that teaching is indeed a management activity *par excellence*. The following classification of managerial skills provides a useful starting point for consideration (Whitaker 1983):

Creating:
- having good ideas;
- finding original solutions to common problems;

- anticipating the consequences of decisions and actions;
- employing lateral thinking;
- using imagination and intuition.

Planning:
- relating present to future needs;
- recognizing what is important and what merely urgent;
- anticipating future trends;
- analysing.

Communicating:
- understanding people;
- listening;
- explaining;
- written communication;
- getting others to talk;
- tact;
- tolerance of other's mistakes;
- giving thanks and encouragement;
- keeping everyone informed;
- using information technology.

Motivating:
- inspiring others;
- providing realistic challenges;
- helping others to set goals and targets;
- helping others to value their own contributions and achievements.

Organizing:
- making fair demands on others;
- making rapid decisions;
- being in front when it counts;
- staying calm when the going is difficult;
- recognizing when the job is done.

Evaluating:
- comparing outcomes with intentions;
- self-evaluation;
- helping to appraise the work of others;
- taking corrective action where necessary.

2. Personality and experience

This category refers to some of those elements in the professional work of teachers which differ from person to person. They are determined both by experience and by the clusters of values and attitudes that have accumulated throughout life and which form a dynamic part of personal and professional behaviour (see Figure 2.1). This combination of aware-ness, experience, intelligence, skill and intention provides us each with an ever-developing potential to act. We draw on these attributes in specific situations to deal with particular challenges and tasks.

Figure 2.1 Factors relating to professional effectiveness.

Experience
We are very much the products of our own experiences and actions, and behaviour will to some extent depend upon the way we have responded to circumstances in the past. We can be said to gain experience when we deliberately learn from the past and use it to guide future thinking and action.

Awareness
This involves being in touch with our own experiences and being sensitive to the effects that our behaviour has on others. Awareness of our emotions and the extent to which they influence our thinking and behaviour is particularly important. Personal and professional effectiveness is likely to increase when we are sensitive to the effect we have on others and modify our behaviour appropriately.

Skill
This is about knowing how to do something and being able to do it to a consistent standard.

Intelligence
Traditionally, intelligence has been associated with intellectual agility, cleverness and the ability to solve brain teasers. In recent years a more comprehensive and enhancing concept has emerged which suggests that intelligence is an innate capacity to adapt, survive and flourish. Denis Postle (1989) suggests that a new concept of intelligence must include intuitive, emotional and physical components as well as purely intellectual ones (see p.141). Postle notes that if we accept this wider definition, four things become clear:

> First, we see that, as well as representing a pinnacle of human achievement, thinking skills such as deduction, inference and reasoning are just one of several, more or less parallel styles of intelligence . . .
>
> Secondly, we find that the powerful self healing, self stabilizing, self regulating intelligence of the human body has been grossly undervalued.

Thirdly, it becomes easier to see that the tremendous attention given to intellect over the last few centuries is an accident of history, a side effect of the dominance of men.

Finally we realize that our excessive respect for intellect reflects a dangerously one sided view that, far from supporting human survival, now threatens it. Hundreds of thousands of people devote their working hours to planning the last day on earth – a catastrophic memorial to intellect divorced from feeling.

Personal and professional effectiveness draws on this more rounded intelligence and increasing evidence suggests that people in leadership and management positions are perceived by others as effective when they behave sensitively in interpersonal situations, have a capacity to handle emotional situations well and are seen to be able to relax and enjoy a full and satisfying life outside the workplace.

Intention
This is the ingredient which transforms capability into action. Unless the components of personal and professional effectiveness are activated in particular situations nothing happens, as potential is available but not used. It is through the exercise of will and intention that energy is released, intelligence applied and skills used.

3. Operational modes
One of the most frustrating aspects of management work is realizing at the end of the day that although you have been exceedingly busy, many planned tasks and activities remain neglected. Over recent years time management has become something of a preoccupation as we struggle to pack more and more into the same amount of time.

Part of the desperation about time and workload arises out of a basic misperception about the nature of managerial work. Most of us see our roles as requiring us to attend to those tasks and activities designated in our job descriptions. We make plans and organize our time to deal with these requirements. What we find, however, as we set out to conduct these tasks is that we are constantly interrupted. During the course of most days we find ourselves engaged in a series of interactions, few of which had been planned. People approach us and make requests. Often these approaches seem friendly and undemanding, prefaced by such phrases as, 'Can I have a word?', 'Have you got a minute?', or 'Are you busy?' The modesty of these requests usually belies their importance. Few of us turn down these requests; in fact we tend to respond to them with willingness and sensitivity. Taken individually, these interactions are usually very brief, seldom longer than five or six minutes and often very much less, but they do create a diversion in our already tightly planned schedule. It is not uncommon to find that a succession of short interruptions has placed our whole schedule in jeopardy. The tendency is to blame ourselves for giving more attention to the apparently urgent than to the important tasks we have set ourselves. We seem to find ourselves preoccupied with incidents and events that conspire to divert us from the real tasks and challenges of our roles. One of the consequences is that we can feel out of control, reacting to events rather than directing them. We can feel guilty because we are so driven by events and worried that perhaps we lack the skills for the job.

What we have here is a classic management dilemma. We have tended to think that good managers are always in control of their destiny and are only effective when they operate in a proactive way, demonstrating supreme control over their actions and the situations in which they find themselves. The reality is quite different. Far from dealing with trivial and apparently minor incidents, these interruptions are crucial to the well-being of the organization, enabling it to function effectively, to deal with its temporary difficulties and problems and to engage in the essential daily work. Research has shown (Minzberg 1973) that management by interruption is a highly effective way of operating, creating countless opportunities for real issues to be dealt with, policies to be highlighted, values to be demonstrated and visions pursued. It is because managers are so good in this incidental mode that so many schools are well run and able to deal with their crises and satisfy the demands made on them.

Figure 2.2 suggests that teachers, as indeed most managers, operate in two distinct but related modes – fixed and flexible. It is often in the flexible mode that managers do their most effective work. In the spontaneity of the moment they are able to deal with the urgent issues, creatively helping others to gain the information they need, resolve their dilemmas and difficulties and receive the encouragement and reassurance that is so often necessary to function effectively.

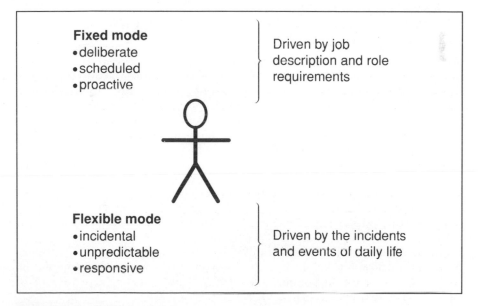

Figure 2.2 Operational modes.

One of the challenges of management work lies in placing these two modes in a realistic balance. Since the flexible mode tends not to be referred to in job descriptions we do not afford it the importance it deserves, nor allocate time for it by not scheduling our deliberate work too tightly. We need to appreciate that being interrupted presents opportunities to lead and manage, to advance the work of the organization by responding to the needs others are facing and by helping them to manage their work more effectively.

TEACHING AS LEADERSHIP

Another useful way to examine the nature of the teacher's role is through the concept of leadership. Teachers can be regarded as exercising one of the most demanding leadership challenges devised by society – the education of the next generation. Leadership can be regarded as that part of a manager's work concerned with helping people to tackle prescribed tasks to the optimum of their ability. It is concerned more with effectiveness than with efficiency and more with quality than with attainment.

As well as considering leadership from the leader's own perspective, it is important to have regard for the needs that we have of our leaders. Good leaders seem to have an infinite capacity not only to satisfy vital needs but also to anticipate them. Such a capacity grows out of four key qualities:

1 Genuine interpersonal behaviour.
2 Warmth, care and respect for those we work with.
3 Empathy.
4 A strong and unshifting belief in the potential of others to grow, develop and change.

All of us are needy, and failure to get some very specific needs satisfied, particularly those that contribute to our pattern of motivation, can result in loss of confidence and enthusiasm; a sense of not being involved and a part of things; a feeling of being unappreciated and undervalued, and a reduction of job commitment and energy. These are expensive losses which few organizations can afford. Good leadership is the delicate process of anticipating these needs in others and striving to satisfy them. This is as true for learners in classrooms as it is for workers in factories or offices. Teaching is an act of discovering what the felt needs of the pupil are and the growth needs they invariably conceal.

Figure 2.3 indicates a range of needs likely to be experienced quite frequently by pupils during the process of learning. Effective teachers are those who are able to reach out to pupils, to appreciate and understand their needs and seek specific and individual ways of satisfying them. Diana Whitmore (1986) asserts: 'If children were to experience adults as welcoming, guiding and supportive, they would discover the wonder of life, the joy of exploring, the beauty of understanding.

As teachers, we can help to create these felt experiences in pupils if we

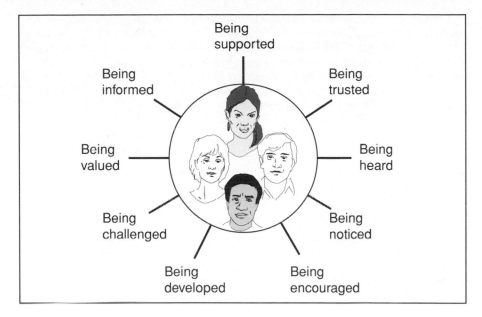

Figure 2.3 Leadership and needs.

seize opportunities, usually in the flexible operational mode described above, to respond to some basic needs:

Trusting – conveying to pupils a belief in their abilities. Resisting the temptation to increase control when things are difficult. Expressing delight at successes and achievements.

Listening – constantly seeking opportunities to listen to pupils' current experiences. Asking questions, seeking information, eliciting opinions, delving into details and showing genuine interest and concern.

Noticing – taking note of contributions and providing regular positive feedback on successes and achievements.

Encouraging – Empathizing with the demands and challenges of the learning process. Providing support for problem-solving and action planning.

Developing – offering practical help for those striving to make breakthroughs in knowledge and skill. Working to create new learning opportunities.

Challenging – building a climate of systematic and continuous improvement. Constantly helping others to seek new angles, new possibilities and new ideas.

Valuing – providing detailed and specific feedback so that all pupils feel a deep sense that their contributions and efforts are valued.

Informing – keeping information flowing freely through the classroom, tutor group, etc. Checking that pupils know what is going on.

Supporting – offering practical help as well as moral support. Getting alongside pupils as often as possible. Providing a helping hand and a listening ear.

There are considerable similarities between effective leadership and effective teaching. Studies undertaken in the United States and Germany (Aspy and Roebuck 1976; Tausch 1978), which set out to determine which particular teacher behaviours were correlated with different types of learning outcomes, produced largely similar results to research into leader behaviour in a wide range of business organizations (Peters and Waterman 1982). In the research into teachers, three particular behaviours turned out to be especially significant:

1 The teacher's ability to understand the meaning that classroom experience is having for each pupil.
2 The respect the teacher has for each pupil as a separate person.
3 The ability of the teacher to engage in genuine person-to-person relationship with each pupil.

It was found that the pupils in classes with teachers who demonstrated these qualities to a high degree made significantly greater gains in learning. The greatest gains of all were in those schools where teachers were supported by heads and senior staff who also exhibited such qualities. In these situations the main outcomes were:

1 Pupils became more adept at using higher cognitive skills and processes such as problem-solving.
2 They had higher self-concepts.
3 They exercised greater learning initiatives in the classroom.
4 They exhibited fewer discipline problems.
5 They had a lower absence rate.

The teachers monitored in these studies exhibited the following key characteristics in their work with pupils:

1 They had a more positive self-concept than low level teachers.
2 They were more open and self-disclosing with pupils.
3 They responded more to pupils' feelings.
4 They gave more praise.
5 They were more responsive to pupil ideas.
6 They engaged less often in formal didactic instruction.

These are very much the characteristics which have been identified in high-quality leaders.

In the world of fast and accelerating change the skills of effective leadership are developed in and through experience. Warren Bennis (1989) notes:

Leaders learn by leading and they learn best by leading in the face of obstacles. As weather shapes mountains, so problems make leaders. Difficult bosses, lack of vision in the executive suite, circumstances beyond their control, have been the leader's basic curriculum.

This suggests a radical revision of the way that leadership has traditionally been conceived. Teachers, like those in other leadership positions, must no longer assume they are where they are because of what they have learnt, but because they have a capacity to learn faster than the rate of change in the surrounding environment.

Eric Hoffer (1985) also emphasizes the importance of learning in the basic approach of effective leaders: 'In times of drastic change it is the learners who inherit the future, the learned find themselves equipped to live in a world that no longer exists'.

This suggests a new vision of the pupil–teacher relationship, one that helps to destroy the idea that teaching is an elitist and specialist occupation. Theodore Roszak (1981) suggests that in every educational exchange it is first of all the teacher who has something to learn. In approaching pupils there are vital questions to consider:

- Who is this child?
- What does he or she bring to this situation?
- What is there here for me to discover that no one else has ever known before?

It is through interactions with pupils, what Roszak describes as 'glad encounters with the unexpected', that we can engage in discovering and empowering each child's learning destiny.

Teaching and leadership are both concerned with helping others to see that something is possible, and supporting them in the process of removing the blocks which prevent them standing on their own foot. It is what Daniel Rosenblatt (1975) describes as 'offering a kind of hope that change is possible'.

Leadership, as with teaching, creates an atmosphere that promotes the taking of small steps towards change, change that is free of shame, fear, guilt, humiliation and degradation.

> There has to be some kind of educational process bringing the art of living into day to day management. There has always been a complete difference between the way individuals relate to their colleagues and the way they relate to their friends and family. In the latter area, kindness, tolerance etc. are not regarded as sentimental and wet, but as making the relationship work. Can one parallel this in business now? The difference between the two sets of attitudes is beginning to narrow and that may be the answer to tomorrow's problems.

This quotation from Francis Kinsman (1991) highlights a key challenge for teachers and leaders – to counter the traditional and unnecessary separation in organizations of the personal and the professional. People are whole beings and are at their best when they feel complete and integrated. The separation into parts of ourselves is one of the most damaging tendencies in human activity.

There are no simple solutions in management because there are no simple problems. If problems were simple and straightforward there would be no need for management in the first place. Leadership is an active response to complexity, an ambitious striving towards achievement in awkward situations. It is a journey of belief and hope and downright determination.

A FRAMEWORK FOR MANAGING

Given the enormous complexity of organizational life and the considerable challenges facing those involved in the management of learning, it is important to develop some way of attending carefully to the intricate details of development while at the same time sustaining a picture of the whole. One way to help this process is to develop conceptual maps or models that show the key elements of the teaching task and their relationship to each other.

The following model attempts to capture the key dimensions of the educational task and the vital elements of organizational life that so affect it (Whitaker, 1993a). It offers a framework that can be applied to a range of perspectives (see Figure 2.4):

- As a guide to classroom organization.
- As a personal planning framework.
- By pupils to guide self-directed learning.
- As a conceptual model of classroom life.
- As a basis for curriculum planning.

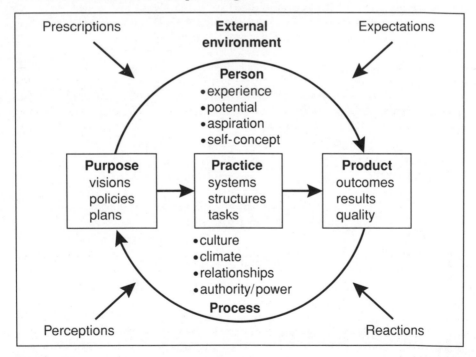

Figure 2.4 A framework for managing.

The external environment

For the pupils in the classroom, and to a large extent the teacher who shares it with them, the external environment consists of those locations which exert force and pressure on activity within the classroom: government legislation, school policy, plans and procedures, rules and regulations and all the hopes and expectations raised by those with a vested interest in educational outcomes – school staff, governors, parents, public opinion and the examination system.

Classroom life is a complex engagement of these forces with those generated by the participants themselves – the pupils and the teacher. Holding these in an appropriate and effective balance is a formidable challenge for any manager. That the external environment is in a state of constant flux further complicates the challenge, creating new tensions and stresses within an already fragile structure. Four particular external forces are worth noting.

1. Prescriptions

Schools, for the first time in their history, are faced with a plethora of prescriptions, setting requirements for their work and creating tighter systems of accountability. These prescriptions have a direct input into the *purpose* element of the model. Teachers, more than ever before, have to plan within a complex framework of educational content and subject targets. How they assess the effectiveness of their pupils' learning is now subject to strict procedures and detailed criteria.

The management of a constantly changing body of prescriptions is a key challenge to both teachers and pupils.

2. Expectations

Less specific, but no less forceful, are the expectations focused on teachers and pupils. Parents have a major interest in how schools are run, an interest which is often confused by the disputatious quality of public debate and the partial stance of the public media. Public opinion exerts a strong influence on schools, both through its local networks of interest and through national debate. Teachers have expectations of each other as well as of their pupils. The behaviour of all those involved in school life is affected by these expectations. Some strive for approval by seeking to satisfy perceived expectations while others, deeming them unreasonable, set out to resist and frustrate them.

3. Perceptions

Public opinion is to some extent informed by the professional dialectic of teaching, but politicians, employers, economists, academics and church leaders also have their disparate opinions to add. In times of economic stress, education becomes something of a social scapegoat. As we move inexorably towards greater structural unemployment, the question of how we should be educating our children for a future which will be very different from the present is bound to occupy those whose responsibility it is to decide the nature of the curriculum.

Pupils constantly find themselves compared with pupils from a previous generation or from another continent. These perceptions can conspire to damage self-esteem and self-confidence and create the sense of being a victim of the system rather than an active agent. Allowed to run unchecked, this can lead to apathy and alienation from a process which should be concerned to create opportunity and optimize potential.

4. Reactions

How pupils are reacted to in the course of their lives critically affects the stance they take to their own learning in schools. Generation gaps and fast changing youth cultures can create problems of understanding and communication. Clashes of values and modes of expression can reinforce antipathies which cause separation and isolation. On the other hand, when pupils are responded to positively with generosity of spirit and with a belief in their abilities and achievements, learning and development is nourished.

These different forces combine in powerful ways to influence and affect the ways that learning is managed in the classroom. No understanding of schooling can be complete without a sensitive awareness of the subtle interplay between these forces and the capacity they have to touch and affect the lives of teachers and pupils alike.

THE PERSON

In the search for management and teaching processes which are truly integrating, it is vital to remember that all organizations are made up of unique and distinctive individuals. A proper respect for individualism is a characteristic of an effective management culture and the leadership challenge is all about the harnessing of different patterns of knowledge, skills and qualities in the pursuit of personal and organizational goals.

The framework highlights four particular elements of the personal dimension.

> *Experience* – all participants, pupils included, bring with them into school their own distinctive and differentiated experience as a rich resource for the organizational endeavour.
> *Human potential* – the concept of human potential serves to highlight the fact that all of us can be more than we currently are, given the right conditions of encouragement and support.
> *Aspiration* – while ambition is often regarded as a somewhat self-seeking quality, the important directional tendency in people is motivated by personal and professional aspirations. The more these can be made explicit and tuned to organizational visions, the greater the likelihood of potential energy being converted into a powerful catalytic force.
> *Self-concept* – the self-concept conditions how we behave and what we do. The successful organization is one that builds self-esteem and self-confidence through an appropriate balance of challenge and support.

The individual is an organization's most important resource. We need to strive to discover ever more effective ways of releasing the human abilities and energies that are available within each pupil in the classroom and to create optimum conditions for personal growth and development.

PURPOSE

The defining of purpose is the first of the three strategic activities required to enable the educational task to be carried out effectively. One of the keys to organizational success is the ability of all participants to define and articulate clearly both the purposes for the specific role they occupy, and the goals and objectives for the organization as a whole. This can help to create a powerful, directional tendency for all those involved in the life and work of the school.

In a fast changing world it is important to keep purpose at the forefront of management and leadership activity so that changes and developments in the prescriptions for learners can be taken account of in designing new programmes and practices and adapting to changing needs. Effective teachers are those who are able to help pupils to understand and articulate clearly the aims and targets for their own learning and to generate a sense of commitment to them.

The vocabulary of planning has become cluttered with a collection of terms that are frequently used interchangeably. It is useful to make some distinctions:

- vision: how we want things to be;
- policy: what we have committed ourselves to;
- plans: the practical activities to implement the policy.

It is significant that in all the wealth of documentation issued by government departments about the National Curriculum, not one publication has been offered to the pupils.

PRACTICE

The second strategic process is concerned with action and the transferring of visions and plans into a range of appropriate tasks and activities. For teachers this involves translating curriculum targets and programmes of study into learning activities and experiences. If visions are to be achieved and intentions fulfilled, then enabling structures have to be created and developed.

Schools have a variety of structures and systems – the curriculum, the allocation of learners to groups and classes, the distribution of resources, the timetable and the specific roles and responsibilities of the staff. There will be many informal systems, some of them temporary and short-lived, designed to enable the school to manage and organize its affairs systematically and efficiently.

The growing tendency in organizational development is to minimize the inhibiting and debilitating features of sharply differentiated hierarchic structures and attempt to create leaner organizational designs with fewer status levels. This involves a greater degree of involvement of all workers in decision-making and the development of collaborative management. Effective managers are those who are able to build and develop flexible structures so that others can carry out the essential activities of the organization with efficiency and effectiveness. Management is the process of enabling the personal effectiveness of others.

There are clear and crucial implications for schools and teachers here. It is in the classroom that children gain their experience and understanding of how organizations work. It is vital that, as teachers, we continue the struggle to create more active, involving and collaborative classroom cultures so that potential is not inhibited and wasted, and so that pupils will gain more positive attitudes about organizational life and their contribution to it. There is much that we can learn from new practices that are evolving in those commercial organizations which are now recognizing the importance of people working together in collaborative teams and partnerships in a climate of trust and encouragement. A great deal more attention needs to be focused on the dynamics of the class as an organization and how learning can most effectively be harnessed and released.

PRODUCT

The third strategic activity is concerned with assessing outcomes and end results. The word *product* is perhaps too material a concept for some, but it refers more to the process of productiveness than to its tangible manifestations. One of the distinctive and challenging aspects of school management is that of defining outcomes and measuring quality. The productive school is one that succeeds in bringing about purposeful and planned change in its pupils and the quality of management and leadership is judged on results rather than intentions. While all good organizations are concerned to serve their customers' and clients' requirements adequately, they are also anxious to devise methods for assessing and evaluating the quality of their services. This is equally true in schools. The Education Reform Act has placed a new emphasis on assessment and evaluation, imposing a set of tight requirements and demanding procedures.

Essentially, the review process is concerned to compare outcomes with plans – to assess how closely results matched declared intentions and reflected the purposes of the school as a whole. This requires, as the lower looped arrow in Figure 2.4 shows, a necessity to look back to the visions and intentions that were set. Effective accountability involves the accurate presentation of information about successes and achievements, and the clear identification of areas of difficulty and concern. The purpose of review is to bring about improvement. It both draws from and contributes to the other dimensions of the model.

PROCESS

This dimension refers to that most vital aspect of organizational life: the way that people interact and relate to each other and the behaviours they display in the working environment. It is concerned with the effective integration of all the individuals referred to in the *person* dimension and includes:

- the ways that values and attitudes are demonstrated;
- how issues of motivation are dealt with;
- how relationships are built;
- how collaboration is encouraged;
- how decisions are made;
- how power and authority are exercised;
- how conflict is resolved.

The culture of an organization is invariably regarded as the outcome of people behaving as they do. Developing culture and climate in the classroom needs to be seen as an intention – the deliberate development of relationships, behaviours and values that are consistent with the declared vision. In this sense it is very much a strategic issue. As teachers, we need to recognize the central importance of organizational culture in our own management and leadership behaviour. Personal effectiveness in management roles is concerned with creating and developing the very best conditions to support the work of others – in this case pupils in a classroom – so that they are encouraged to work to the optimum of their capability. It involves maintaining a psychological environment which is high in challenge but also ready with support. At the personal level, effective managers create for themselves appropriate work habits, an efficient work environment and pay attention to their own well-being and sense of fulfilment.

In schools, organizational culture is important at two levels. Firstly, there is the management culture within which plans are made, decisions taken and the work of the school organized. Secondly, there is the culture of the classroom – the climate of values and behaviour which so affects the capacity of pupils to learn successfully. There needs to be comparability between the two. One of the key purposes for management is creating the optimum conditions for human potential to be released. One of the most vital tasks for school leaders is to work at building and developing these two related cultures into a cohesive and interdependent climate of endeavour.

3

Classrooms and Schools

When people participate in organizational life, they are significantly affected by the dynamics they encounter and contribute to, and behave in ways designed to protect and advance appropriate self-interest. Some of the dynamics that arise in organizational settings can seriously impede and inhibit our capacity to be effective and to realize and utilize the full range of our skills and abilities. In successful organizations the impact of these dynamics is quite different – they activate and enhance personal effectiveness.

Just as in the organization of work in factories and offices, so in schools we have tended not to appreciate the powerful effect that organizational dynamics have on learners. Many of the causes of serious underachievement can be attributed to organizational factors rather than cognitive ones. These elements can inhibit the capacity of pupils to realize their potential for learning. Teachers too can find themselves deflected from the primary function of managing pupil learning by the pressures and demands of purely organizational issues.

In recent years, with an ever accelerating rate of change, there has been a concerted struggle to discover and define new organizational structures and to create a new deal for the individuals who participate in them. There is a new concern to replace many of the inherited organizational traditions that exploit the individual and diminish human dignity, with practices that are altogether more life-enhancing and more successful in bringing the best out of people.

From a traditional preoccupation with product, we are discovering the importance of attending also to process. In the new management paradigm, the key question becomes: how can we help people to be as effective as they are capable of being and to be as successful as they want to be? The following observations apply as much to classrooms as they do to schools.

ORGANIZATIONAL LIFE

When we enter an organization, we cease to be free agents, and subject ourselves to a range of contractual requirements and institutional obligations. We accept defined roles with boundaries that specify the functions we are expected to perform, and become part of an elaborate hierarchy of dependent relationships. This involves a considerable challenge to our powers of adjustment and accommodation, often requiring us to accept things we feel uncomfortable about or uncommitted to. What we often experience in organizations, whether as employee or pupil, is a severe challenge to our directional tendency as we encounter impediments to our hopes and aspirations, lack of interest in our needs and disregard for our anxieties and concerns.

A key function of those with senior responsibility in organizations is to manage the match between the needs and requirements of the institution with the needs and aspirations of each of its individual participants. Perhaps it is because this is so difficult that so little concern has been shown for it. But since organizational life is inevitably complex, difficult and frustrating, there is all the more reason to apply energy and imagination to its management. When serious mismatches occur we create dissonances and dysfunction, and the organization fails to optimize its available potential.

The struggle for match needs to be considered in relation to a set of key factors:

- purposes and intentions;
- values and attitudes;
- roles and relationships;
- practices and behaviours;
- power and authority.

Purposes and intentions

People tend to work best when they feel a strong sense of commitment to clearly defined purposes. A sense of ownership is sometimes used to describe a powerful association between individual and organizational goals. When organizational aims are defined by a minority of senior staff and imposed on the others as a requirement, then there is often a weak sense of association, and compliance rather than commitment is the likely outcome. Therefore, the deliberate management of intentions becomes a major management task requiring the active, if sometimes disputatious, involvement of all those who will be required to serve them. Because this process can be messy, involving the compromising of cherished ideals, it is often avoided. A poorer end product is traded for a quieter and more prescribed life.

Values and attitudes

While an individual teacher's work will be conditioned by the attitudes, beliefs and ideas that are brought to bear upon it, so the work of the school as a whole will be conditioned by the ways that individual value systems relate and interact with each other. Each participant in organizational life can be considered as having a personal value system consisting of:

- values: specified and prized opinions;
- attitudes: more or less settled modes of thinking;
- assumptions: taken-for-granted ideas and opinions;
- ideals: high personal concepts and visions;
- beliefs: ideas accepted as truths;
- prejudices: preconceived opinions.

This value system has a powerful effect. Not only does it determine how an individual thinks and feels, it affects behaviour particularly in relationships. New relationships are very much about testing out interpersonal value systems for similarities and differences. Clashes of values may inhibit the development of the relationship, while similarities of attitude may serve to extend or deepen it. The decision to end or continue an interaction will often be determined by the sense of comfort or discomfort that is experienced as the two value systems interact. Extended across a wider pattern of relationships in an organization, this process becomes complex and frequently confusing.

Roles and relationships

It is through the exercising of roles and the building of relationships that the management of an organization is done. In countless daily interactions, some exceedingly brief, decisions are made, ideas exchanged, possibilities explored, problems dealt with and concerns expressed. The extent to which we can successfully perform our roles and responsibilities will depend on how well we feel we can transact business with others, whether colleagues on the staff or pupils in the classroom. We prefer to engage with those colleagues with whom there is a high degree of commonality, and disengage from those whose values threaten us or cause discomfort and anxiety. When we are new to an organization we are prepared to negotiate and adjust as we strive to build effective working relationships, and to compromise values if necessary to maintain politeness and a comfortable interpersonal climate. In long-established situations in the staffroom or classroom, relationships are more likely to settle into a number of patterns:

- intimate and enjoyable relationships;
- diffident but polite relationships;
- strained and difficult relationships;
- hostile relationships.

In a large organization all these combinations are likely. These profiles will condition relationships and determine interpersonal behaviours at both the personal and the professional level.

Practices and behaviours

In organizations where work functions are complex, requiring some degree of personal autonomy about style and operation – learning and teaching would both fall within this category – issues of conformity and nonconformity sometimes arise. Where a particular house style of practice is developed by the participants themselves, then there is often a high degree of attention to methodology and technique. In professional organizations such as schools, styles and practices in teaching are often regarded as the concern of the individual, although the same is not true about learning. Approval or disapproval of practice by senior staff often depends on whether the practice is in tune with their preferred method. Far too often there is a conspiracy to avoid attention to practice, creating awkward tensions among colleagues who work in contrasting ways.

Power and authority

A major determinant of personal behaviour in organizations is the way that those placed in the upper levels of the organizational hierarchy behave to those placed lower down. In schools this applies to the relationships between senior staff and their colleagues and between teachers and pupils in classrooms. Research has demonstrated (Rowan 1988) that when people are over-controlled and over-supervised they feel mistrusted, and this produces a withholding of energy, enthusiasm and commitment to the task in hand. Hierarchies have been found to produce a range of inhibiting effects on those in the middle and lower levels:

- feelings of inadequacy;
- inability to express oneself;
- inability to influence anyone;
- feelings of being shut out;
- increase in cynicism;
- increase in destructive feelings;
- feeling that one has either to dominate or be dominated;
- feeling that to conform is the safest way forward;
- feeling that intolerance and exploitation has to be accepted;
- feeling that new ideas must only come from the top;
- feeling that those at the top are not interested in these feelings and that there are no easy ways of communicating with them.

John Rowan (1983) has suggested that in traditional triangular hierarchies those who occupy the top create a layer of control mechanisms to separate them from the very much larger lower layer. The hierarchical elite have to work hard to make sure that those who occupy the lower sections do not break through the control layer and overwhelm them. The appalling tradition of management–worker relationships we have inherited in this country makes the challenge of designing and operating more participative and democratic management systems very severe indeed.

In noting attempts to create alternatives to this inheritance, Charles Handy (1989) observes that clever organizations do not work in the same ways that organizations used to work. They have different shapes and different working habits. They have different age and gender profiles and are creating new assumptions about how power and authority can be exercised.

In the attempt to make sense of organizational life we need to be aware of the range of pressures that act together to define what we do and how we do it:

- prescriptions – what we must do;
- expectations – what we ought to do;
- situations – what we need to do here;
- predilections – what we want to do.

Prescriptions
These are requirements – things that are established by law and contract. In recent years legislation has significantly increased the prescriptions for both teachers and learners in schools. A great deal of energy is needed to manage the accountability of these requirements and demands.

Expectations
Although not backed by law, these forces are no less powerful in determining how we carry out our daily work. They derive from a variety of sources:

- the customs and traditions of the organization;
- the client community – pupils and parents;
- the institutional hierarchy – governors, senior staff, colleagues;
- vested interests – professional associations, pressure groups, OFSTED, partner schools;
- public opinion and the media.

Role behaviour is powerfully determined by expectations, since the pressures and influences that produce the *oughts* and *shoulds* derive directly from the environment in which we work. We want to please people, to satisfy their reasonable expectations of us and to experience approval for what we do. A great deal of pressure and stress is experienced both by teachers and pupils in striving to satisfy other peoples' demands, trust, hopes and expectations of us.

Situations
These are the immediate and momentary pressures arising out of day-to-day activity. They derive from the business of keeping the organization functioning, and are created in the constant round of interactions, incidents and events that characterize most days in school. Each day we find that we take on tasks and activities that we had not anticipated and for which we will not have budgeted time. These require us to operate almost continuously in the incidental and flexible mode described in Chapter 2. Situational pressures tend to interrupt planned work created by the prescriptions and expectations referred to above, often causing a crisis in workload and time management.

Predilections
These are the pressures created by our own ambitions and aspirations. Many of us experience an uncomfortable tension between the demands of the system – the prescriptions, expectations and situations – and our own ideals, values and visions. When there is insufficient space or time for our

own concerns and interests then commitment is compromised, self-confidence is damaged and working effectiveness is reduced.

Each of these four types of pressure is experienced in schools by both teachers and pupils. Effective management and leadership is concerned with creating a psychological climate in which these differing demands can be kept in balance and duly respected. When external demands increase, a vital function of leaders is to sustain commitment and attention to individual and collective predilections, thereby helping every member of the organization to value and honour their goals and commitments and keeping self-confidence and self-esteem buoyant.

Organizational life presents challenges both to individualism and to individuality. It is important to be clear about the distinction. Individualism is the tendency to promote individual concerns over the collective good. Individuality is the capacity to promote personal integrity within a collaborative setting.

Individualistic organizations are characterized by:

- professional isolation;
- little dialogue between colleagues about practice;
- lack of attention to professional change and development;
- wide variations in professional practice;
- habitual patterns of working alone;
- little attempt to build agreed and cohesive professional policies.

These characteristics are common in a wide variety of organizations and they also summarize the inherited tradition of classroom culture. We should not be surprised that life in organizations can promote such individualism, given the pressures and complexities that abound within them. Life in organizations, like life in families, is seldom plain sailing.

Individuality on the other hand is an important organizational ingredient. The skill of organizational management lies in harnessing individuality, idiosyncrasy and sometimes eccentricity to the common purpose. Effective teamwork is the successful blending of disparate forces and the creating of a vibrant sense of interdependence. A tight control of monolithic structures tends to reduce individuals to *company people* with a significant loss of flair, enterprise and commitment.

One of the difficulties of creating effective and successful organizations lies in the lack of preparation for collegiality and collaboration. In families, we have been controlled and supervised. In schools, we have been marshalled and directed within a framework of rules and requirements often reinforced by explicit disciplinary codes. By the time we enter organizational life as management partners we may well have lost whatever collaborative skills we might have developed, and find ourselves struggling through structures of direction, control and dependency. When eventually we reach senior positions we are confused by the ambiguities and complexities that make leadership such a tantalizing and frustrating activity. We are agents of our own high ideals and intentions, but also victims of our own socialization and experience.

INTERPERSONAL FACTORS

In order to conduct business in an organization it is necessary to work with and through others. This requires the creating of relationships which are exercised through interaction and transaction. We become part of a complex framework of dynamic relationships:

- one to one;
- groups, teams, units, cliques, departments, sections;
- individual to group;
- group to individual.

How well we conduct our day-to-day business very much depends on how interactions are managed and how we experience the behaviour of those we encounter.

In the process of observing others – listening to what they say and watching what they do – we can begin to sense the nature of their experience. But we all have the capacity to dissemble – to say and do things which are not congruent with what we are experiencing and feeling. This can lead to confusion, ambiguity, mixed messages and misunderstanding. To be more effective in our relationships we need to be aware of, and sensitive to, the complex nature of the interpersonal landscape between ourselves and others. It is important to note the range of interpersonal factors that combine to make us what we are and how we behave in different communication situations. Our uniqueness as individuals is contributed to by the combination of factors (see Figure 3.1) (Whitaker 1993b).

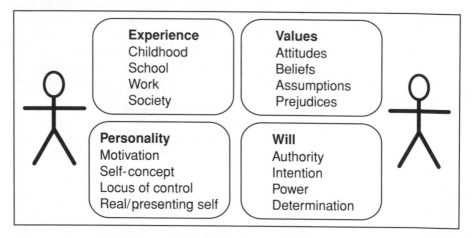

Figure 3.1 The interpersonal landscape.

Experience
We each bring to our professional lives a unique set of experiences from childhood, our life in schools, in our relationships, at work and as members of society. We have been formed and moulded by these experiences and how we have responded to them.

Values

Throughout our lives we have been developing attitudes, beliefs, assumptions and prejudices. While these are rarely rigidly fixed, some will be firmly held and will affect the decisions we make in our lives and the ways in which we communicate with those we meet.

Personality

In addition to experience and values, our personalities are affected by our unique pattern of motivation – needs and aspirations – and how we strive to satisfy them. The strength of our self-concept will depend on how successful we feel ourselves to be in meeting the challenges we face in our lives. Those of us with an 'internal' locus of control are more able to make for ourselves decisions affecting our lives, whereas those of us with an 'external' locus will constantly seek the approval or permission of others to determine our choices and decisions. A further important factor is the extent to which we present ourselves to the world as we really are – with our fears, frustrations, anxieties, insecurities, guilts and fantasies – or as we would prefer others to think we are.

Will

In the end our behaviour will depend on the ways in which our intentions are empowered into action and the extent to which we experience an inner authority to serve our needs and aspirations. Without will and determination we are unlikely to make an impact in the social and professional worlds where relationships and communication are so vital.

Building and developing relationships is a process of matching the elements of our own unique world with that of others. The greater the similarities, the greater the likelihood of an open and satisfying relationship. Most of the time our behaviour is purposeful, designed to meet needs and satisfy aspirations. In comfortable relationships where we feel a positive sense of connection to the interpersonal landscape we tend to strive for harmony between our inner world and our behaviour – we become more open and trusting to the other person.

In difficult and uncomfortable relationships we experience a sense of tension and dissonance in the interpersonal landscape. This can create feelings of anxiety which can result in behaviour designed to protect our inner world from attack and judgement – we become more closed and defensive.

Clearly, the process of communicating is immensely complex and there is a great deal to try to do in such a short time. We cannot plan every communication incident in advance since we do not know when the majority of them are likely to arise, or exactly how the other person will react and respond. But with those that we know we are going to initiate we can try and take some of these important factors into consideration as we prepare.

ORGANIZATIONAL CULTURES

The term *human resource management* was coined to help managers to appreciate and understand that organizations are essentially networks of human relationships, and that structures and systems need to be designed which optimize and enhance personal effectiveness. The extent to which leaders and managers are able to do this determines the nature of organizational life.

Two contrasting forms of organization culture can be considered: the synergetic organization and the entropic organization.

The synergetic organization is exciting to enter. There is an atmosphere of vitality and interest with a great deal of open listening and talking, lively debates and discussions. People feel trusted by their senior colleagues and are supported to experience a sense of achievement and influence in their daily work. There is a concern for quality and excellence with a constant eye to improvement in the future.

The entropic organization, on the other hand, is depressing to enter. There is an atmosphere of lethargy and apathy. There is a great deal of whinging and gossip about participants and particularly about senior staff. People feel disapproved of and tend to view suggestions for development as personal criticisms. While people feel frustrated and disillusioned with the state of affairs there is a grudging sense of inevitability about the *status quo*.

For participants, these different kinds of organization, whether they be a school or the classes within it, can create quite distinct experiences and produce quite different results.

These are not judgements of two different kinds of people but rather descriptions of two polarized positions. It is not uncommon for a participant from an entropic organization to thrive and flourish on taking up a post in a more synergetic organization and for enthusiastic and successful participants in a synergetic organization to find themselves dragged down and demoralized fairly soon into a new job in an entropic organization.

This analysis can also be applied to classrooms. As we have already seen from research into pupil behaviour in classrooms, some pupils can thrive in one type of·classroom culture and significantly underachieve in another.

The important point is that both these extreme examples of organizational culture are creations of human activity. Both are built and developed by people with clear intentions and high ideals. What differs is the way they go about achieving them. How we lead and manage in organizations determines whether we create conditions which enable partners to be at their best, to express their enthusiasm and interests, to practise individuality, to take risks with new ideas and possibilities or establish situations which cause colleagues to suppress their vitality and skill and conceal their potential for success and achievement.

In circumstances of fast change and development, organizational culture can come under severe pressure. In their study of the ways that different organizations respond to pressures exerted by the external environment, Miles and Snow (1978) generated three distinct types of behaviour:

- *Defender* organizations that strive for stability by discouraging competition.
- *Analyser* organizations that are alert to new possibilities but only if viability can be established.
- *Prospector* organizations that respond well to turbulence and uncertainty, striving to find new opportunities by sustaining an innovation edge.

These descriptions can also be applied to managing in schools and classrooms. Defender management is about clinging on to what has always been known and avoiding situations which require new ideas, skills or competencies. Defender cultures are characterized by a determination to sustain the *status quo* and pursue a 'business as usual' strategy. Analyser management accepts that some new knowledge and skill may be necessary but only if there is no alternative. Prospector management begins with the assumption that progress into the future can only be sustained on the basis of continuous, systematic development. Prospector cultures strive for an innovative edge in the changing environment, recognizing the importance of flexibility and adaptability. It is this approach which is at the heart of the synergetic organization.

An interesting and practically useful analysis of culture and change is provided by Murgatroyd (1988), who draws parallels between the dynamics of families and the culture of organizations.

He points to four styles of relationships as being especially significant in forming a cultural identity:

1 Enmeshed – in which the participants think and behave as one unit.
2 Connected – in which there is a strong sense of connectedness between participants, a respect for individuals and a high capacity for flexibility and adaptation to change.
3 Separated – in which self-interest takes precedence over the group, creating inevitable power struggles. Any change needs to be legitimized separately by each individual.
4 Disengaged – in which the organization becomes a production economy of independent participants and there are few personal or social ties.

This analysis provides a useful framework with which to consider classrooms and the extent to which relationships tend towards either separation or integration.

Murgatroyd also offers four descriptions of the capacity of an organization to change:

1 Chaotic – in which the organization responds to change in an unstructured and fruitless way.
2 Flexible – in which the organization responds in a considered way with imaginativeness and flexibility as events unfold.
3 Standard – in which the organization responds with a routine procedure and is reluctant to use new or risky strategies.
4 Rigid – in which the organization responds in a fixed way – usually 'No!'.

It is interesting to consider what would happen, for example, in an enmeshed culture with a rigid response to change. Trade union disputes of the 1970s give some insight into the difficult management challenges created when group cohesion and solidarity is combined with a single agreed response to offers and proposals. A separated culture with chaotic responses to change could be a rock band where individual aspirations become more important than the future welfare and success of the group and where the individuals cannot agree how to adapt their musical offering to changing tastes and fashions. On the more positive side it is significant to note how often failing or struggling organizations such as theatre companies or football teams can survive when, under new management, they develop a strong sense of collaboration and connectedness and a flexible strategy to the changing environment in which they operate.

The implications for managing in schools and classrooms is clear. If we want to create synergetic learning cultures that enhance and optimize pupils' potential to learn, develop and grow, then a great deal of understanding, skill and energy needs to be devoted to the task of culture building. Edgar Schein (1985) has observed: 'the only thing of real importance that leaders do is create and manage culture . . . the unique talent of leaders is their ability to work with culture'.

A vital factor in this process is determining the relationship of trust to control. Handy (1976) suggests that for people to feel trusted, the controls exercised over them must not be experienced as invasive of appropriate autonomy and self-direction. In schools, trust must be seen as an experience of the pupil, not an assertion of the teacher. Trust can only be said to exist if people feel trusted by those in authority over them and able to extend their own trust.

Handy (1976) has also developed the notion of the motivation calculus to emphasize the importance of acknowledging individual choice and decision-making in organizations (see Figure 3.2). The E factors represent the amount of energy, effort, excitement and expenditure an individual decides to invest in any activity. The motivation calculus is the mechanism by which we decide how much E to invest.

This concept highlights a number of key elements that need to figure in management behaviour at the interpersonal level, and in the development of a school and classroom culture supportive of human potential, endeavour and achievement:

1   The work that we do needs to respond to deep needs for satisfaction within ourselves.
2   The work that we do needs to provide opportunities to satisfy aspirations and achieve results.
3   Energy, effort, excitement and expenditure are decisions of individuals, not the inputs of managers or leaders.

Managers are in the business of helping to satisfy needs, and this demands a sensitive attention to the thoughts and feelings of the people involved. Effective managers are those who have a capacity to sense a pattern of needs in those they work with and to adapt their working style

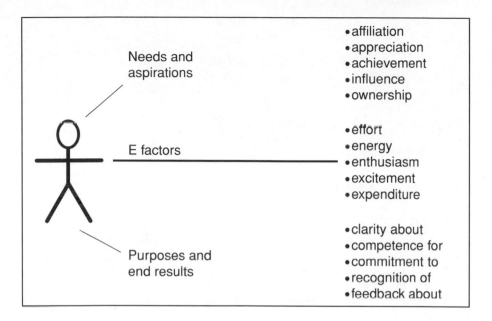

Figure 3.2 The motivation calculus.

accordingly. Motivation is a key consideration in management and it is useful to be aware of three components:

1   The needs to be satisfied.
2   The aspirations to be achieved.
3   Self-esteem.

In managing, treating all people the same is a recipe for difficulty and disappointment. The guiding principle should be to treat people appropriately, according to their perceived needs and aspirations and with a sensitivity to their self-esteem.

There are challenging times ahead as we begin to focus on the important but intricate issues of management and culture in schools, and as we develop the skills of harnessing the enormous potential that pupils bring with them to their learning.

4

Aspects of Learning: A–Z

This chapter contains a range of items about various aspects of the learning process. They represent many of the ideas I have encountered in my work with pupils and teachers over the past twenty-five years or so. Most of the entries are concerned with practice – how various aspects of learning can be managed in the classroom. They are not intended to constitute a separate and alternative curriculum, but rather to be incorporated, as appropriate, into the practices and methodologies teachers use in all phases of learning and in any subject area. Many teachers will recognize aspects of their own approach and many of the ideas presented have been in use for many years.

I hope readers will find the selection both interesting and stimulating. It offers an agenda for consideration, and practical possibilities for development. The selection reflects my own particular professional journey in education and is not intended to be comprehensive.

Since the selection defies an easy thematic classification it has been arranged in alphabetical order. I have avoided a complicated cross-referencing structure, preferring to leave the reader free to make connections and pursue specific lines of enquiry. A complete list of the entries is included in the index.

ACCOUNTABILITY

Accountability, the process of accounting for what we do and how we exercise our responsibilities, is very much to the fore in our lives at the moment, particularly in work situations where the relationship between rights and responsibilities is most tested. Essentially, it involves the creation of a relationship of trust between individuals and groups of people, where the nature of the trust is explicitly stated and agreed. In the classroom it is desirable to develop a climate of mutual accountability between teacher and learner. This can help to establish an appropriate structure for learning and teaching and involves:

- negotiating agreements;
- making explicit statements of learning aims and purposes;
- working within agreed structures and boundaries;

- working to timetables and meeting deadlines;
- providing appropriate accounts of work done and results achieved.

This style of mutual accountability involves a dynamic interplay between teacher and learner:

The teacher – defines requirements, resources, time available and support;

The learner – expresses specific needs, particular interests and individual hopes;

Together they – agree the terms of reference for a piece of work, a programme of study, a curriculum assignment or a learning task.

Learners are more able to exercise accountability, effectively when the teacher has helped them to:

- define precise learning purposes for each piece of work undertaken;
- create a clear vision of what the tangible end results of the piece of work will look like and the specifications that have been agreed;
- determine the discrete activities that will be needed to complete the work;
- produce a plan of the sequence of these activities;
- review the outcomes when the work is completed.

What often happens on the completion of a piece of work is that the teacher assesses and makes judgements about the work. This can discourage accountability, inhibit self-responsibility and reinforce dependence on the teacher. Learners are more likely to develop self-discipline, reliance and a real sense of responsibility if the teacher engages in a mutual examination of completed work, where the precise agreements between the teacher and the learner become an essential part of the evaluative process.

Pupil profiling and records of achievement are an important ingredient in this process of mutual accountability, although they are very much the summative part of it. Effective accountability is built, exercised and developed through the daily interactions of classroom life.

ACTUALIZING TENDENCY

There is within us all a basic capacity to strive for fulfilment. As human beings we share this powerful feature with other species. Unlike most other species, however, we have a unique ability to damage and inhibit this powerful force in ourselves. While daffodils do not seem to have difficulty being successful daffodils, or cats being fully functioning cats, most of us do seem to experience the most extraordinary problems being people. Perhaps it is the long journey to adulthood that is the problem. The extended dependence of children on adults creates for us from our earliest years a seemingly endless series of conflicts which challenge individuality and authenticity in the struggle to make ourselves acceptable in the eyes of others. Although parental love is searing in its intensity it is often conditional. We have been led to believe that our success as parents and as teachers depends upon moulding our children into acceptable forms.

Carl Rogers (1980) has defined the actualizing tendency: 'In every organism there is an underlying flow of movement towards constructive fulfilment of its inherent possibilities.'

The learning process is about attuning to this flow and channelling it in appropriate directions. Our work as teachers is perhaps more than anything else a striving to ignite the actualizing tendency in all the pupils we work with. For many of us this will involve a radical reconstruction of the assumptions upon which our present approach to learning is built. It means never accepting the apparent limitations of a learner's abilities, but of striving to unlock the barriers to learning that previous experience has helped to create, and discovering the unique and individual combination of approaches and experiences that will lead learners to success.

AFFIRMATION

This is the process of positively communicating to others those aspects about them which please and satisfy us.

Effective learning is more dependent on learners feeling good about themselves and their innate capacity to learn than we have traditionally assumed. For the teacher this means getting below the ritual shallowness of traditional reward systems. For the learner it means increasing their capacity to disclose feelings and talk through learning experiences with both teachers and their friends.

It is through experiences of affirming and being affirmed that we become more aware of our personal power, our capacity to affect and contribute to the personal growth of others as well as ourselves.

If we think back to our own schooling we can probably recall failures, discouragements and put-downs. Perhaps knowingly or unknowingly we continue to carry mental and emotional scars of these experiences, with the result that we inhibit our own capacity for growth, learning and development. Affirmation is crucial to successful learning. If we are to learn successfully we need to know that our efforts are appreciated by others and are worthy of being appreciated by ourselves.

Being an affirming teacher involves being open and honestly appreciative of those qualities in learners that we value and want them to value for themselves. Its chief purpose is to create in each learner a feeling of being valued for who they are, as well as for what they do. Affirmation has many positive benefits:

- it helps to clarify and reinforce our strengths;
- it deepens relationships;
- it increases awareness of our growth;
- it compensates for the negative messages that we accumulate in our daily lives;
- it creates the possibility of celebrating our lives and achievements;

- it encourages us to work hard at those aspects of our learning we wish to succeed at;
- it strengthens and releases creative energy for learning;
- it helps to develop that necessary belief in ourselves.

It is important to make a distinction between affirmation and praise. Praise is often directed to end results and successful outcomes; affirmation needs to be directed to the skills and qualities that bring about these achievements.

AGGRESSION

Most of us display forceful and attacking behaviour towards other people from time to time but, unless we have been extremely fortunate in our childhood, we will have had little opportunity to understand our aggressive tendencies and the pattern of painful emotions that accompany them. Anger and aggression tend to be disapproved of in our upbringing and after a certain age positively discouraged. We quickly learn to suppress both the behaviour and the complex and confusing emotions that accompany it. Suppression of these natural and normal feelings can be deeply damaging to our psychological well-being and is likely to contribute to difficulties in effective learning.

Emotional education seeks to provide opportunities for learners to increase awareness of their behaviours and to understand the pattern of feelings and emotions that are related to them. With young children we can support this process by helping them to concentrate on the felt experience rather than the behaviour itself. When we encounter aggressive behaviour it is useful to:

- create an opportunity to talk with the learner about the behaviour;
- encourage the learner to talk about the incident;
- listen with full attention;
- accept and acknowledge the feelings as natural in the circumstances;
- identify the feelings and give them a name;
- listen and reflect while the problem is explored and a resolution found.

One of the difficulties with repressing these hurt and negative feelings is the danger of coming to believe that only 'I' experience them, and others do not. This further reinforces a sense of unworthiness and inadequacy. There is much we can do to help learners remove this sense of inner isolation. Helping them to share emotional experiences provides the realization that being aggressive and feeling angry are common and regular features of most people's lives.

One of the important purposes for personal and social education as a dimension of all learning is to help pupils more creatively to articulate and explain the aggressive and angry feelings that will be experienced during the normal course of school life. Failing to acknowledge the sometimes deep and complex feelings that are aroused during learning is to risk jeopardizing the learning itself.

ANGER

We live in a society where one of the most natural emotions we can experience – anger – is dealt with in the most unimaginative and unhealthy ways. Displaying anger has come to be associated with weakness of character, and displays of it are regarded as a sign of immaturity. This means that there are few appropriate avenues for its expression available to us. Thus in situations where anger is not recognized as a natural part of personal experience, it is likely that the emotions and feelings which give rise to the anger will be ignored by others and not dealt with by the individual.

In his exploration of anger, Theodore Rubin (1969) writes:

> Too often anger is not seen as basic or human. Anger is easily the
> most maligned and perverted of feelings and responses. Although
> there is an enormous range of 'angry problems' nearly all people
> have some difficulty handling anger. The price paid for the distortion
> of a basic emotion is incalculable. Poor mental health, poor physical
> health, damage to relationships – especially to parent: child
> relationships – and even that most malignant of human diseases –
> war – are the wages of distorted anger.

Clearly it behoves us as educators to develop more creative approaches to the management of anger as a normal part of healthy learning and growth.

We are often angry with ourselves because we have let ourselves down in the presence of others, and have created the possibility of others reinforcing a perceived belief in our own inadequacies. This adds to a general feeling frequently developed in childhood and schooling that we are not good enough, and that we fall short of the expectations of significant others in our lives and society in general.

As teachers, we need to help build a new understanding of the way that suppressed anger can seriously impair the capacity to learn and inhibit the actualizing tendency within each of us. If we can recognize that anger is a perfectly natural response to the inner experiencing of our lives, we are more likely to be sensitive to its occurrence in the learners we work with.

Developing a skilful capacity to respond creatively and with sensitivity to feelings of anger, resentment and outrage in learners is a vital quality in effective teachers. Positive and sensitive responding involves:

- accepting that feelings of anger and their associated behaviours are a natural part of normal development and growth;
- conveying to the learner this acceptance by acknowledging the presence of anger and avoiding body language and facial expressions which might convey disapproval;
- inviting and encouraging the learner to articulate the experience by disclosing the emotions and feelings involved;
- reflecting these expressions and insights back to the learner;
- helping the learner to own and take responsibility for the anger and its associated behaviour;

- helping the learner to identify the specific trigger points of the anger and to explore possible solutions to the difficulties involved.

ANXIETY

Feeling uneasy and concerned is a universal phenomenon in human experience and can serve to prevent us from running headlong into danger. It can also inhibit us from responding to opportunities and taking our chances in life. Over-anxiety can become a distressingly debilitating behaviour. When not dealt with creatively it has the capacity to inhibit and sometimes substantially reduce our abilities to operate successfully. Often linked to painful experiences in the past, it works by anticipating difficulties, frustrations and embarrassments in future activities.

The recognition of anxiety is of particular concern in the learning process which is about a continuous process of change, a constant moving from the known to the unknown. Successful learning involves taking risks and trying things out, and it is this vital aspect of learning that can be seriously damaged if learners are not helped to accept and handle their anxieties creatively and confidently.

Part of being a good teacher is anticipating the likely causes and starting points for anxiety, and then helping learners to increase their awareness of worry and concern. Typical situations which can create anxiety are:

- learning tasks which are not well matched to the abilities of the learner;
- teaching which is inadequately or inappropriately presented;
- tasks which are vague in terms of purpose and aim;
- tasks or experiences which do not allow sufficient time for the learner to reach the task objectives.

Taking anxiety into account is a vital part of building effective working relationships with learners. Teachers can provide positive and sensitive support by being alert to the signs of anxiety – for example, body language which suggests worry, difficulty and frustration, and by developing a sensitive capacity to accept anxiety as a natural and essential part of the learning process.

The reflective and experiential learning approach sets out to acknowledge this aspect of development. The learning cycle described earlier is designed to create opportunities for learners to identify and work through their worries and concerns. Each learner will display an individual and separate pattern of anxiety behaviour and the teacher will need to become familiar with it. Good teaching is not about pandering to anxiety, but making decisions about the right balance between challenge and support in the design and facilitation of learning.

APPRAISAL

Appraisal is now part of the professional environment. The introduction of appraisal into the education service has been greeted with some suspicion because it has been seen as a system of judging the worth of an individual teacher's performance. This is very unfortunate and unnecessary, because appraisal has the potential to be a highly powerful aid to personal and professional development. It is also important to realize that appraisal is something we have always done. We are forever appraising situations, working out costs and benefits, estimating risk and identifying more effective ways forward. For most of us, appraisal has served as a largely unstructured reflection on our experience, and an important means of learning from and through those experiences.

If a structured process of appraisal is an aid to professional development and the learning of teachers, it is important to ask how it can be utilized in the service of learner development. It is just as important for pupils to submit to systematic review aspects of their learning as it is for their teachers. A useful technique of carrying out a personal appraisal is to use a form specially prepared for the purpose (see Figure 4.1). Using a process such as this involves the learner in listing those features of a specific piece of learning which are felt to be successful and going well, and then to list difficulties and frustrations. The next stage is to take each of the points and to identify strategies for the future – things that have worked well can be repeated and refined, things which have proved difficult need alternative strategies or perhaps can be eliminated altogether. At this stage, working in peer partnerships or critical friendships increases the value of appraisal as a means of development and growth. Such a process can bring more precision and insight to profiling and records of achievement.

Parts of my learning which are going well:	Ways I can continue and build on these successes:
Parts of my learning I am finding difficult:	Ways I can overcome these difficulties and frustrations:

Figure 4.1 Appraisal review sheet.

Just as teachers work in appraisal partnerships to explore experience and make plans for the future, so too should pupils, learning to support each other in the complex business of learning and developing. In such appraisal partnerships it is possible to create a safe, supporting yet challenging climate in which each partner in turn can experience an enhanced capacity to examine and explore aspects of their learning life. In particular such a process can help learners to:

- reflect on and describe their learning experience;
- gain insights and understandings;
- develop ideas and concepts;
- examine attitudes, values and beliefs;
- review previous targets;
- assess outcomes and results;
- identify successes and achievements;
- confront difficulties and challenges;
- recognize areas for development;
- make plans for change.

In an educational culture which has traditionally placed so much emphasis on pupils competing with each other, it is not easy to envisage the implications of pupils collaborating with each other in the pursuit of their learning aims and aspirations. Adapting the essence of the appraisal process for use within the classroom would help to build a more enhancing and collaborative culture, and enable pupils to learn more deliberately from their experience.

ASSERTIVENESS

In our work with learners it is very important to provide opportunities for them to develop behaviours which are effective in situations of potential conflict. Assertiveness is interpersonal behaviour which enables us to maintain self-respect, satisfy our needs and defend our rights without either being aggressive or submissive.

A great many of the interpersonal conflicts we meet in our lives arise because as individuals we have not acquired appropriate behaviours to cope with them. Conflicts occur in a variety of situations, ranging from the need to make a complaint to that of trying to settle a serious dispute at home. Conflict also seems to be an increasing feature of school life, with interpersonal tension seriously hindering the capacity to learn effectively.

In conflict situations we have a tendency to incline to one of two behaviour styles. If we are submissive we retreat from honestly expressing our feelings, needs and concerns and allow other people to deny our rights and ignore our needs. If we are aggressive we express our feelings, needs and concerns at the expense of other people by speaking loudly, by being rude, abusive or sarcastic, and sometimes by resorting to physical aggression.

Assertive behaviour avoids both of these unhelpful approaches to conflict situations. It allows us to express our opinions, ideas, needs and concerns clearly without hostility or apology, standing firmly but sensitively for what we believe in. The key elements of the assertive stance are (Whitaker 1993b):

1 Listen to the other person with full attention and respect.
2 Summarize what you have understood the other person to have said.
3 Explain how you feel about what they have said – a disclosing statement about your feelings.
4 Listen to the other person's response to what you have said. Often your disclosure will have had a strong effect on them and they will moderate the way they are communicating, often apologizing for upsetting you.
5 Repeat the attentive listening, continue summarizing and explaining how the other person's message or point of view is affecting you.
6 Offer a suggestion that might help the other person to achieve some of their own aims while serving your own needs.

Effective behaviour is never that simple however, and dealing with conflict by formula is not to be recommended. What is essential, if we are to avoid falling into either the aggressive or submissive trap, is to develop a capacity to own and express our feelings in conflict situations. Doing this and responding empathetically to the other person is more likely to reduce tension and create the possibility of a peaceful resolution.

The capacity to disclose feelings is fairly natural in young children, but it tends to have diminished by adulthood, particularly in males. The schooling process needs to nurture this natural capacity, rather than to subdue it, and this means that the feelings dimension of learners' lives must be regarded as equally important as their thoughts and ideas. Our work in classrooms needs to provide opportunities to develop assertiveness and to help learners to use it with skill and understanding.

ASSUMPTIONS

In our attempt to construct reality in a world overloaded with phenomena of every description, we tend to incorporate ideas and beliefs on insubstantial information. We can assume that something is so on the basis of personal perception, and fail to take account of other perceptions which add to the shared reality of which our own views are only part.

A radical critique of the education system must take account of commonly held assumptions about schooling and the learner's role within it. Few would argue with the notion that schools are there to prepare learners for life, but what is in contention is the way that such preparation is conducted. Children learn very quickly in their school career that hard work and good marks are the first indispensable step on the road to success. A. S. Neill (1968) has suggested that schooling is based on the assumption that a child will not grow and develop unless forced to do so, and that those good habits which have not been forced into us in childhood will not develop later on.

Carl Rogers (1983) has suggested some other assumptions implicit in our educational system:

- Learners cannot be trusted to learn.
- An ability to pass examinations is the best criterion for selection and judging potential.
- What a teacher teaches is what a pupil learns.
- Knowledge is the steady accumulation of facts and information.
- An academic procedure, e.g. the scientific method is more important than the idea it is intended to investigate.
- Pupils are best regarded as manipulative objects, not as persons.

A useful insight into the power of assumptions was provided by Douglas McGregor (1960) who highlighted the powerful effect that assumptions about personhood can have on work and motivation. He posed two contrasting sets of assumptions about people in organizations, referred to as Theory X and Theory Y. In relation to learning in schools his theory can be summarized as:

Theory X
People dislike work and try to avoid it. They have to be bribed, coerced and controlled and even threatened with punishment to perform adequately. Most people lack ambition, prefer to be led and wish to avoid responsibility. By nature people are resistant to change.

Theory Y
People do like work and don't have to be forced or threatened. If allowed to pursue objectives to which they are committed, most people will work hard and not only accept responsibility but actively seek it. People have a natural ability to change and adapt.

Teachers proceeding from a Theory X position will tend to build structures and systems designed to:

- direct the efforts of pupils;
- control their actions;
- modify their behaviour to fit teaching requirements.

They will also adopt interpersonal behaviour towards pupils that is characterized by:

- persuasion;
- reward or punishment;
- instruction and command.

Teachers who espouse Theory Y assumptions will tend to build structures and systems designed to:

- make it possible for learners to develop;
- seek responsibility;
- take risks;
- set ambitious targets and challenges for their own learning.

For many of us, past experience in families, schools and the workplace has been, unless we are exceptionally lucky, predominantly of the Theory X kind. As a result of this, part of our career path into teaching may be motivated by a desire to avoid the controlling forces of Theory X being exerted on us, and perhaps also to be among a smaller group in society who hold power to control others. An important element in the development of teachers is a capacity to develop an awareness of the way that Theory X experiences have affected us and formed our behavioural tendencies. For many, the greatest challenge is balancing an intellectual commitment to Theory Y with an experience that has conditioned us in the dynamics of Theory X.

ATTITUDES

Attitudes are combinations of concepts, information and emotions that result in a predisposition to respond favourably or unfavourably towards particular people, groups, ideas, events or objects.

They are referred to a great deal in the literature of the curriculum, particularly in the guidelines of some subjects. There is often a lack of clarity about what attitudes really are and how they feature in the growth process. When the subject matter of learning involves the exploration and examination of human issues and concerns it is especially necessary to be clear about how attitudes relate to the subject matter being taught.

We use attitudes to help structure our view of reality, and they often serve as temporary props during particular stages or phases of growth and learning. In helping learners to form and develop their attitudes and to utilize them in their thinking, we need to take account of three particular factors:

- attitudes are learnt through formal and informal interaction;
- all attitudes are continually open to modification and change according to experience;
- acquisition and modification of attitudes originate in human interaction, both passive and active.

This suggests that if the schooling process is to succeed in helping pupils to form and develop their attitudes, then our work in classrooms needs to create opportunities for pupils to engage in more profound interactions – for example, through group work, drama and role play.

Two particular types of attitudinal behaviour which arise when issues and concerns are the subject matter of classroom learning are prejudice and stereotyping:

Prejudice: an attitude which has a particularly heavy emotional loading favourable or hostile to people, groups, ideas, events or objects.

Stereotyping: attitudinal behaviour which results when generalizations are drawn from limited evidence or experience.

Learners need to be helped to develop awareness of these particular attitudinal positions. In helping them to do this we should take account of:

1   Balance: the balance of thinking to feeling in a particular attitude.
2   Needs: the relationship of an attitude to an individual's motivation
      structure.

In an attempt to encourage clarity in our work on attitudes we sometimes place too much emphasis on logical reasoning and fail to give adequate consideration to feelings. A balanced attitude has both rational and intuitive elements in it. Some further definitions will help emphasize this:

> An attitude is a mental state of readiness, organized through experience, exerting an influence on your response to situations with which it is related.
> An attitude is an organized and consistent manner of thinking, feeling and reacting to people, groups, situations or events.
> An attitude is what I know or believe, plus how I feel, plus what I am inclined to do about it.

In our management of the learning process we need to create opportunities for pupils to engage in learning activities which allow for the dynamic process of attitude acquisition and modification. Many of the experiential techniques referred to in these pages are particularly effective for this.

Attention to attitudes is at the very heart of the reflective and experiential learning process. Reflection involves the exploration of attitudes in the light of experience. Personal and professional change becomes possible when we are prepared to modify and develop attitudes to allow for new behaviours.

One of the key roles of an educator is to help learners develop a skilful capacity for critical self-examination. In the reflection stage of the experiential cycle it is useful to provide opportunities for working in pairs and structuring critical friendships.

AWARENESS

Awareness is the process of getting in touch with our own behaviour and experiences in order to learn more about ourselves and how we function in various situations.

Education in terms of the schooling process is often regarded as a preparation for life. It is argued that certain specified learning experiences are a necessary precondition for successful living after a period of statutory education. There is good sense in this, but so strong has the notion of education as training become that little or no attention is given to the life force of the learners who are subject to the training. We need to recognize that learning and living are largely inseparable. Learning is not a preparation for life, it is life, and, as teachers, we should be concerned to make it a process in which the lives of the learners are enriched and invigorated.

A useful way of assisting this process of enrichment is to devote specific time in our work with learners to cultivate awareness. There are three aspects of awareness that concern us:

1   Awareness of the outer world – actual sensory contact with objects

and events in the present through what we see, hear, smell, touch and taste.
2   Awareness of the inner world – actual sensory contact with inner events in the present through what we feel both physically and emotionally.
3   Awareness of fantasy activity – all mental activity beyond present awareness and experience.

The first two kinds of awareness encompass all that we can know about our present reality as we experience it, here and now in the present moment of our lives. The third kind incorporates such internal activity as imagining, interpreting, guessing, thinking, comparing, remembering and anticipating.

If, as Paulo Freire (1972) suggests, we should relate formal learning to the life force of each individual, we need to find ways of doing this in the classroom. Cultivating awareness involves pausing at key moments during a lesson and inviting learners to focus inwards on their experiencing of the activity, clarifying the intellectual and emotional processes at work. This provides an opportunity to identify how well we are managing the activity, what sorts of questions it raises, the feelings evoked, the attitudes and values involved and our relationship to the learning in terms of motivation and achievement. Brief interactions in pairs or small groups can help learners clarify their thoughts and feelings and check out with others how they are dealing with the issues.

BEHAVIOUR

In the context of schooling, behaviour is a term we tend to use to refer to the extent to which learners conform to or deviate from accepted social and institutional norms.

The history and traditions of schooling have inclined us to a view of learner behaviour which devolves around control. Teacher management of learners frequently focuses on classroom control and dealing with pupils who are difficult and disruptive. It is only very recently in the history of education that there has been any attempt to consider behaviour from the learner's point of view. The development of a pastoral dimension, the provision of counselling services in some secondary schools and the emergence of personal and social education mark a shift in thinking from behaviour as an issue of control to behaviour as an expression of need.

We urgently require a new set of assumptions about learner behaviour if the liberation of the learning process from its repressive traditions is to be successful. The following propositions are offered as part of this debate:

* Behaviour is purposeful. It is an outer expression of an inner need.
* Behaviour tends to be consistent with inner experience.
* Behavioural difficulties in classrooms, as elsewhere, can usually be traced to difficulties in human relationships.
* Learners are social beings who can only be understood holistically and in relation to the group to which they are striving to belong.

- The need to feel a sense of belonging to social groups and organizations is a major human need and motivator.
- Through relationships and interactions, pupils strive to satisfy their need for a sense of belonging.
- If this sense of belonging is satisfied then behaviour will tend to be constructive; otherwise it will deviate from acceptable norms.
- Feelings of inadequacy, discouragement, alienation and a fear of rejection are major causes of learning failure and deviant behaviour.

We need to be aware and sensitive to these powerful motivational forces. If pupils' attempts to gain attention, to feel acknowledged and to achieve a sense of belonging are not met successfully, then they will tend to try out behaviours which extend beyond the threshold of acceptability – either by withdrawal and retreat or by aggressive and disruptive activities. In both cases the behaviours are purposeful – to avoid the pain of being discounted, disapproved of and alienated.

It is with the experience of being a learner that teachers need to be concerned. The pains and struggles of living and being are very much on the agenda of the learning process. We must seek to balance an attention to the outward journey in learners' lives with a concern to help them come to terms with and understand their inner journeys too.

Although behaviour is for the most part intentional, it is rarely purposeless. Most acts of behaviour are designed to serve inner needs – either to protect us from physical, emotional or psychological danger or to advance specific drives, hopes or aspirations.

It is in childhood that we develop the skills of dissembling – behaving against our own best judgements. As we find that our instinctive behaviour does not meet with adult approval and acceptance we have to modify it to get what we want, and to do this we have to modify our behaviour to give them what they want from us. Adult love of children is frequently conditional – *I will love you if you behave as I want you to be.* This is often disguised by adults through the message: *I am doing this for your own good.*

For children, this process is both confusing and disorienting. As children, we are led to believe that if we find this process difficult then there must be something wrong with us, so we further complicate matters by keeping these dark secrets and pretending that we are all right.

R.D. Laing (1967) has noted the important distinction between behaviour and experience (see Figure 4.2). This distinction is at the heart of the very complex process of managing pupil behaviour in classrooms. Part of the enormous challenge for teachers is appreciating the difference between what learners experience and how they behave, and helping them to understand this important relationship for themselves.

BELIEFS

Beliefs are ideas we want to put our trust in, and as such are that part of our understanding we accept as true.

A key purpose for personal learning is to awaken learners to the world of beliefs. Developing a sturdy but flexible set of beliefs is a natural part

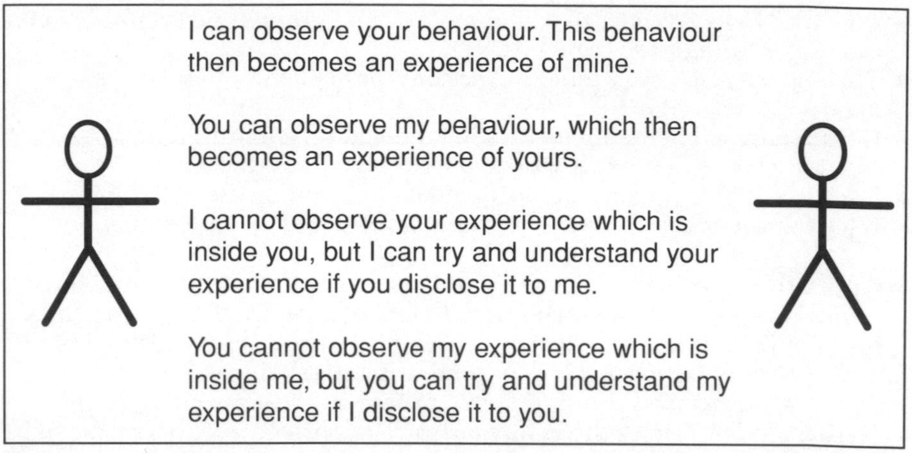

I can observe your behaviour. This behaviour then becomes an experience of mine.

You can observe my behaviour, which then becomes an experience of yours.

I cannot observe your experience which is inside you, but I can try and understand your experience if you disclose it to me.

You cannot observe my experience which is inside me, but you can try and understand my experience if I disclose it to you.

Figure 4.2 Behaviour and experience.

of human experience and development. Beliefs form a vital part of our intellectual and moral framework for understanding the world and our experience of it.

The role of the teacher in assisting this process is one of creating opportunities for beliefs to be considered, grappled with and submitted to critical analysis and review. In our work with learners we need to support the development and adoption of beliefs by creating a climate that supports this process. Firstly, we need to accept and encourage a respect for diversity and a recognition that beliefs are personal and individual frameworks for understanding and living in the world. It is useful to help learners appreciate the differences between cultural beliefs (those that form part of religious and cultural traditions) and personal beliefs (those that develop as part of our individual attempts to construct reality against some system of explanations and understandings).

It is in this area of personal beliefs that learners will experience struggle. The belief system of the home and school are often in conflict, presenting complex dilemmas and issues of loyalty. The tension between the adult belief system and the pupil belief system can impose stresses and strains on both teachers and pupils. There are no easy routes to reconciliation. As in the wider world, it needs a deep capacity to accept diversity, to understand and appreciate differences and similarities and a sensitivity to the inevitable struggles that are created in this complex area.

Beliefs develop as we extract meaning from our own experience and place it in relation to other and sometimes older wisdoms and understandings. Learners need opportunities to authenticate their thinking, to explain their understanding and to grapple with meaning.

Attention to beliefs can accompany work in the whole area of attitudes and values and will feature particularly in work carried out in religious education, personal and social education and the humanities, but the whole area of beliefs will impinge on most areas of the curriculum.

BILINGUALISM

As a society becomes more diverse, so an increasing number of teachers will be faced with the challenging issue of bilingualism. Essentially this involves the recognition that in any group of learners the language of transaction may not be the first language of all the learners taking part, and for a few it may be their third or fourth language. Indeed, the truly global learner has the capacity to operate at some level in many languages and the capacity to operate in more than one language is an indication of the potential of human aspiration and capability.

This does not mean that teachers should be multilingual, but that certain fundamental considerations need to be present in creating an effective learning environment:

1   An assumption that languages other than that of the formal transactions are present in the learner group.
2   That there is no hierarchy of languages. All are equal.
3   The central importance of the learner's first language – the language of home and family.
4   The need to create among all learners a respect for language in general and for all languages in particular.
5   The interdependence of languages and how they grow and develop through interaction with others.
6   The vital relationship of language to culture in describing and sustaining cultural history and traditions.
7   The need to celebrate and honour all languages.

In practical terms teachers need to be aware of the language profiles of the learners they work with, to affirm the bilingual and multilingual abilities of learners, and seek to use linguistic diversity as a rich resource in the classroom.

Language is developed through transaction, and in the multilingual classroom there need to be numerous opportunities for interpersonal dialogue between pupils for the language skills to be developed.

BRAIN

One of the problems with established patterns of education, and particularly with didactic and instructional methods of teaching, is the understanding of the way the brain works. During the past ten years or so research has discovered that the brain is infinitely more complex than we had ever assumed. One of the key discoveries is that we have two upper brains rather than one and that they operate in different ways and with different purposes (see Figure 4.3).

Traditional teaching methods have placed an almost obsessive emphasis on those functions that are located in the left hemisphere of the brain – giving great attention to the memorizing of facts, the search for single correct answers and logical sequence. Research has also shown that where learners are encouraged to utilize a specific mental area, particularly those located in the right hemisphere, this improves

| Left
hemisphere | Right
hemisphere |
|---|---|
| language
logic
number
sequence
linearity
analysis | rhythm
music
images
day-dreaming
colour
connections |

Figure 4.3 Hemispheres of the brain.

performance in other areas (Buzan 1982). In other words, where learners are encouraged to engage the brain functions of imagery, imagination and rhythm in the pursuit of knowledge and understanding, then learning is more successful. Two of the so-called *great brains* – Leonardo da Vinci and Albert Einstein – are examples of achievers who worked through an elegant synthesis of left and right brain activity.

Clearly this has fundamental implications for the ways in which we organize learning in formal educational settings. It gives added emphasis for the creation not only of broad and balanced curricula, but broad and balanced teaching methods. The so-called elite academic subjects like mathematics and science also need to activate the right brain dimensions of learners, providing more opportunity for experiential and active learning methods than has traditionally been the case.

Another crucial consideration is that we have also underestimated the capacity of the young to achieve far more than we have ever thought possible. This awesome potential also improves with age, and the belief that mental activity declines as we get older is not supported by evidence. We now know that if the brain is stimulated, no matter at what age, it will continue to increase its capacity. This is not to say that a concern for the left brain and its functions is wrong, but rather that it is incomplete. The left brain works better when it is fully supported by the right. It is the powerful synthesis of the left and right hemispheres that is likely to achieve higher standards of academic achievement.

Research into the working of the brain continues. An even greater interest is now focused on the nature and working of the mind. Mind is used to describe how the functions and structures of the brain are used and its almost limitless capacity to invent new and unique pathways to understanding. As teachers, we should be more concerned with the minds of our pupils than with their brains, noting how each uses the brain to develop individual and unique mind patterns to cope with cognitive processes. These are developed through experience, and modify as new and more complex cognitions are presented. The mind is never fixed. An active mind is turbulent and busy, constantly striving to cope with new data, new relationships of ideas, new experiences and new classifications of knowledge. One of the joys of working with young children is watching the awesome process of mind development.

The very best teachers place enormous trust in the capacity of their pupils' minds to deal with information, knowledge, concepts and ideas. Teaching set rules for perception and conception does nothing to encourage the flexibility of the mind to discover its own unique solutions to specific problems.

BRAINSTORMING

This fairly well-known way of generating ideas in a group is not always carried out systematically. It was invented to counter the tendency in the western intellectual tradition to draw conclusions and make decisions by dispute. As soon as one person puts forward an idea or suggestion there is a tendency for the rest to search for defects and faults in it. Brainstorming is concerned with generating possibilities rather than with nit-picking and fault-finding. Education is badly in need of an alternative to this inhibiting tradition and good use of this technique can help to provide it.

To produce the best results it may be approached in the following way:

1 Set up a flip chart or large piece of paper that can be seen by all members of the group.
2 Identify the task e.g. 'List possible themes for the next inservice day'.
3 One member of the group writes down suggestions verbatim.
4 Allocate five minutes to list as many ideas as possible. All suggestions are valid and no suggestion should be queried or challenged in the initial listing.
5 After five minutes, or when ideas cease to flow, discussion, classification and clustering of the ideas can take place.

There are many benefits to this activity:

* it easily involves everyone;
* it is integrative – the ideas stem from individuals but the group owns the collection;
* all available experience is drawn on;
* it encourages creativity, imagination and lateral thinking.

As well as serving to generate a large collection of ideas in a short time, this method can also be used to improve the quality of interpersonal living in classrooms, particularly by focusing on the intuitive and emotional dimensions of learning and living. It is an activity which not only encourages creative thinking but stimulates creative feeling, and learners need far more opportunities for this side of their learning to be developed.

Simply asking a group or class to brainstorm how someone might feel in a particular situation can demonstrate a range of responses. This is good because it helps pupils to understand that, while others do have different emotional responses, others have the same or similar ones. Work in counselling reveals that adults have 'bottled up' their feelings in the mistaken belief that no one else could possibly feel the same way.

Lists produced by brainstorming of this sort can provide endless agendas for group discussion work, talking in pairs and personal writing. Learners should be encouraged to use personal brainstorming in their own individual work.

CAREERS EDUCATION

One of the key aims for any effective education system should be to help individual pupils to make choices about their lives and futures.

Traditionally, careers education has been concerned to facilitate the movement of pupils from school to work and to achieve the best relationship between abilities, skills and interests and paid employment. Associated with this approach has been the focusing on decisions which involve commitment to a single career life. The emergence of large-scale unemployment during the past twenty-five years has done much to challenge traditional notions of work, career, employment and retirement.

Rapid and far-reaching changes in society are affecting the ways that working life will be conducted in the future. In *The Future of Work* (1985) and *The Age of Unreason* (1989), Charles Handy has done much to define the likely patterns of the future. He suggests that the single continuous career will be replaced progressively by a portfolio approach to work, involving self-employment, paid employment, community work and continuing education. The tendency will be towards a more fluid and flexible workforce with a greater focus on providing small-scale services and a greater utilization of individual talents and abilities. With longer life spans and earlier retirement it will be increasingly necessary to conceive of a working life well beyond the traditional forty years.

Employers will strive to find effective ways of minimizing costs while maintaining quality of service or product. They will be desperate to avoid the personal and financial problems created by redundancy and anxious to develop staffing which is capable of change and adaptation. Handy notes the increasing trend towards what he calls the 'shamrock organization'. The first leaf will consist of *core workers* – a very much smaller group of people than in the past who will be at the heart of the business and on permanent contracts. The second leaf is described as the *contractual fringe*. Organizations will make increasing use of specialists, largely self-employed individuals or groups who will be contracted in to do work which does not justify a full-time permanent contract. The third leaf is the *flexible workforce*, perhaps the most rapidly growing section of the employment market. These people will be part-time and temporary workers who are called in as and when necessary to plug gaps, cover for absences or carry out occasional functions.

The implications for learning and teaching in schools are profound. Not only will it be important to promote new assumptions about a fast changing future, but teachers will need to recognize that they are educating for uncertainty. The skills we prize today may well be redundant tomorrow.

In our work with learners we need to place an increasing emphasis on:

1   Learning how to learn – constant retraining and development.
2   Developing flexibility and adaptability.
3   Decision-making skills – exercising choice.
4   Working with and through change.
5   Envisioning the future – trend spotting.
6   Self-management.
7   Interpersonal effectiveness.

In a fast changing world, all teachers need to be career educationalists – helping learners to plan and prepare for their personal futures. Far too many pupils leave school dependent on employees to create and provide work. Careers education in school has to be concerned with a shift in assumptions so that pupils are increasingly helped to see the opportunities inherent in the self-employment option, and to acquire the skills and abilities to create constantly developing portfolios of work.

CHANGE

The twentieth century has been the most eventful in history, and the pupils now in our schools will live the whole of their adult lives in the twenty-first century. During the latter part of this century the pace of change has increased dramatically and we now inhabit a world that is characterized by rapid and accelerating change.

One of the key assumptions upon which our traditional orthodoxy in education has been built is that teaching in schools is concerned with the transmission of knowledge, knowledge that will remain valid throughout our lives. A. N. Whitehead (1931) observed over sixty years ago that such an approach would only work if the time span of major cultural change was greater than the life span of individuals. But now:

> We are living in the first period of human history for which this
> assumption is false . . . today this time span is considerably shorter
> than that of human life, and accordingly our training must prepare
> us to face a novelty of conditions.

It is with this notion of novelty that schools need to be concerned, and the curriculum will require significant development if pupils leaving school are to be equipped with the skills and abilities to make their way in social, technological and economic situations that have not yet been envisaged. Commenting on the problems that will face the citizens of the twenty-first century, Alvin Toffler (1971) identifies three key purposes for schooling:

1   The process of learning how to learn. Pupils need to learn how to
    access complex data and information easily, but also how to
    manipulate it in a wide variety of contexts. Pupils must learn how to
    discard old ideas and know when to replace them. The sacrosanct
    nature of traditional school knowledge must be challenged.
2   We must help learners in the increasingly complex problem of
    building relationships, an aspect of personal development
    traditionally ignored by the schooling system.

3 Changes in the nature of society will multiply the types and complexities of decisions facing individuals. Therefore education must face the issue of over-choice and pupils will need to be helped to take greater responsibility for the management and direction of their lives and learning than ever before.

Another problem of attempting to sustain a knowledge-based model of school education is that of curriculum lag. If we continue to present a knowledge base built during our own education and training, then we will fail to deal with the current and emerging reality of pupils' lives – we will be concerned only with their history.

A key challenge for teachers is that of preparing the young for a world that cannot be envisaged, a world characterized by constant and accelerating change. The aim of education therefore becomes one of inculcating and developing capacities for learning and relearning that are flexible, adaptable and multi-dimensional.

CHOICE

Effective learning is dominated by choosing, and yet the processes involved in sensible and responsible decision-making have rarely featured in the curriculum for learning in schools.

One of the purposes behind the move from a teacher- to a learner-centred model of education is a determination to reduce the sort of teacher dependence characteristic of a schooling system based on instruction. The realization that learners are equipped with a huge capacity for learning which is only likely to be harnessed if the right environment for learning can be created has presented the need to help learners to accept and develop increasing responsibility for their own learning. This involves the skilful and responsible exercising of choice.

A useful concept to help our understanding of this process is that of the *locus of control*. Rotter (1966) suggests that it is possible to distinguish two particular control dynamics in human behaviour. The first of these identifies those people who feel very much in charge of themselves and agents of their own destinies as *internals* – their locus of control is within themselves. Those who feel they have very little control over what happens to them are referred to as *externals* – their locus of control is perceived as being outside themselves. Evidence by J. E. Phares (1976) makes it very clear that those who operate with an *internal* dynamic are better able to make choices in their lives, take responsibility for their own actions and the consequences of them, and are better able to cope with failure and learn successfully from it. In particular, Phares discovered that internals:

● have greater self-control;
● are better at retaining information;
● ask more questions of people;
● notice more of what is happening around them;
● are less coercive when given power;
● see other people as being responsible for themselves;

- prefer those activities which require skill than those involving chance;
- have higher academic achievements;
- are more likely to delay gratification;
- accept more responsibility for their own behaviour;
- have more realistic reactions to their own successes and failures;
- are less anxious;
- exhibit less pathological behaviour.

The majority of these outcomes would be on most teachers' lists of desirable attributes in learners, yet for far too long the schooling system has been pursuing an approach to learning which reinforces an external dynamic – a belief that other people are responsible and that only the teacher is in a position to make decisions about an individual pupil's learning.

The implications from this research are clear. When learners are able to accept responsibility and choice in their learning they are likely to be more successful. As teachers, we need to cultivate an *internal* dynamic in our classrooms, and discourage that most limiting condition – teacher dependence.

CIRCLE WORK

This is a way of organizing a group experience where the goals are interpersonal awareness and the development of social interaction skills. The idea is for the group – it could be a whole class – to sit in a circle and share ideas, insights, experiences or present feelings. It provides effective training in active listening and opportunities for each group member to be heard by others. Early agendas, while pupils tune in to the idea, should be fairly safe and simple, like going round the group sharing favourite holiday experiences, television programmes or musical tastes. Later, as trust begins to develop, the group topics can involve pupils disclosing feelings within the context of the lesson subject under consideration.

The basic format is for the teacher to suggest a topic and then pass round the circle inviting each person in turn to share an observation, an idea or a feeling. Those who do not want to contribute allow their turn to pass without comment. In managing circle activities it is important to:

1 Allow time and space for the activity. Work in the round if at all possible.
2 The younger the learners, the smaller the circle and the shorter the circle time.
3 Emphasize circle time rules on each occasion:
    (a) everyone who wants a turn gets one;
    (b) everyone who shares thoughts and feelings gets a hearing without interruption.
4 Make the task clear. Ask the group if they understand. Give examples of your own.
5 Don't worry about silences; sometimes they have benefits. Learn to read them and watch non-verbal behaviour in the group.

6   Do take your own turn, which is either to share or to pass. There are
    good reasons for this:
    (a)   it provides a model for pupils;
    (b)   you become an equal sharing member of the group;
    (c)   it helps learners to see you as a person and not a role.
7   Responses to contributions should be reflective and empathetic, not
    judgemental or moralistic. Encourage pupils to develop good feedback
    techniques by reflective summarizing, particularly when feelings are
    involved.
8   Try not to close a circle until everyone who wants to share something
    has had the chance to do so.

It is important to emphasize that circle work is not a discussion, but a
structured exercise in disclosure, sharing thoughts and feelings, active
listening and empathetic reflecting. It can be used profitably in any
subject area and is an excellent way of increasing pupil involvement and
helping them to learn with and through each other.

Through regular practice in circle work, pupils acquire the important
disciplines necessary for effective collaboration and learn to avoid the
competitiveness so often associated with badly managed discussions,
where the emphasis is on argument rather than reflection and disclosure.

CLASSROOM CLIMATE

This can be defined as the quality of classroom life as reflected through
the relationships between the teacher and the pupils and among the
pupils themselves.

It is increasingly recognized that one of the key features contributing
to effective learning in pupils is a positively supportive classroom
climate. The prime responsibility for creating this rests with the teacher,
and much will depend upon the assumptions about pupils and their
learning which have contributed to the forming of a particular teaching
style.

Traditionally, classrooms have been regarded as places where pupils
undertake the tasks necessary to prescribed learning. Interpersonal
behaviour has tended to be between the teacher and the class as a whole,
with some interchanges between the teacher and individual pupils. This
tradition assumes a passive rather than an active learning process. If we
are to make the schooling process relevant to the lives that pupils
actually lead, then the classroom needs to become a place where aspects
of their lives can be brought to the fore. This involves creating in our
classrooms an emphasis on interpersonal living, so that pupils have the
opportunity to develop an awareness of the effect that the classroom
experience is having on them.

Canfield and Wells (1976) observe:

> Students have a vested interest in the emotional environment of the
> classroom. Teachers and students should sit down together and
> freely discuss cooperation and competition, trust and fear, openness
> and deceit, and so on. These and many other topics discussed in

classroom meetings help create the kind of climate that fosters total pupil growth.

A positive classroom climate tends to develop when teachers behave with a facilitative style. This can be fostered through positive communications at a variety of levels, and teachers need to encourage pupils to bring to their learning a synthesis of physical, emotional, intuitive and intellectual well-being. It is crucial to employ teaching strategies that develop a sense of pupils being fully involved in their own learning.

In general terms a positive and encouraging classroom climate is created when teachers:

- enjoy relationships with their pupils;
- express their own needs and wishes to pupils;
- are understanding and accepting of pupils;
- foster and encourage warm and friendly relationships between pupils;
- spend more time listening to pupils than talking to them.

In specific terms, the classroom climate can be facilitated by maintaining interpersonal communication at a positive and caring level. Examples of this style of communicating are:

- dealing with important interpersonal issues when and as they arise, not leaving them until later;
- talking directly to pupils, rather than about them to the class as a whole;
- speaking to pupils with courtesy, care and consideration;
- being aware of the importance of eye contact and non-verbal communication;
- avoiding the common blocks to effective communication – judging, criticizing, preaching, commanding and moralizing.

Although in most primary schools these days classroom furniture is arranged to facilitate pupil interaction, a great many secondary school classrooms are still arranged in a formal pattern of rows with desks all facing one way. If our classrooms are to become interactive workshops, then furniture needs to facilitate that purpose. New schools are increasingly reflecting this trend, with carpets, some easy chairs, screens, quiet and private areas and a presence of plants, lively and interesting displays and flexible layouts.

When all pupils face the teacher, interactions between pupils become more difficult. Pupils need to communicate directly with each other, not only via the teacher standing at the front. Above all this requires that seating arrangements facilitate easy eye contact.

Some useful questions to reflect on about classroom climate are:

1 How would I describe the classroom climate I create?
2 What are my assumptions about pupils? How do they govern my relationships?
3 How do I behave to pupils I don't like?
4 What sort of interpersonal behaviour do I encourage in my classroom, both formally and informally?

5   How would I describe my teaching style?
6   How much of myself do I disclose to pupils?
7   How do I deal with interpersonal issues in my classroom?
8   How do I organize the furniture to try and create a more interactive environment?

Developing an effective classroom climate needs to be a constant feature in programmes of professional development and can be a very useful focus in the appraisal process.

CLASSROOM ORGANIZATION

There is a vast amount of literature about the organization and management of learning in classrooms. For those teachers concerned to join the shift from a teacher orientation to a learner orientation, there needs to be an alternative set of preconditions for effective classroom work.

An effective model for the organizing of learning needs to take account of four key factors:

1   What the learning purposes and objectives are.
2   What the teacher will do.
3   What the learners will do.
4   The environment in which the learning will take place.

The successful management of learning depends upon the effective interplay of these key factors. The following checklist may be useful in planning.

Learning purposes and objectives

1   Which particular learning objectives is the activity designed to serve?
2   What specific knowledge, skills and attitudes are expected to be developed?
3   How will these objectives and purposes be communicated to the learners involved?
4   How do these particular objectives relate to what the learners have previously experienced?
5   How do the learning objectives relate to activities and experiences which are to follow?

What the learners will do

1   How will each of the four components of the experiential learning cycle be catered for?
2   Which specific activities will the learners undertake to:
    (a)   engage in new learning material;
    (b)   reflect on this activity;
    (c)   draw conclusions from this reflection;
    (d)   plan to incorporate this learning in the future?
3   How familiar are the pupils with the activities involved? What explanations will be necessary?

4   What is the plan for managing the sequence of activities involved?

What the teacher will do

1   How will I introduce the lesson and help to clarify the purposes and objectives involved?
2   How will I organize the activities and the transition from one to the other?
3   How will I cater for individual needs and interests during the activities?
4   What particular facilitation style will I adopt in managing these activities?

The learning environment

1   How will I set up the room in which the learning is to be conducted?
2   What resources and equipment will I need to provide?
3   What materials will I need to prepare?
4   What sort of psychological climate do I want to create for these particular pupils and these specific activities?

A wide range of management skills are involved in managing classroom learning. The process is not unlike managing a medium-sized business. Perhaps too much attention traditionally has been focused on the teaching aspects – the management of pupil behaviour – and not enough on the leadership aspects: the empowerment of pupils' learning potential.

CO-COUNSELLING

The management of reflective and experiential learning draws heavily on techniques and practices developed over recent years in the fields of counselling and psychotherapy. Counselling, like experiential learning itself, is designed to help the individual more fully to develop self-awareness and bring meaning to experience.

Co-counselling is a technique which can profitably be adapted for use in learning situations. It involves the creation of active and empathetic partnerships to reflect on and explore aspects of the learning process and of participants' personal experience of them. The techniques can be used in most subject areas and with any age group of learners.

The technique is best used when there is a need for learners to think through and clarify aspects of their learning – either particular parts of subject material, or their reactions to and understanding of a particular learning experience. In English, for example, pupils might be invited to talk to their partner about a particular character in a play or novel; in humanities, to express the human costs of governmental decisions; or in art, to share their understanding and appreciation of a particular painting. Such a process helps to clarify thinking, draw conclusions, gain insights and express feelings.

It is important to make a distinction between this technique and conversation or discussion. Co-counselling involves the alternating of roles – talker and listener. The purpose of the interaction is to enable the talker to reflect on and articulate thoughts, ideas and feelings in relation to a learning experience or activity. The role of the listener is to assist this process by giving sensitive and undivided attention to the talker. Even five minutes each way can allow considerable understanding and insight to be developed.

Pupils need to be helped to develop the basic counselling skills of active listening and empathetic responding (see Counselling, p.90).

COMMUNICATIONS

Much of the literature of organizational communication is relevant to classroom life. It is through the interpersonal dimension that a successful classroom climate is built and developed and optimum conditions for effective learning established.

With the increasing recognition that teaching is more than the simultaneous instruction of a group of learners, comes the need to use the insights of organizational theory and psychology. A classroom has most of the significant features of an organization and it is worth considering the learning process in relation to our understanding of what contributes to success in organizations in general and apply these findings to the classroom. Among the features of organizational communication that contribute to success are:

- establishing vision and purpose;
- integrating the efforts of all involved;
- building a healthy climate of relationships;
- making high-quality decisions.

There are a number of implications for the classroom. Firstly, the need for the whole class to understand the learning purposes of the moment and to share some common sense of direction. Secondly, all members of the learning group need to see themselves as participants in the achievement of both common and individual goals. Thirdly, all learners need to recognise that, together with the teacher, they share the responsibility for establishing interpersonal conditions conducive to effective learning. Finally, the success of the group will depend upon the quality of decisions that are made about objectives, choice of working practices, the details of end-products and how the evaluation will be carried out.

All this demands that we come to regard classroom life as a series of practical workshops where there are high levels of interpersonal communication, and where much of the learning stems from transactions between learners. The learners of the future will need a vastly wider repertoire of interpersonal activities to facilitate learning and more highly-developed communication skills than pupils in school have traditionally been encouraged to develop.

As we shift our teaching styles from predominantly information-distilling processes to the facilitation of largely self-directed learning, the need will emerge to provide training in a wide variety of communication skills:

- clarifying and expressing learning purposes;
- active listening;
- managing disclosure and feedback;
- working in critical friendships;
- high-quality group work;
- counselling and co-counselling;
- making presentations.

Recent debates about the content of the English component of the National Curriculum have indicated the traditional obsession with the rules of language and with performance in language. A sadly and dangerously neglected area of the curriculum has been that crucial area of social learning, where language plays such a vital part in personal and interpersonal development. We need to give increased attention to the dynamics of language in such areas as relationships, understanding, awareness, sensitivity, openness and directness.

COMMUNITY

Community has become an increasingly important focus in education in recent years. While attempting to increase neighbourhood involvement in the management of schools, and to provide relevant learning opportunities for a wide range of local needs, community education is also to do with education for community. Schools focus their key learning objectives on the most precious resource of any community: its next generation.

This involves helping learners to develop a strong sense of place and location, not simply in the geographical sense but also in terms of the human achievements and aspirations of its members. There is often a tendency for the younger generation to feel isolated in, and alienated from, their communities – to feel victimized both by outsiders who make decisions on their behalf and also by the adult community members who often fail to assert the needs and determinations of the community itself.

Part of good community education is the preparation for responsible and active citizenship, and this is best achieved by helping the young to discover valid roles and responsibilities in the directions that the community decides to take. This requires active participation in local affairs and an opportunity to learn with and through the community. All schools, wherever they are located, need to cultivate a *community-conscious curriculum*. This can be conceived as a curriculum in which the following seven key points are firmly embedded and reflected in the teaching programmes:

1 *Raising awareness* by helping learners to understand the dynamics of the community, how decisions which affect it are made and who the democratic participants are.
2 *Promoting learning* that uses the real live experiences of the community for case studies. In the early years of schooling the theme of *people who help us* should focus on a whole range of community members, not simply shopkeepers and doctors, and in later secondary

work pupils should be encouraged to undertake live projects in the community which bring real benefits to the locality.

3 *Developing responsibility* that helps young people to recognize and accept responsible roles in the community, including membership of community bodies which welcome the opinions and aspirations of the young as a central part of the community's concerns.

4 *Celebrating diversity* which recognizes that the community is not a single cohesive unit but a cluster of varied interests, concerns, cultures and hopes. A successful community is one which not only recognizes this fact, but seeks actively to learn from, and celebrate, the rich opportunities contained in diversity.

5 *Increasing choice* through the democratic involvement of the young in community affairs, thereby helping them to exercise responsible personal choices in activities which affect others, and collective choices that bring benefits to all.

6 *Giving power* which enables young members of the community to recognize and exercise their power to influence and achieve changes for the better.

7 *Achieving change.* A community-conscious curriculum is one that sees the end result as bringing about changes that increase the opportunities for all in the community, which builds community self-esteem and empowers the community to act as the agents of their own destiny.

COMPETITION

The schooling system inherited by the present generation of learners has been built on the assumption that a competitive ethic is a key motivator in learning – that the struggle to be a winner will bring out the best in everybody. Since by definition most will lose in such a system and many may never win, this harmful notion needs changing.

Fisher and Hicks (1985) observe:

Many of our interrelationships and institutions are characterised not by co-operation but by the competitive ethic. While this may bring out the best in some people, it does tend at the same time to militate against co-operative initiatives, whether local or international, causing human problems and conflicts to be seen primarily as contests to be won – violently if necessary – or at least not lost, rather than as common problems which can be solved by the interested parties acting together.

Part of the problem with traditional schooling has been the preoccupation with learning as an individual process. There are still classrooms which regiment learners at individual desks and forbid talking – even when human communication is the subject of study! The acquisition of knowledge, the development of understanding and the promotion of skills need to be seen as common goals which are best individually achieved when the interested parties work together, with and through each other. Collaborative learning is used extensively outside the schooling system, in training programmes and inservice education, but it has yet to be seen as a key to the learning process for pupils in schools.

In a competitive schooling culture, much of the energy that pupils could use for productive subject learning is expended on how to cope with and avoid the humiliating excesses of win/lose learning. For those who are never going to come first, the objective becomes one of striving to at least not come last and thereby be the scapegoat and the most despised. Above all, a reliance on a competitive ethic inhibits that essential ingredient of reflective and experiential learning – the opportunity to reflect with others in order to test out ideas, compare experiences, clarify meanings and plan new strategies.

COMPUTERS

The 1980s witnessed the gradual introduction of computer technology into schools. During the 1990s we will continue to witness a steady expansion of information technology in the learning process, and by the turn of the century few parts of the educational process will be unaffected and untouched by it. Many who first encountered computers in their adult lives have a mistrust of some aspects of technology and may well continue to suffer from the debilitating and limiting condition of *technofear* – extreme anxiety aroused by high technology apparatus. On the other hand, pupils of all ages have demonstrated an easy and happy capacity to incorporate computer assisted learning (CAL) into their range of learning strategies.

Some teachers hold the view that a steady expansion of high technology will reduce the learning process to robotic dimensions, with pupils engaging in endless communication with visual display units. This is an unjustified concern, for recent history has shown (Naisbitt 1984) that as technology takes over an increasing range of functions in our lives, there develops a corresponding need to compensate with an increase in more human activities. The increase of word processing has been accompanied by an increase in the sale of high-quality fountain pens; an increase in databases has been accompanied by bumper sales of books in all categories. As *high tech* increases in our schools, so has *high touch* – and more personal and interactive processes are likely to emerge.

Information technology and effective learning are highly compatible. Computers are tools which can be organized to facilitate learning and to enable learning time to be used more efficiently. What we need to do in our teaching is to help learners to control the technology, rather than be controlled by it. More efficient use of technology can free learners from endless repetitions of practices and processes to engage in the all-important interpersonal aspects of learning. Word processing can enable pupils to produce high-quality documents more efficiently than longhand writing, and data searches will be able to locate and print information more efficiently than ever before. Storing information on disks will replace the need to keep endless notebooks of information and facilitate retrieval and revision for examinations.

CONCEPTUAL MAPS

With an increased understanding of how the two hemispheres of the brain function has come the realization that not all learners structure their thinking in the linear and sequential patterns so actively promoted in traditional learning. It is important to encourage learners to experiment with different ways of structuring their ideas, organizing their planning and seeking solutions to their problems.

In making notes, for example, it is important to realize that the mind does not always work best in sequential mode and indeed works in a whole variety of ways involving word association, visual memory, key concepts, felt experience, and so on. When we invite learners to make notes, draft ideas or make preparations for particular projects we should utilize the mind map technique developed by Tony Buzan (1988):

> Rather than starting from the top and working down in sentences or lists, one should start from the centre or main idea and branch out as dictated by the individual ideas and general form of the central theme.

In *The Brain Book*, Peter Russell (1980) emphasizes how this approach maximizes the optimum functioning of both hemispheres of the brain, but enables the powerful force of visual memory to be utilized in ways that lists and sentences cannot match. In using conceptual mapping as a key tool in the learning process, Russell recommends the following precise processes:

1   Print words rather than using script. This gives a clearer visual image and facilitates remembering.
2   Key words should be printed on a line and each of the lines joined to other lines to give structure to the pattern.
3   Coloured images are much better remembered than black and white ones.
4   Centres and subcentres can be given depth by using three-dimensional shapes, providing the map with a more solid visual structure.
5   Use other visual images rather than words. This also facilitates remembering and stimulates creativity.
6   Use arrows to link and associate different areas in the pattern.
7   Groups of words can be outlined or their background shaded to hold them together as a unit.

The effectiveness of this process is also emphasized by Gabriele Rico (1983). He refers to the technique of *clustering* – where a key word is used to evoke clusters of ideas and associations:

> As you spill out seemingly random words and phrases around a centre you will be surprised to see patterns forming until a moment comes – characterized by an 'aha!' feeling when you suddenly sense a focus for writing.

In all these methods, the emphasis is on spontaneity – the antithesis of much that reductionist processes have held dear. The purpose of the techniques is to stimulate intuition and to generate a range of ideas and possibilities. It is vital to let ideas pour forth without censorship or deliberation (Goldberg 1989).

For too long, pupils have been dependent on official or correct classifications and taxonomies of knowledge and ideas. In the creating of effective learning, it is crucial to help pupils to develop their own classifications, not as alternatives or rivals to the official, but as a means of extending the mind in its struggle for insight and understanding.

The use of conceptual mapping in the ways outlined here enables a wide variety of memory processes to be stimulated. Since mind maps tend to fix ideas in memory far more successfully than lists or blocks of prose, they are an excellent learning tool.

CONFIDENCE

Developing confidence is a vital building block in successful growth and learning. The ubiquitous presence of the phrase 'lacks confidence' on so many school reports indicates how lightly the issue has been treated in traditional schooling.

Lack of confidence develops when learners constantly receive messages that their work is not good enough, that they are not trying hard enough or that they lack what it takes. Messages such as these have a crushing effect on self-esteem and tend to inhibit the tendency to reach out and take risks – so vital to successful learning. While the message that is sent is usually: 'this work is not good enough', it is often received by the pupil as: 'I am not good enough'. Learning failure comes to be associated with personal failure and, when consistently applied, reduces the capacity for full functioning in learning and other vital areas of living.

One of the challenges for teachers is the inherited obsession with precociousness (fast learning). Child management has traditionally set itself against precociousness, emphasizing the need for modesty, the avoidance of pride and the importance of self-effacement. In the process of growing up, far too many of us learn to doubt our own skills and abilities, developing uncertainty about our worth and potential. We tend to believe what other people say about us.

Helping learners to develop sturdy self-confidence is a key task for teachers. We all start life with an awesome capacity to learn successfully. We learn to shut down this capacity because the feedback we frequently receive from the significant adults in our lives has such a crushing effect on our self-concept, inclining us to reconsider ourselves as less able than we really are. If confidence is lacking, effective learning will be problematical. Far too often, cognitive interpretations are offered to explain learning difficulty or reluctance, when attention to learning confidence and self-esteem would be more profitable.

In our attempts to build confidence in the pupils we work with, we need to be particularly aware of the part played by:

- Motivation – the striving to satisfy needs and achieve goals.
- Success – helping learners to build on their achievements rather than constantly drawing attention to their failures.

- The giving of specific but non-judgemental feedback on the outcomes of learning.
- The need for pupils to disclose doubts and anxieties created by some learning tasks.

Learners need affirming in the belief that they can learn successfully, and that the role of their teachers is to provide a secure environment, appropriate structure, proper resources, clear leadership and positive encouragement.

CONFLICT

The traditional view is that conflict is difficult and disruptive and needs to be avoided at all costs. Many of the problems of discipline and disruption in classrooms are due to the sustaining of this belief. An alternative view of conflict would be that it is a natural consequence of human interaction, and that its causes need to be confronted and resolved in creative ways. Regimes which do not tolerate dissent usually sustain control through oppressive and life-diminishing means. It is vital for learners to be afforded opportunities to deal creatively with conflicts that arise in the course of classroom learning.

Conflicts arise naturally between learners themselves and between learners and teachers. Introducing conflict management strategies into the learning process is an important role for the teacher. There is a growing literature on the theory and practice of conflict resolution and it is an important area for professional development.

Let us look first at conflict prevention and control. One way to reduce needless conflict is to create a learning climate which encourages the following behaviours:

1 Reflective listening – to another who is upset or angry and who needs to deal with emotional overloading.
2 Assertive disclosure – making it possible for those with strong emotional needs to express them without fear of disfavour or retribution.
3 Awareness – of behavioural issues and situations which tend to give rise to conflict.
4 Letting off steam – helping people to have their flare-ups and release tensions without everybody feeling they also have to be upset about it.
5 Increasing the quantity and quality of emotional support for those in states of tension and agitation.
6 Increasing tolerance of those with short tempers and the tendency to flare up. Recognizing that anger and resentment has antecedents in our earlier experience.
7 Some appreciation of the costs and consequences involved in not creating effective ways of managing potential conflict situations.

A regime of prevention will not remove all conflict. When used poorly, preventative regimes can encourage denial, avoidance and dominance in the attempt to inhibit conflicts from arising. Preventative methods are best for dealing with what can be called *non-realistic conflict* –

issues arising from ignorance, error, prejudice, displaced hostility and poor organizational structures. *Realistic conflict*, which arises out of genuine clashes of needs, goals or values, needs resolution strategies to deal with it.

Conflict resolution is difficult for many because it starts with emotions and feelings rather than with reasons: 'When feelings run high, rational problem solving should be preceded by a structural exchange of the emotional aspects of the controversy' (Bolton 1979).

In attempting to deal with another person in a conflict situation or to help two protagonists to resolve their dispute, the transaction needs to be built upon three key principles:

1 Treating the other person with respect.
2 Listening for the other person's experience.
3 Stating clearly personal needs, views and feelings.

In helping learners to develop these conflict resolution skills it is useful to build the following assumptions which underlie the principles outlined above:

1 Each of us has equal rights and responsibilities.
2 We all face difficulties which we need help and support to resolve.
3 Sometimes strong feelings of anger, resentment and mistrust will feature in our relationships with others – and these are to be expected.
4 Dealing with interpersonal disputes in an open and creative way is much better than avoidance, denial and repression.
5 The skills of conflict prevention and resolution are well worth acquiring and developing.

Conflict is communication that involves a clash of values, attitudes, beliefs, rights, ideas and understanding. It is the state that exists when differences and disagreements seem beyond resolution.

In many organizations people strive to avoid conflict, usually because their experiences of it are so painful. Since we have not developed effective communication skills to manage conflict, we can often feel inept, oppressed and angry when we find ourselves clashing with colleagues.

It is important to stress the inevitability of conflict. Few schools, if any, will have staff and pupils who are united in their values, beliefs, philosophies and perceptions. In a complex and busy organization, difficulties will arise constantly throughout the day.

Healthy and effective organizations are not necessarily those where there is an absence of conflict. Indeed, complacency can set in where there is too much cohesion and not enough conflict. Pascale (1991) has suggested that people are often at their creative best when they cannot have their way, and that it may be necessary on occasions to stimulate some conflict in order to activate creativity and commitment – creating discord to blow a fuse but not a gasket.

The key to handling conflict creatively is recognizing its inevitability. The absence of conflict can suggest that excessive power is inhibiting expression, creating a failure to give attention to the difficult and frustrating interpersonal tensions that arise in complex organizational situations.

CONNECTIONS

A key tradition in schooling has been the *naming of parts* – the capacity to name things and attach labels to objects, people or places in the belief that such identifying is itself learning and understanding. This belief continues to be sustained, with high prestige being attached to people who demonstrate simple feats of memory on quiz programmes and being offered the accolade of 'Mastermind' or 'Brain of Britain'.

More important than simply having knowledge and being able to recall it at will is the capability of being able to manage it in the pursuit of useful objectives and further learning. Pike and Selby (1988) provide a vivid insight into the changed circumstances of the modern world through the description of Emily, a 14-year-old living in a village in North Yorkshire.

> On first impression, Emily's world may seem small, enclosed and save for its beauty and relative remoteness, unexceptional. If we dig a little deeper, however, we discover a personal world rich in connections with the wider world.

The story goes on to describe how most of the objects in Emily's life build a pattern of connections across the world and how her own life is inextricably linked into a vast global interdependent network:

> Like Emily, almost all of us are caught up in a network of links, interactions and relationships that encircle the planet like a giant and intricate spider's web so that the wider world is a pervasive and ubiquitous element in the routines of everyday life.

It is this systemic reality which demands that as teachers we help learners to understand that knowing how the world they live in works demands the capacity to see relationships and to make connections. Merely knowing the names of things provides little help in the striving for insight and understanding.

Systems theory has helped us to see the world in terms of both particles and connections. It is the ways in which the particles connect that is often the most significant, and in most systems it is the relationships between the varied parts that matter most.

One of the challenges presented by the rigid classification of subjects is the freeing of conceptual and imaginative thinking outside this sometimes restrictive framework. While the development of cross-curricular themes goes some way towards overcoming rigid subject stratification, it is vital to help pupils to understand that classifications are for convenience, they are not reality itself.

CONTROL

For the traditional educator, control is the means by which classroom behaviour is regulated. It involves the exercise of personal power and authority, and the regulation of individuals through systems of rewards and punishments. For the person-centred teacher, control is more an issue of creating and maintaining optimum conditions for effective learning. This is a participative process involving teacher and learners working together.

Control is oppressive where arbitrary rules and conditions are imposed on pupils to the detriment of learning. Control is liberating and enhancing when used to create opportunities for self-management and self-regulation. Much depends on the teacher's basic assumptions about learners and beliefs about the best conditions for effective learning. McGregor's Theory X/Y (see Assumptions, p.62) is of particular relevance here.

One of the crucial elements frequently referred to in the analysis of organizations is the presence or absence of trust, and it is central to the debate about power in relation to leadership. Handy (1976) illustrates the trust/control relationship by suggesting that the sum of trust plus control is always constant. An increase in leader power and control causes a decrease in the subordinate's perception of trust:

$$CONTROL + X = TRUST - X$$

But if the leader wants to increase the trust then it is necessary to relinquish some control:

$$TRUST + Y = CONTROL - Y$$

Handy further observes that giving trust is not easy because:

1 It requires having confidence in the subordinate to do the job.
2 Like a leap in the dark, trust must be given if it is to be received.
3 Trust is a fragile commodity; like glass, once it is shattered it is never the same again.
4 Trust must be reciprocal. It is no good a superior trusting subordinates if that trust is not returned.

In classroom life, the issue of control is at the heart of what we do. Other sections in this chapter provide practical help in determining the sort of classroom management ethic to strive for.

CO-OPERATION

Co-operation is the other side of the competition issue discussed earlier (p.82). Although conducted in the collective setting of the classroom, learning in schools has focused on the individual working alone and separately from others. Although group work has become a more common feature of classroom organization in recent years, the stress on the individual has continued, so that achievement is measured in the nature of the individual's contribution rather than in the process of co-operation or the collective end result.

Many of us find working with others more difficult than working on our own. Because we have been trained to place reliance on our individuality, to watch our backs and to be wary of the intentions of others, we tend to see group work as yet another arena for competition. Co-operating with others on a common task requires additional skills, qualities and attitudes than those we bring to individual work.

Fisher and Hicks (1985) suggest that three qualities need to be fostered if a co-operative climate is to be achieved in the classroom:

1 *Self-respect* – through which pupils come to value their own abilities and achievements and have confidence in them.
2 *Communication* – listening to and conveying ideas clearly, both verbally and non-verbally.
3 *Empathy* – sensing the experiences and feelings of others and being able to convey this.

In addition to the creation of conditions conducive to participation and co-operation, it is necessary to look for opportunities when collaborative working in groups is likely to produce more satisfying learning experiences and more productive learning outcomes.

COUNSELLING

There is a growing interest in the subject of counselling, both as a means of building effective relationships with pupils and as a tool for more sensitive leadership and management. While counselling is fast becoming a new profession, with codes of ethics and professional accreditation, it is important to recognize that at heart it is a very basic and non-professional activity.

Counselling works from the assumption that those with problems and anxieties have the resources to deal with them quite adequately themselves, but that help is often needed if those resources are to be activated. Most of the time, when people share their problems they are not seeking advice, solutions to problems or even reassurance. They simply want to be heard, to have their point of view acknowledged and their feelings accepted. Most of us in the course of our lives have become so used to being offered other people's solutions to personal anxieties and concerns that our own problem-solving skills have never been fully developed.

Counselling-type relationships have a highly important part to play in the learning process and reference has already been made to co-counselling as a powerful technique to use with pupils. Some specific time needs to be found to help pupils to develop the interpersonal and communication skills necessary to the technique. In addition to the skills of active listening, three particular qualities are prerequisites for successful interpersonal helping (Rogers 1967):

- warmth;
- genuineness;
- empathy.

Warmth
This quality is well summarized by Murgatroyd (1985):

1 A person comes to you for help.
2 If they are to be helped they need to know that you will respect their experience and understand their problems and feelings.

3   Whatever your own feelings about who they are and what they have done, you will accept them as they are.
4   If they sense you are both accepting and understanding of their experience and will not be judgemental, they will be more able to disclose their concerns and problems and be open to the possibilities of change and development.
5   If, however, they feel you have a vested interest in their change and that the relationship is conditional upon that, then they may experience pressure and reject the help.

Genuineness

This quality refers to the capacity to be open and direct with the other person. Once we start to play the role of counsellor and stop being ourselves, we lose authenticity and the relationship suffers. This means we have to be as honest and open as we expect the other person to be. When this happens a genuineness communicates itself and the relationship grows. Without this quality there can be little trust between the two.

Empathy

The concept of empathy is central to effective interpersonal communication. In general terms it is the ability to convey to other people a deep understanding of their problems and feelings. It involves the sensing of the emotions of the other person and being able to communicate this sensing back to them. In attempting to increase our capacity to be empathetic it is necessary to recognize two aspects:

1   Receiving messages from the other person and being able to sense the feelings of the experience involved.
2   Conveying this 'sensing' back to them.

There are some considerable challenges in developing counselling skills. Virtually all the management models we have inherited in organizations have been of the controlling, supervising type. If we are genuinely concerned to be helpful and encouraging, we will need to take our own communication development seriously, recognizing the crucial importance of the counselling stance.

Rogers (1967) has said that the true benefits of such a helping relationship can be achieved if:

I can create a relationship characterised on my part by:
- a genuineness and transparency, in which I am my real feelings;
- a warm acceptance, and prizing of the other person as a separate individual;
- a sensitive ability to see the world as the other person sees it.

Figure 4.4 shows one approach to the management of a counselling relationship which does have a useful application in the context of the classroom life. It offers a sequential process designed to establish interpersonal ease, to proceed through the identification and exploration of key learning issues, to the considerations of future directions and the setting of targets.

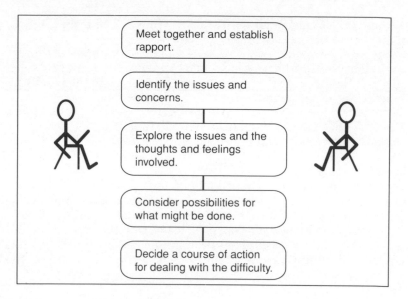

Figure 4.4 The counselling process.

While it is vital for the teacher to be able to adopt a counselling stance when appropriate and necessary, it is also important for pupils to be helped to develop the essential skills and qualities for themselves. In many ways the quality of learning depends upon it.

CREATIVITY

It is through our creativity that we are able to reach out into the world, to satisfy our needs and strive to satisfy our hopes and aspirations. Combined with those more instinctive and conditioned drives, it gives us the impetus to be ourselves and to make a mark on the world. Creativity is often thought of as the soft option in learning – an alternative to intellectual activity. 'You can do a painting when you have finished your maths' is a comment sometimes often overheard in primary schools. Such a view is sustained by the structure of the National Curriculum which places the hard cognitive and traditionally elite subjects at the core of the curriculum with precedence over others.

The issue is not what status so-called creative subjects should have in the curriculum, but how creativity can be appropriately and more usefully harnessed in the pursuit of all learning. Creativity is at the heart of all intellectual excellence. Most of the great achievers in the *academic* disciplines – science, mathematics and history – have been imaginative, curious and intuitive as well as intelligent. Both Da Vinci and Einstein relied on right brain functions as well as left.

Theodore Roszak (1981) reflects:

> I have seen my daughter's exquisite choice of the creative life treated with indifference in every school she has attended in three countries.

She has taken a rich and delicate talent into her school life – a talent which has carried her mind to the study of music, poetry, drama, history, literature – only to have that talent treated as non negotiable currency by her teachers. Until at last, school became a bore and a burden for her, an agonizing irrelevancy from which she begged to be liberated at the earliest practical legal moment.

One of the great strengths of reflective learning is its capacity to create opportunities for creativity to be released in all learning situations. Employing the learning cycle described in Chapter 1 allows and encourages all the attributes and capacities of the learner to be harnessed in the pursuit of learning objectives. We need to accept creativity as an inextricable part of the academic and cognitive domain and a vital prerequisite for a more holistic approach to learning.

Relegating creativity to a lower status than rationality produces incompleteness. We cannot realize our potential if we are only utilizing a portion of the resources available to us.

CRITICAL THINKING

A vital part of becoming a powerful and effective learner is that of being able to think critically. This process is described by Stephen Brookfield (1987) as having four distinct features:

1   The ability to identify and examine the assumptions underlying human ideas and behaviour that are usually taken for granted.
2   Recognition and awareness that the nature of ideas and behaviour are powerfully affected by the context in which they occur.
3   The capacity to imagine and explore alternatives to existing ways of thinking and living.
4   Exercising reflective scepticism in the face of claims to universal truth or the ultimate explanation.

In other words, the practice of critical thinking enables us to do our thinking for ourselves – to employ relevant information, to weigh evidence, to take account of context, to challenge generalizations and insubstantial assumptions. Above all, it encourages us to submit ideas, theories and experiences to a rigorous examination in the pursuit of meaning and understanding.

In offering guidance and advice to teachers, Brookfield suggests a number of strategies for teachers:

1   Build the confidence and self-esteem of learners by valuing their attempts at critical thinking.
2   Listen attentively to learners as they grapple with the learning process. Critical thinking develops best through sensitive interaction and discussion, where participants place the understanding of others' ideas and experience as highly as their own.
3   Provide deliberate support for those engaged in the process of critical thinking. There is a danger that, as teachers, we focus only on the subject matter of critical thinking rather than on the process itself.

4   Act as a mirror by reflecting back to learners their attitudes, rationalizations and habitual ways of thinking.
5   Motivate learners to think critically by affirming the existence of ideas that may be tentative and only partially formed.
6   Engage with pupils in regular review and appraisal of critical thinking so that progress can be assessed, successes identified and difficulties dealt with.
7   Foster the development of critical thinking networks by providing many opportunities for learners to engage in discussion and group work where emerging critical thinking strategies can be tried out.
8   Be critical teachers by undertaking a variety of facilitative functions – being advocates for missing perceptives, adversaries to propaganda, recorders of sessions, mediators in conflict and general resource persons.
9   Help learners to develop awareness of their critical thinking by helping them to face up to their preferences, biases, habits and blockages.
10 Model critical thinking by demonstrating the key characteristics of that thinking in our own behaviour: clarity, consistency, openness, communicativeness, specificity and accessibility.

It is important for pupils not to confuse critical thinking with criticism. We are encouraging rigorous thinking about critical issues, not thinking in order to criticize.

CULTURE

Culture has a wide range of meanings, some of which are particularly important in the context of learning. In the wider sense, culture refers to a set of ideas, assumptions, beliefs, customs and traditions developed over generations by groups of people united by their place of origin and residence. Part of the preparation for responsible global citizenship should be the development in young learners of an increasing appreciation and understanding of the world as a system of interconnecting parts, so that learners come to appreciate the huge potential contained in the richness and variety of cultural diversity.

This aspect of culture needs to be a strong focus in the work we do. It involves us being more careful in our selection of examples, images and resources in order to reflect variety and diversity in the world, and to try and build appreciation and respect for those cultural aspirations and achievements which are different from our own.

Within organizational settings, culture refers to the cluster of human attributes present in the school or the classroom, the assumptions that people hold about the organization, and the pattern of behaviours which arise as a consequence of them. It is often summed up as 'the way we do things round here'.

As teachers, we need to be aware of our own cultural assumptions and the extent to which these become pervasive in the classroom context. We need to be careful to create opportunities for variety to be celebrated and learned about, and we need to help learners to establish their own frameworks for developing an understanding of the cultural factors that affect their own lives.

CULTURAL SEEDS

One of the most significant spurs to effective learning is the captivating idea which ignites within our consciousness and sets in motion a dynamic and energetic spate of enquiry and research. Seymour Papert (1980) has coined the phrase 'cultural seeds' to describe this phenomenon. He observes:

> . . . children learn to speak, learn the intuitive geometry needed to get around in space, and learn enough of logic and rhetoric to get around parents – all this without being 'taught'. We must ask why some learning takes place so early and spontaneously while some is delayed many years or does not happen at all without deliberately imposed formal instruction.

The answer to this puzzle lies, says Papert, in the notion developed by Piaget that children are builders of their own intellectual structures. Children, like builders, need materials to build with and these materials – both physical and mental – need to be provided in abundance as the child gradually builds its own intellectual structures. The key, Papert argues, lies not only in providing a material environment rich in resources and materials but one in which the adult participants, both teachers and parents, are seen by children to be engaging with significance and pleasure in that environment. The cultural seeds are often caught when an activity is perceived by children to be especially profitable and rewarding to the adults around them. Children will have no difficulty in constructing a mathematical intellect if they are immersed in 'mathsland', where mathematics is played at, discussed, celebrated and enthused over.

There are huge implications here for the way we construct and operate learning environments. But it is not enough simply to create space for the interests and enthusiasms of learners; it is vital to be ever alert and watchful for those moments in a learner's life when they recognize, sometimes quite overwhelmingly, that they are in the presence of a big idea. Too often these moments remain unrevealed, and many learners are not aware that the cultural seed that has attached itself within their imagination has any learning implications at all. Our only hope as educators is to work sensitively with their experience, and in recognizing their current preoccupations, learn to nourish and cultivate their seeds – providing the light and space in which these seeds may grow.

There is often no logic about cultural seeds and their germination within us. Browsing through a magazine, a chance encounter, watching someone absorbed in their endeavour, can create a crystallizing essence, potent with possibility and opportunity. The learning climate needs to make welcome such serendipity – providing an ever-present incubator in which cultural seeds can grow. Some seeds bring forth a life that is short but intense, others a blooming which is lifelong, a journey of discovery and development.

CULTURAL TOXINS

These are the dangerous and pernicious beliefs that take hold within us and conspire to inhibit learning and stifle the development of potential:

- I don't have an ear for languages.
- I'm tone deaf, I can't sing.
- I don't have a head for figures.
- I could never learn to play the violin.

During our learning lives, lack of initial success in a learning task can lead to a sense of failure if others disapprove of our efforts, or even express disappointment at our lack of immediate success. If repeated and reinforced, these apparent deficiencies become identity as we repeat these beliefs like superstitions. Papert (1980) uses the example of difficulty with mathematics to illustrate this:

> If people believe firmly enough that they cannot do maths, they will usually succeed in preventing themselves from doing whatever they recognise as maths. The consequence of such self sabotage is personal failure, and each failure reinforces the original belief. And such beliefs may be most insidious when held not only by individuals but by our entire culture.

In *The Drama of Being a Child* (1987b), the psychologist Alice Miller extends the argument into what she calls 'toxic pedagogy'. This starts, she suggests, in toxic theology, where God, having created people in his own image, has created the view in parents that they have the right and duty to mould their children in their own image. Thus as well as passing on to their children their biological genetic structure, they attempt to implant their psychic genetic structure – neuroses, toxins and all. For children the message they receive is clear: 'Only if you look, talk, behave and be like I want you to be will I accept, value and love you'. In short, Miller suggests, bringing up and educating children is a process of unwittingly but unconsciously killing off their real selves. The basic, pulsing, potent life force which is their unique individuality is being forced out of them.

It is against this background that teachers are challenged to operate. In some senses the learning process is something of a rescue operation, where the teacher strives to help the learner rediscover and reactivate the inner vitality and authenticity of self and individuality which an alien world has often unwittingly conspired to destroy.

DANCE

It is surprising, given its prominence in both popular and high culture, that dance has such a lowly place in the curriculum of most schools. Perhaps it is because of its popularity and its association with the intuitive and expressive rather than the intellectual capacity that it has been denied an adequate place in the formal learning process.

One correspondent at the time of the 1987 General Election wrote to the Conservative Central Office: 'I was very interested in your manifesto, but it doesn't say anything about dancing.'

Writing in *Person/Planet*, Theodore Roszak (1981) reflects on the attempts he and his wife made to find a school which did take dancing seriously. At every turn they encountered the same intellectual monopoly:

> Again and again, when I find myself in the midst of educational controversy I come back to one fixed point of reference. 'But my daughter is a dancer . . .'. And because she is a dancer there has been no place for her in the supposed best of schools. Further, I ask what if she had chosen to be a rhapsodic poet, a visionary physicist, an unconventional healer, a circus clown, a yogi, a wood carver, a prophet, a magician, a clairvoyant, a social crusader, an eccentric inventor, a fool of God? What place would there have been for her then? Even less than nothing. An outer darkness of contempt and prejudice.

It is perhaps significant that most pupils know better than to ask such questions of their careers teachers.

The dictum 'healthy body, healthy mind' is often used in defence of physical education. What we have failed to see in our obsession with the cognitive is that the physical and intellectual are inextricably linked in the holistic system which is the self, and that to separate the parts hierarchically is to rob the system of its essential order and unity so that it becomes dysfunctional. As we have already seen, the balancing of right with left brain functions optimizes the capacity to learn. Successful learning stems from a happy integration of the parts, bringing body into rhythm with the mind and spirit.

Dancing is a vital and exuberant means of self-exploration and self-expression. It taps into our deepest emotions and intuitions and provides perhaps the healthiest and most enjoyable means of keeping fit and integrating the four attributes: emotional, intellectual, intuitive and physical.

DATABASES

The increasing rate of change in information technology will bring about many revolutions in education. Prominent among these will be the way that knowledge-based information is stored and retrieved by learners in classrooms. There are two key factors to take into account. Firstly, there is the increasing difficulty of publishing valid and up-to-date information in book form. The accelerating pace of change in world events, scientific advance and social fashion create a validity gap between a book being conceived and its being published. This gap is often two years, during which time the subject the book sets out to explore becomes history.

The second issue is to do with the rapid development of the technology by which information is managed. Computer-based storage of information can be updated quite easily and downloaded into a school or pupil's own information storage system using telecommunication equipment. It will not be very long before schools and classrooms have their own fax machines, database terminals and word processing units. With the introduction of compact disks in place of the less capacious floppy disks will come the opportunity to store vast quantities of information previously only accessible in printed form.

For the learner in tomorrow's world, the whole business of managing information will be of a new order. It is essential that we welcome this technological advance and its potential to facilitate powerful learning. There are parts of learning that will remain untouched by technology – the human interactions so vital to successful growth and development – but we do need to help learners acquire and develop the skills of using technology as tools for their learning. Increasingly sophisticated software packages are being developed which offer expanding opportunities to free time from undemanding, repetitive and routine activity to more fruitful and enriching pursuits.

DECISION-MAKING

Education is decision-intensive. Survival, let alone success, in the highly complex world of the twenty-first century will depend upon each of us having high-level abilities in self-management, whether in workplaces or in our personal lives. In a world of over-choice, the capacity to make consistently high-quality decisions is a prerequisite for effectiveness.

It is a pity that the skills of decision-making are seen only as appropriate to programmes of management training for senior workers in organizations. They should really be in the curriculum for schools right from the start of the formal educational process. The journey to self-responsibility will not be achieved if we concentrate only on the content of the curriculum and not on the processes involved in being an effective learner. Every day, pupils in classrooms exercise choices, select responses and make decisions. Unless they are very lucky, they are unlikely to have been taught what the specific ingredients of intelligent choosing or decision-making consist of. The educational system will never success-fully assist the journey from dependence to independence without opportunities to acquire the skills that accompany successful self-management in a modern world.

It is useful to have a working model of the decision-making process to present to learners, so that they can both learn to be more systematic and have a framework against which to review their decision-making experiences. One such framework involves the following sequence of activities:

1 Identify the issue for choice or decision.
2 List all relevant factors.
3 Specify the criteria the decision will need to satisfy.
4 Develop alternative choices.
5 Match alternatives to criteria.
6 Choose the best match.
7 Implement the best solution.
8 Review the choice in the light of experience.

There are many variations of this framework in the growing literature of self-management and development.

A great deal of hesitancy and uncertainty arises when we have to make choices because we lack the simple skills of being systematic. It is not enough only to give attention to decision-making skills in so-called life skills lessons, since it is in the very process of learning itself that we begin the business of exercising choice and making decisions. Without skill, this involves haphazard guesswork and arbitrary selection, thus jeopardizing effective learning and self-management. Management training begins in the nursery.

DESIGN

The principles of design have much to offer to the learning process in general as well as to specific areas of the curriculum. At the heart of the design process is a systematic sequence of activities:

1 Identifying needs and opportunities.
2 Generating a design proposal.
3 Planning and making.
4 Appraising and evaluating.

This is an alternative framework to the decision-making process described earlier. This particular outline offers a guide to most areas of work and certainly stretches way beyond design-specific activities. The framework could just as easily guide a primary pupil undertaking a piece of research in history as another faced with the manufacture of a working model.

The skills of learning involve a capacity to use such planning frameworks as this in a systematic way in a variety of situations. Our capacity to learn effectively in later life, when the supportive structures of schools and colleges have been removed, will largely depend on our capacity to utilize systematic processes. Reflective and experiential learning deliberately sets out to help learners experiment with planning frameworks, and eventually to design and experiment with their own.

DIARIES

Keeping a diary is an important reflective learning activity. Unlike most pieces of writing done at school, a learner's diary is personal and private, only to be shared with others by agreement.

Rather than the somewhat dry approach of recording events in narrative, we should encourage learners to use their diaries in diverse and creative ways:

• making lists;
• drawing;
• making flowcharts and mind maps;
• recording quotes;
• raising questions;

- noting reactions and feelings;
- developing ideas;
- making jottings;
- recording experiences;
- planning tasks and activities.

Unlike the general notebook or jotter that is often provided for pupils, a diary is an altogether more purposeful document. It belongs to the pupil and should be given high status in the learning process. It should also be the best quality notebook that the school can provide, and ideally pupils should have the opportunity to choose their own from a selection of sizes, formats and colours.

Pupils should be given time each day for diary work. Providing it in each lesson is even more powerful, and an indication that a school is really taking reflective and experiential learning seriously. It might be argued that five minutes' diary work in a fifty-minute lesson cannot be afforded, but reflective time can result in more effective time management and therefore more productive learning.

Given time and encouragement, learners can be helped to appreciate how valuable personal writing can be. Not only does a diary provide a safe and personal place to record the substance of reflections about learning, it is also a place where pupils can register their joys, delights, fears, frustrations and aspirations, thus developing a powerful self-awareness and the integration of themselves with their learning.

DISCIPLINE

Discipline is a powerful concept in the schooling system. For most pupils it has come to be associated with the punishments that might follow transgression from formal rules and requirements. That the development of discipline has become so closely linked with punishment is unfortunate.

While discipline has an important academic connotation – the discrete principles governing the study of a particular subject – it more generally refers to behaviour, and the development of awareness of what is appropriate in different contexts. The tradition we have inherited is that discipline has to be set by teachers, rigidly enforced and supported as necessary by sanctions and punishments if pupils are to learn success-fully. Perhaps in the past this had more to do with producing an obedient workforce than it did with developing human potential and aspiration.

Becoming self-disciplined is an experiential journey involving the making of connections between cause and effect – between what we do and its impact on others. It is a difficult journey for most children, full of hazards and inconsistencies in which what they are urged and required to do by one set of influential adults often seems to be contradicted by another.

In free, liberal democracies, issues of human rights and responsibilities are central to political activity. Discipline is a process of striking a balance between freedom to serve our own best interests and respecting the need to do this without contravening the rights and interests of others. Learning to be self-disciplined is not easy for children in a world characterized by so much aggression, dishonesty, cheating, oppression and injustice. Harsh regimes of discipline have always been the hallmark of totalitarian tyrannies. We must not make schools institutions in which the traditions of free thought, tolerance and respect for the dignity of the person are suspended. Nor must we exclude children from the framework of human rights and responsibilities that apply to adult generations.

Currently in schools, we are struggling to move beyond the traditional assumptions that children need to have discipline forced on them and that retribution and harshness serve their best interests. At the same time as they are introducing new curricula, teachers are also striving to develop more humane and effective approaches to discipline in which pupils do not feel crushed and alienated, but where they do feel involved and encouraged to release their learning energies in appropriate ways.

Many schools are now exploring positive discipline and behaviour management systems which set out to acknowledge and reward the positive rather than simply punish the negative. Developing new assumptions and practices is difficult, and schools may encounter some opposition as they attempt to build cultures of co-operation, respect, trust and mutual self-interest.

Personal and social education has a vital part to play in helping learners to appreciate that the world they live in is full of ambiguities and contradictions, and that both success and survival depend upon a sturdy capacity to adapt quickly to different situations and circumstances. There is no simple way to be self-disciplined in a complex world. An essential part of the schooling process is to help pupils to appreciate, understand and work with the inevitable confusions, ambiguities and complexities of the world in which they live.

DISCLOSURE

The capacity for personal disclosure – the process of sharing our thoughts and feelings with others – is a vital element in the process of understanding ourselves and making sense of the world in which we live. While self-disclosure is a natural part of interpersonal living, it is important to give it special attention in the learning process. Since learning involves a continuing process of taking in new ideas, developing attitudes, acquiring skills and generally attempting to extend competence, it is essential that we have opportunities to explore the way that learning impacts upon our inner world of thinking and feeling.

Structured disclosure is the complementary part of feedback described later (see p.118). A helpful device to understand the processes involved in disclosure and feedback is the Jo-Hari window (named after its originators Jo Luft and Harry Ingham) (see Figure 4.5). This illustrates how the Jo-Hari window is made up, producing four distinct personality areas:

Open – that about us which is known both to ourselves and to others.

Hidden – that about us which is known to ourselves but not to others.

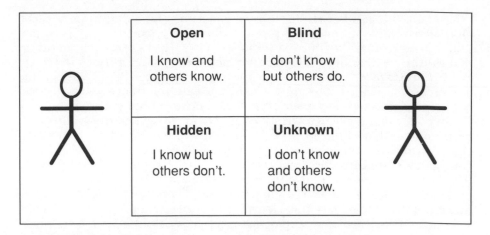

Figure 4.5 The Jo-Hari window.

Blind – that about us which is known to others but not to ourselves.

Unknown – that about us which is unknown to both ourselves and others.

Personal awareness is increased and the potential for development enhanced when two communicative activities are employed:

1 *Disclosure* – a willingness to communicate information about ourselves to others.
2 *Feedback* – a willingness to receive and take account of information supplied by others about our behaviour and its consequences.

The purpose of creating structured opportunities for disclosure is to provide a safe context in which learners can express and explore the experiencing of their learning. This is best conducted in structured pairs, where each partner in turn acts as talker or listener (see Co-counselling, p.79).

The psychologist Sidney Jourard (1971) sees appropriate disclosure as a symptom of a healthy personality. Through disclosure we have the opportunity to open up our inner being to the world, and in the process of so doing, to bring greater meaning and understanding to our existence.

When I say that self disclosure is a means by which one achieves personality health, I mean that it is not until I am my real self that my real self is in a position to grow.

This involves, Jourard argues, making ourselves known fully to at least one other human being. When we conceal and repress our anxieties, frustrations and concerns as well as our joys, achievements and ambitions we arrest our personal development. The learning process, especially for the young, is attended by a constant state of flux in our inner world. It is this flux that needs to be dealt with in the vital reflective component of experiential learning through such processes as co-counselling, circle work and group activities.

In helping learners to develop skills of self-disclosure it is useful to distinguish between *You* statements and *I* statements. The first focus on the other person – 'You just don't understand', while the second focus on the sender – 'I am finding it very difficult to explain this'. In helping learners to express and explore the nature of their learning experiences through disclosure it is best to help them develop proficiency with *I* statements.

DISCUSSION

Discussion has long been used as a device to help learners clarify ideas, engage in structured argument, explore alternatives and compare their attitudes with others. In some schools, discussion has been a token gesture in the direction of active learning, while in others it has been abandoned as disruptive and potentially chaotic. The same can be said of a great many of the discussion groups that adults engage in; that they are called meetings lends them a spurious tone of respectability and purpose.

In *A Guide to Student-Centred Learning*, Brandes and Ginnis (1986) describe a discussion activity during an English lesson:

> They were totally absorbed in what they were doing. They stayed on task for the full 40 minutes, without a break, without any further motivation from Ruth [the teacher].

The authors compare this experience with another:

> I had been working in a school where the kids were completely subdued and repressed; in each of six lessons that I visited, they were afraid to ask a question, express an opinion or in any way to challenge the teacher or each other. I found that depressing.

The teacher in the first example had developed four key aims for discussion work:

1   To develop confidence in verbal skills and expressing personal opinions.
2   To be able to listen to another's point of view.
3   To appreciate and understand another's concepts, or a problem, or an historical or political event.
4   To take responsibility for one's own learning about a topic.

Brandes and Ginnis also observe that far too often as teachers, we look for consensus and agreement, as though the purpose is to get learners to view things from the same standpoint.

> On the contrary, I think it is our duty to encourage freedom of opinion, questioning of values, challenging of moral standpoints, and the students have an inalienable right to their own ideas.

Robin Richardson (1982) suggests that certain conditions need to be fulfilled if discussion activities are to have purpose and value for learners.

1 Learners need to work in small groups of between two and six members and the group needs to be seen as the focus by the teacher, not the individual pupil.
2 There needs to be a specific outcome specified within a set time and that the outcome needs to be achieved through discussion – the exchange of viewpoints and information.
3 Rules of procedure need to be agreed which encourage all the pupils to take part.
4 Some activity or task needs to be undertaken in addition to talking, listening, writing and reading.

Perhaps one of the reasons why discussion activities are sometimes so difficult to manage is that pupils have not developed the skills and disciplines that are so essential to their success. Among these are listening carefully to others in order to sense the feelings involved and understand the thoughts. Circle work can help to build these skills and is an excellent way to introduce discussion to pupils with little previous experience. Disclosure is also important. Pupils need to be helped to appreciate that discussions are not necessarily concerned with argument or with consensus. They are a powerful means for exploring ideas and possibilities in an environment of respect, shared interest and concern.

DRAMA

Play is one of the central building blocks in the education of young children. Somewhere around the age of 7 or 8 it seems to disappear from the repertoire of classroom activities. It is unfortunate that the word 'play' has associations with recreation, enjoying yourself and a supposed lack of purpose. Play is often the hardest work that young children do, and they bring to it great concentration, intellectual application and creative endeavour.

Writing about the role of play in adult learning, Laurie Melamed (1987) says:

Through play (the work of children) the individual learns to concentrate, to exercise imagination, to solve problems, to try out new ideas and to develop a sense of control over his or her life. Discovery and intensity are combined with exhilaration and enjoyment, an integration which many adults envy. Are these attributes of playful learning forever to be denied to adults?

Not only are they frequently denied to adults; they are denied to most learners in the post-infant stage of schooling.

Drama has the potential to come closest to the functions described by Melamed. Once we overcome the association of drama with theatre and the staging of productions, we begin to see how important drama is in the curriculum of learning. Essentially drama provides a deliberate setting in which we are able to explore *as if* . . . situations. For example: 'What would happen if when you got outside the shop you found you had been given change for £5 instead of £10?'

The subsequent exploration of this situation in dramatic role play allows us to explore the possible ways to resolve the problem, to understand the issues involved and to see things from another person's point of view. In many ways it is similar to the sort of modelling economic forecasters engage in when they attempt to predict what effect a 1 per cent rise in interest rates would have on a cross-section of the population.

When in science we ask pupils to imagine the dilemmas of a research chemist, or in history to gauge the impact of the declaration of war, we are engaging in the world of drama. We sometimes benefit from physically acting out these situations in the search for meaning and understanding, but it is important to remember that we are constantly *acting out* inside our own heads. How much more valuable this activity could become in the learning development of pupils if we afforded it time in the curriculum.

DRAWING

It is unfortunate that drawing has become the prerogative of the art lesson, or reduced simply to a means of illustrating written work. Far too often, drawing is regarded as a skill which, by the secondary stage of education, few pupils consider themselves good at. However, when drawing is used as an activity of exploration it can deepen awareness, clarify and resolve internal struggles and tension and release considerable energy for learning and growth.

When words are difficult, drawing is an excellent way of helping pupils to get in touch with the inner dimensions of being. It can be used to help them get below the surface reality of their lives to the deeper meanings hidden below. Drawing is a powerful means of enabling pupils to create maps of consciousness which are so important to their learning and growth (Oaklander 1978).

If drawing is to be used effectively, it is important that both teacher and pupils are able to suspend traditional assumptions. Graphic skill is of little importance when drawing is used in this exploratory way. For this reason it is useful to start with abstract drawing. One way of doing this is to ask pupils to create their own personal logos. In pairs or small groups, pupils can then discuss how these logos reflect attitudes, values, personality, moods and hopes.

Drawing can be used effectively as a small component within a lesson. It is particularly useful when the lesson content has focused on feelings, attitudes or values. Used for a few minutes before discussion activity in small groups, it can help pupils work out their reactions to some lesson content or learning experience and order their thinking and feelings about it.

A five-minute drawing activity could be initiated in the following ways:

- Draw how you felt yesterday and how your moods changed during the day.
- Draw how you feel after seeing a film.

- Draw how you would feel if you were a mother receiving bad news.
- Draw the relationship between the two main characters in a drama.

As important as the drawing is the talk that follows it. Pupils should be encouraged to share the experience of the drawing through description and explanation, but only as far as they feel able. This discussion work is best organized with pupils in pairs, each pupil working with a partner they trust and relate well to.

Figure 4.6 Drawing – 7-year-old girl.

By way of example, the drawing illustrated in Figure 4.6 was done by a 7-year-old girl after the imaginary journey described in the section on Guided visualization (p.133). The girl was very keen to talk about the picture and the following summary is the gist of what she said:

> My place has three houses. One is for me. That one (on the left) is for my dad and mum and that one (on the right) is for my sisters. That's me looking out of the window. When my dad parks his car there I know he has come home. I planted those flowers. There are big trees in the back garden.

In the process of talking about drawings with pupils it can be helpful to seek further clarification. *What* and *how* questions are particularly useful, but *why* questions which seek for reason and interpretation are best avoided. In the example quoted above such questions as:

- What is it like in your house?
- What do you do when you want to talk to your sisters or your mum or dad?
- How do you manage in the house all on your own?

can help the pupil focus on the wider or deeper issues of the subject matter under consideration.

EMOTION

Many school brochures and curriculum statements make assertions about developing pupils emotionally. Few schools have a policy document for emotional development and, when asked about this, often claim that emotional development is part of the hidden curriculum, or that it happens incidentally in school assemblies and in other curriculum work. Clearly, we have inherited an education system in which the mind and its working is submitted to deliberate and systematic training and the emotions are left largely to themselves. In their descriptions of scientific enquiry, learners are urged to remain detached and objective. Yet we continue to relate the story of Archimedes, who having gained an insight into the displacement of water is purported to have leapt from his bath in a state of great excitement crying 'Eureka! Eureka!'. Hardly the behaviour of the detached and rational scientist we are urged to become. Most of the great scientists in history have succeeded by striking a happy balance between passion and detachment in their work. Why then do we discourage learners from expressing amazement, a sense of awe and wonder, or a passion for enquiry in their scientific writing?

There is an urgent need for an emotional curriculum which will both acknowledge the inextricable relationship between thinking and feeling, and set out deliberately to educate us in the management of our emotional lives. Arts education does address the great emotional elements of life – love, death, jealousy and betrayal; but where in the curriculum is there a place for helping pupils from their earliest days to understand and cope with the painful struggles of living – conditional love, envy, jealousy, rejection, fear, exhilaration, sadness? Personal and social education and life skills have followed the lead of active tutorial work in bringing such issues into the classroom, but largely as a space in tutor time in secondary schools.

Most adults reflecting on their school days remember how they felt – their fear of certain teachers, their love and admiration of others. They remember feelings of anxiety, anticipation, insecurity and dread. Biographical literature is full of such recall. The link between learning and feeling is powerful and inexorable. This link needs to be recognized by all teachers, whatever their subject or phase. Pupils need to be helped to understand that learning, like other great endeavours in life, is an interplay of joy and pain – an alternating dance of success and failure.

Reflective and experiential learning builds on the assumption that successful learning requires the energetic harnessing of all human attributes – intellect, emotions, intuitions and sensory experience. The cognitive obsession of the western intellectual tradition has imposed on learners in school an unhealthy and imbalanced approach where intellectual activity is regarded as the only correct domain. Not only does this place an incorrect priority on one particular aspect of our personhood, it is also severely damaging to our full capacity to learn. Bringing a feelings dimension into the learning process is a high priority for the schooling system.

In order to create an appropriate balance, a number of changes to traditional assumptions will need to be achieved:

1 Raising awareness that feelings and emotions are as relevant to learning as thinking.
2 Recognizing that in our classroom work we need to provide time and space for attention to the inner lives of learners so that they are more easily able to make sense of their experience and understand it.
3 Providing learning experiences that integrate knowledge, feelings and experience.
4 Extending our repertoire of teaching methods and techniques that give a learning focus to the feelings and intuitive aspects of being.
5 Developing the environment for learning, both in schools and classrooms, so that psychological as well as physical safety is regarded as paramount.
6 Recognizing that future aptitude is about our capacity to *be* in the world and that we need help to develop emotional and intuitive capabilities as well as intellectual and physical ones.

EMPATHY

There is evidence that empathy is a key quality for teachers, correlating more significantly than any other teacher behaviour with improved classroom performance in pupils (Rogers 1983). In other words, when a teacher has the ability to sense the meaning that classroom experience is having for pupils, and communicates this sensing to them, the pupils' capacity for learning increases.

The concept of empathy is central to effective communication. In general terms it is the ability to convey to another person an understanding of how they are feeling about issues in their current experience. It involves the sensing of the emotions of the other person and being able to communicate this sensing back to them. Basically it stems from being a good listener and responding to their comments with sensitivity and understanding.

The basic concept is set out in Figure 4.7. It is useful to make a distinction between the different levels of conveying interest in another person (see Table 4.1).

Table 4.1 Levels of interest and involvement

Apathy	Sympathy	Pity	Empathy
Lack of interest or concern in the other person's concerns:	Close identification and involvement with the other person's concerns:	Condescension at the other person's concerns:	Conveying an understanding of the other person's concerns:
'I don't care.'	*'Oh, I really am sorry.'*	*'You poor thing.'*	*'It sounds as if you found that very difficult.'*

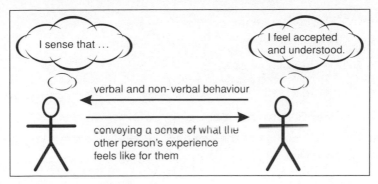

Figure 4.7 The empathetic stance.

Empathy is the process of:

- Engaging with the verbal and non-verbal behaviour of the other person in an interaction.
- Attempting to enter their perceptual world in order to feel at home in it.
- Sensing what it is like to be the other person with their experiences and concerns.
- Conveying to them, through verbal and non-verbal communication, a sensitive and caring appreciation and understanding of what it must be like to be them.

The greatest temptation is to convey to the other person what the concern looks like from our own point of view rather than from theirs. In many situations, offering our own opinions can lead to frustration, with the other person feeling increasingly misunderstood. The empathetic stance is intended to convey to the other person that their messages are understood, that the accompanying feelings are sensed and accepted.

The difficult but important part of this reflecting skill is being able to stay with the pupil's agenda and not interpose with ideas and points of our own. The following example illustrates this:

Pupil: I'm really sick and tired of being picked on all the time.
Teacher: You seem to be saying that some of the staff are picking on you more than they do on others.
Pupil: Yes, they've really got it in for me.
Teacher: That sounds as if you feel that they have deliberately decided to single you out for attention.

The teacher stays with the pupil's concerns and feelings, checking out whether they have been sensed correctly. By reflecting back what has been said, the teacher is helping the pupil to come to terms with those feelings. Only when the pupil's feelings have been brought out and sufficiently explored can coping strategies and plans of action be considered.

Developing the reflecting skill
To help develop effective empathetic responding it is useful to try some of the following opening responses:

- What I think you are saying . . .
- So you feel that . . .
- If I understand you correctly . . .
- From your point of view . . .
- Correct me if I am wrong but . . .
- So, as you see it . . .

Learning to behave in an empathetic way with pupils involves:

1 Frequently checking out that we have accurately sensed how the pupil is feeling.
2 Watching out for both verbal and non-verbal signals that offer clues and insights.
3 Listening for meanings and feelings expressed in the pupil's words.
4 Being sensitive to changes of feeling and meaning.
5 Being able to enter the perceptual world of the pupil and feeling at home in it.

Mistakes to try to avoid

In trying to develop a more empathetic quality with pupils we need to be aware of those verbal behaviours which frequently result in effective communication becoming frustrated:

1 Directing the other person and keeping talk on our agenda.
2 Judging and evaluating the other person's statements, often implying a failure to live up to certain standards.
3 Moralizing, by telling the other person how he or she should be living.
4 Diagnosing, by labelling the other's feelings.
5 Reassuring, by trying to make the other person feel better but ignoring the feelings involved.
6 Advising, by offering ready-made solutions.
7 Interrogating, by asking excessive questions in an aggressive and intrusive manner.
8 Interpreting, by trying to explain away the other person's problem.

Although interpersonal living will undoubtedly improve if we are more empathetic with each other, its specific techniques are not appropriate in all situations. Conversations, for example, would become somewhat frustrating if all we did was to reflect back what we had just heard. In the context of the classroom however, the teacher and the pupil are in the sort of relationship where empathetic behaviour in the teacher does have a significant effect upon the quality of pupil learning.

EMPOWERMENT

This is a concept closely related to the actualizing tendency referred to earlier. It concerns the capacity of individuals to take increasing responsibility for the satisfaction of their needs. It differs from motivation, in that empowerment places the emphasis upon the individual for creating his or her own conditions for growth, for defining challenges and for setting goals and targets. Central to this concept are a number of key assumptions and values (Hopson and Scally 1981). These include the following:

1 Each person is a unique individual worthy of respect.
2 Individuals are responsible for their own actions and behaviour.
3 Individuals are responsible for their own feelings and emotions and for their responses to the behaviour of others.
4 New situations, however unwelcome, contain opportunities for new learning and growth.
5 Mistakes are learning experiences and are seen as outcomes rather than failures.
6 The seeds of our own growth are within us. Only we ourselves can activate our potential for creativity and growth.
7 We can all do more than we are currently doing to become more than we currently are.
8 Awareness brings responsibility and responsibility creates the opportunity for choice.
9 Our own fear is the major limiter to our growth.
10 Growth and development never end. Self-empowerment is not an end to be achieved but a constant process of becoming.

Those who operate in a self-empowered way are characterized by:

1 An acceptance that change and development are the natural order of things and that change is to be welcomed rather than shunned and avoided.
2 Having the skills to initiate change and the capacity to learn new skills and ideas.
3 Taking personal responsibility for actions and behaviours.
4 Making clear goals for themselves and developing action programmes to meet them.
5 Being action-biased.
6 Frequently reviewing, assessing and evaluating their own progress and seeking feedback from others.
7 Being concerned to see others taking greater responsibility for their own lives.

In the well-managed classroom many pupils will be operating in self-empowering ways. Striving to create a climate which is person-centred, motivating and empowering is one of the most important elements of effective teaching. The pursuit of such positive ideas is likely to avoid the situation described by Lieberman and Hardie (1981):

> There is a lot of pain in human systems that doesn't have to be there.
> There is a lot of hope, aliveness and joy ready to flower when
> members of the system can learn to nourish these positive qualities.

ENCOURAGEMENT

One of the often repeated principles of education is that effective learning is facilitated by structuring success. Encouragement is the process of helping others to take the risks in living and learning that lead to success. In attempting to explain the various aspects of encouraging behaviour it is necessary to distinguish between praise and encouragement (see Table 4.2).

Table 4.2 Praise and encouragement

Praise	Encouragement
Emphasis on:	Emphasis on:
● control	● ability to be effective
● evaluation and judgement	● motivation
● approval	● appreciation
● conformity	● experiment and risk
● dependence	● independence
● standards	● aspirations

Generally speaking, interpersonal behaviour will tend to be received as encouragement if it conveys the following messages:

● You are effective and capable.
● I enjoy the way you do things.
● I value what you contribute to the organization.
● I support your goals for the future.
● Like me, you find some aspects of the work difficult and frustrating.

Praise is a reward based on achievement, whereas encouragement focuses on an individual's resources and assets and the way they are utilized towards self-improvement. Praise is often used as a method of control to get others to conform to our wishes, whereas encouragement seeks to help a pupil develop self-acceptance and a feeling of being worthy. Praise is external motivation: encouragement kindles inner motivation.

Most of us employ both encouraging and discouraging behaviours in our personal lives. In our relationships with pupils we need to develop a positively encouraging dynamic. This means deliberately pursuing encouraging strategies and avoiding discouraging ones (see Table 4.3). It is easy to be encouraging to those whose work and responses please us, but much more difficult to those whose attitudes upset us.

Table 4.3 Strategies for encouraging and discouraging

Discouraging strategies	Encouraging strategies
● ineffective listening	● active listening
● focusing on negatives	● focusing on positives
● threatening	● accepting
● humiliating	● stimulating
● disinterest in feelings	● concern for feelings
● emphasis on competition	● emphasis on co-operation

One of the main differences between a positive, healthy organization and a depressed and dysfunctional one is the way that people support and stimulate each other, sharing in each others' successes and achievements, providing support in difficult situations and showing concern for each others' welfare and well-being.

In discouraging environments there is a tendency for people:

- not to listen to each other;
- to engage in a high level of negative thinking, complaining and moaning;
- to behave as if in competition with each other;
- to show little concern for people's feelings.

More healthy environments, on the other hand, exhibit the following features:

- people show an interest in each other and listen with attentiveness;
- people are positive and optimistic, they tend to see problems as challenges;
- a strong tendency for people to be supportive and co-operative and to show an obvious enjoyment of collaborative activity;
- people's well-being and welfare is a high priority for management and leadership.

Most organizations, of course, display elements of both, but there is no doubting which type of human environment most people prefer to work in.

In attempting to develop our capacities to be encouraging, it is worth focusing on some key aspects of the encouragement stance:

1. Valuing people

Merely noting achievement is praise. Encouragement involves valuing all aspects of the pupil and accepting them as they are, in an unconditional way with no strings attached.

2. Conveying confidence

Verbal and non-verbal behaviour is designed to demonstrate a belief in pupils and their skills and abilities and that they will carry out the work they have agreed to successfully. An absence of checking up is particularly important.

3. Building self-respect

As well as demonstrating our own appreciation, encouragement is about developing self-respect and self-confidence in pupils, helping them to achieve a sure sense of their own worth. This reinforces the self-concept and can help to overcome a tendency towards over-modesty or self-disbelief. We can help others to become more aware of their skills and qualities by offering them specific and detailed feedback on their successes. This is far better than vague and generalized praise which only produces temporary good feelings.

4. Supporting change

These days, most of us are engaged in the constant struggle to change and develop. In the fast changing world of education this can produce both resentment and stress. Encouragement helps to focus effort on internal goals and aspirations and to help pupils see that while they are making progress they may also be experiencing doubt.

5. Identifying personal resources

This is about helping pupils to raise their own awareness of their skills and qualities. Many of us try hard but have doubts that we are being effective. This can breed low self-confidence and a reluctance to be more assertive in the exercising of our skills and competences. Receiving feedback on the positive and beneficial consequences of our efforts is a vital means through which we develop confidence and courage to strive further.

6. Invoking energy and commitment

Sometimes pupils need encouragement in order to activate their skills and qualities. This is particularly true when self-confidence and personal commitment are at a low ebb.

The benefits of working in a climate of encouragement are much more than feeling appreciated. It is about developing more courage to tap into our awesome potential and to rise above inhibiting self-disbelief. Since we live in an error-obsessed society, it is all too easy to adopt a safe and cautious approach to life and work.

END RESULTS

If we are to enable pupils to acquire good working habits and develop successful learning and life management skills, it is vital that these are introduced early in the schooling process and developed throughout. One of the aspects of good learning that is not always dealt with well is that of defining clearly for pupils the precise outcomes of the activities they are asked to undertake. Far too often, work instructions are framed in general terms: 'Write an essay', 'Produce information about . . .', 'Carry out a survey of . . .'. Pupils may be given little indication of the precise requirements of the task, yet their outcomes are marked and assessed against a strict and precise marking schedule.

The stage of preparing pupils for self-directed activity or task work needs to be tackled with care and precision. It is at this crucial planning stage that the nature of the end result is largely determined, and it is vital that they do not embark on detailed work without knowing on what criteria they will be assessed.

When work is being planned it is useful for learners to formulate a statement that completes the following sentence stem: 'When I have finished this task, what I will end up with is . . .'. The greater the detail specified, the clearer will be the pupil's vision of what is intended.

Having a clear and detailed vision of the specifications required in an end-product offers a structure which increases the purposefulness of the activity and which provides a clear sense of direction.

FACILITATION

The use of the word 'facilitation' attempts to strike a new balance of power between the teacher and the taught. Traditionally, the capacity of the learner to learn has depended upon the power of the teacher. But teachers cannot force or even give learning to others. Rather, the process needs to be seen as one of activating the pupil's own powerful learning potential and supporting it appropriately with information, experiences, resources, support and encouragement. We need to see our teaching as a process of ministering to this powerful learning potential and of maximizing the actualizing tendency within each and every one of our pupils.

To achieve this facilitation stance we need to move away from definitions which classify teaching on a traditional–progressive continuum (Bennett 1976) or, according to the instructional mode – class enquirer, individual monitor, group instructor (Galton and Simon 1980). While these help in the analysis of such a complex process as classroom teaching, they give insufficient attention to the vital ingredient – the nature of the relationship between teacher and pupil.

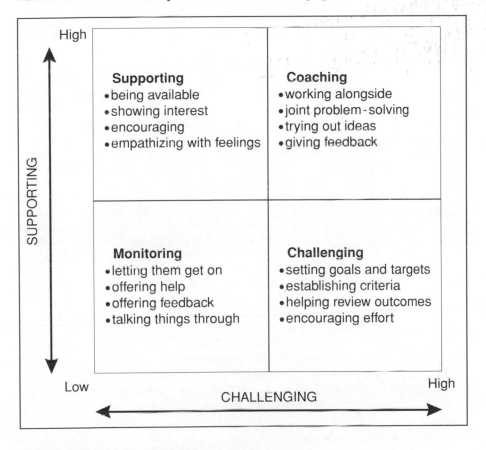

Figure 4.8 Framework of facilitation styles.

In terms of how we operate in the design and organization of learning experiences, it is important to recognize a range of approaches. One way of constructing a framework is to consider the styles of approach in relation to teacher directiveness and teacher support (see Figure 4.8). Such a model helps us to respond to the different learning needs of the pupils we work with. We also need to remember that pupils are likely to respond to all these styles at some time or another and the skill of the teacher is in selecting the appropriate style at any particular moment of intervention. Even in a single lesson in a specific subject area, a pupil might have specific needs for supporting, monitoring, coaching and challenging.

As we learn more about the complex processes of human development and learning, we will develop more appropriate, sensitive and empowering methods of teaching. Much insight and understanding of these processes can be gleaned from the burgeoning literature of leadership, consultancy and counselling.

FAILURE

One of the most powerful limiters to human growth, development and learning is the fear of failure. Failure has been used as a criterion for selection and categorization rather than as a model for learning and growth. Setting perfection as a requirement is perhaps the single most wicked thing that the education system has done to all the generations of learners that have experienced it. This obsession among teachers and parents of wanting children to be perfect has produced more misery, despair, neurosis and learning dysfunction than can probably be imagined. It is no wonder that against the standards of human potential the outcomes from the schooling system are so modest.

Getting things wrong is one of the most powerful means of learning. When we get things wrong we realize that particular strategies may not work and so we test further, eventually discovering what does work. The scientific method is built on a system of trial and error, where the systematic elimination of variables produces correctness in the end. Yet with pupils in school we want them to get it right first time and in their best writing. Even a cursory glance at the notebooks of great scientists, composers, poets and artists show almost without exception that success is a painstaking process of trying it out, changing it, trying it again, modifying it, improving it and refining it. Far too many of us have had a love of learning irretrievably damaged by experiencing our best efforts at reading, writing, drawing or explaining disparaged, rejected as inadequate or in need of improvement. And because we are the creators of our efforts it is ourselves as learners and as people that we come to perceive as inadequate, shameful and ultimately unsuccessful. John Holt (1969) suggests that most children in school fail. They do so, he claims, because they are afraid, bored and confused:

> They are afraid, above all else, of failing, of disappointing or
> displeasing the many anxious adults around them, whose limitless
> hopes and expectations for them hang over their heads like a cloud.

They are bored because the things they are given and told to do in school are so trivial, so dull, and make such limited and narrow demands on the wide spectrum of their intelligence, capabilities and talents.

They are confused because most of the torrent of words that pours over them in school makes little or no sense. It often flatly contradicts other things they have been told, and hardly ever has any relation to what they really know – to the rough model of reality that they carry round in their minds.

This is a harsh indictment of the system of schooling we have inherited, that which places obedience and respect for social order above the development of creativity, intelligence, truth, kindness and sensitivity. The very best that we can do for learners is to help them build on the already powerful learning process that they have built in their pre-school life, a process constructed on both trial and success as well as on trial and error. What each child has learnt has not been achieved first time, but through determination, effort, risk, courage and enormous skill.

FEAR

Fear is a major obstacle to learning A S Neill (1968), writing in *Summerhill*, said, 'The absence of fear is the finest thing that can happen to a child'.

Fear is the anticipation and expectation of painful experience. It is an emotion we acquire as the result of entering a dangerous and hostile world where learning the hard way – through pain and discomfort – is still regarded by many as the only way to achieve success.

Building a climate for learning which is free from fear is a major aim of the person-centred educator. Indeed, part of the process of reflective learning is the opportunity to raise awareness of our fears and anxieties in learning and to find ways of responding to them positively. For the teacher, this requires some specific and deliberate stances towards learners:

1 Striving to avoid whenever possible the arousal of fear in pupils.
2 Sharpening the skills of recognizing when learners are struggling with fear and are uncertain how to deal with it.
3 Helping pupils to accept that fear is an emotion they will experience from time to time, and that it can be confronted effectively and worked through.
4 Providing opportunities for pupils to review their learning experiences and identify those parts of their learning which tend to create fear and anxiety.
5 Listening actively to pupils as they struggle to express fears and concerns.

We cannot eliminate fear which is a necessary way to protect ourselves and manage safety. What we can do is to help pupils to appreciate that fear is purposeful, and that there is no need to feel ashamed of it.

Disclosing fears and anxieties in a safe psychological climate is a sure way to minimize its limiting and inhibiting impact on learning.

FEEDBACK

Reference to the Jo-Hari window (see Disclosure, p.101) will remind us that personal development requires attention to that blind area of our personalities. We need to seek from others information about ourselves of which we are unaware but they are not. This involves a conscious attempt to obtain feedback.

Receiving feedback is what the schooling process is all about. As parents and teachers, we give it to children all the time, yet very often with insufficient sensitivity to the individual who is to receive it. As teachers, we need to remind ourselves of the qualities (referred to in Chapter 2) which make for effective learning, and try to relate our feedback to the needs and personality of the individual. In a relationship which is warm and trusting, most pupils will be prepared to receive feedback and some will consciously seek it.

In giving feedback it is necessary to be aware of some of the psychological implications of giving others information about themselves and their behaviour. Many of us have difficulties both in giving and receiving such information, yet feedback has enormous potential for improving skills, qualities and performance.

During the process of socialization, behaviour is modified through feedback, usually of the corrective kind. The upbringing of children tends to be characterized by corrective and controlling interventions by adults based on error feedback. Children are told when they are 'naughty' or have behaved badly and this information is sometimes accompanied by punishment of a physical, emotional or psychological kind. When children are given success feedback it is often because they have conformed to adult expectations and requirements. This pattern established by parents in childhood is extended in the educational system and reinforced in work settings through hierarchies of status and position. It is not surprising that feedback is associated with criticism and conditionality. We need to be sensitive to the background and experiences that have made people the way they are and determined their patterns of behaviour:

- difficulty in accepting responsibility for behaviour;
- fear of making mistakes;
- difficulty with uncertainty and change;
- assuming that others know best;
- self-doubt and lack of confidence in ability;
- fear of success and reluctance to set personal goals for development;
- suspicion of 'experts' and those in positions of authority.

If feedback is to help the process of learning it needs to be managed in ways that will benefit the receiver.

Occupying a role which requires the giving of feedback presents real challenges. Managing it successfully depends upon the application of some basic skills and strategies.

We can provide feedback to pupils for a number of purposes:

1. To confirm successes and achievements

Feedback of this type provides clear and concrete information about specific behaviour and its consequences. After receiving feedback of this kind a pupil knows:

(a)   what they have done well – the *task;*
(b)   how they did it – *application* and *skill;*
(c)   the successful consequences – *achievement.*

This information enables the pupil to continue repeating and developing the behaviours which have been successful.

2. To help overcome problems and difficulties

Feedback of this type is essentially different from criticism. It is not concerned with passing opinion on performance or with designating blame, but with supplying clear and concrete information about specific behaviour and its consequences.

After receiving feedback of this type a pupil knows:

(a)   what they have done – *task;*
(b)   how they did it – *application* and *skill;*
(c)   the problem encountered – *difficulty.*

This information enables the receiver to modify and change behaviours that have resulted in difficulties.

3. To give pupils information about the effects and consequences of their behaviour

This combines both previous types of feedback and helps people to see more clearly the relationship between behaviour and its consequences. The aim is to provide sufficient information to meet the development needs of the receiver and enable appropriate choices to be made and decisions to be taken.

Our success in using feedback to build confidence and to develop skill will depend to a large extent on a capacity to avoid the recourse to judgement. Far too often feedback is judgemental – praise is positive judgement and criticism negative judgement. Our socialization has been a process of being found fault with, and improvement has been concerned with correcting these faults. Too frequently for comfort this judgemental approach has focused on aspects of personality in rather general ways: 'You're so untidy', 'You really will have to try harder'. Such comments rarely provide the detailed information on which any form of improvement can be built.

If feedback is to be effective, two particular conditions need to be created.

1. Motivation
The pupil receiving the feedback needs to be motivated to improve and is therefore needy of the information which will help this.

2. Moderation
The amount of feedback provided needs to be sufficient and not excessive. It should be matched to the perceived capacity of the pupil to take account and act upon it in significant ways. Feedback is essentially a sampling process, involving the selection of significant aspects of behaviour for comment.

In offering feedback four further factors need to be remembered.

1. Be specific and concrete
This involves commenting on only those behaviours which have been directly observed – what was seen and what was heard. It is essential to avoid discussion or comment of what the pupil is like or to make comments based on inferences or assumptions. Deal in facts by concentrating on specific and concrete incidents.

2. Be brief
Limit feedback to a few key observations. Too much information can cause confusion and frustration. Start with one or two key observations and then allow the receiver to respond. In this way disclosure and feedback can work creatively together.

3. Be descriptive
Stick to the factual detail of what has been seen and what has been heard. It is important to appreciate the distinction between behaviour and experience. We can observe the behaviour of pupils but cannot know their experience unless it is disclosed. In giving feedback, provide a factual description of behaviour but avoid speculation about the thoughts and feelings of the pupils. By offering specific and factual description we are providing information which invites a responsive approach to key issues and concerns.

4. Be reflective
This involves offering information in a way that enables the pupil to respond through disclosure. It also involves listening with full and undivided attention to these responses. The key is to encourage the pupil to reflect critically on experience and to identify ways of improving and developing. Handled badly, feedback will tend to close down rather than stimulate the reflective capacity.

Seeking feedback on behaviour is also a vital part of teacher growth and development. The Jo-Hari window is a useful device for considering teaching style and the way we behave with pupils in the classroom. Becoming a more effective teacher depends very much on being able to push the boundaries of the known area into the hidden and blind areas.

One positive and effective way of seeking feedback on our teaching is to invite a trusted colleague to spend some time observing our classroom at work. This observational monitoring, while part of the planned process of teacher appraisal, should not be regarded as an assessment procedure but rather a means of discovering more about our personal and professional strengths and weaknesses. To get the most out of it the teacher being observed needs to identify the key areas for observation and monitoring. The areas need to be defined quite precisely:

- During the next hour could you monitor the amount of time I spend with each pupil.
- During this lesson could you make notes about the ways I deal with pupil enquiries.
- What I really want to know more about is what goes on in the groups with which I am not personally working.

Such an open and outward approach to the business of working with pupils in the classroom is to be encouraged. Each lesson we monitor is a new opportunity to learn more about how to become a more effective facilitator of pupil growth and learning.

FIELDWORK

It is curious that since schooling is a deliberate preparation for adult life so little of it is conducted outside the classroom. In New York in 1972, Fred Koury established 'City as School'. This was created for pupils who were unsuccessful in their regular schools. The students would learn by working in the community but also fulfil the requirements of the New York City Board of Education Diploma. A whole network of learning centres have been established throughout New York – organizations of a business, cultural, civic or political nature – and students spend between twenty-five and thirty-two hours per week at one or more of the centres. This is community education extended well beyond the often narrow boundaries defined for it in Britain:

> The variety of ways in which the resources of the community can enable its high school students to learn experientially reflects the many facets of the community itself . . . a boundless resource commonly ignored by educational ventures.
>
> (*Education Now* 1988)

The introduction to the 'City as School' catalogue states:

> Learning at an external resource is not like learning in a classroom. Working with a professional chef in a restaurant or with a legislation aid in a politicians office or with the staff of an art museum is, in each case, a unique opportunity to learn by doing . . . Each learning experience is set up by the resource staff and evaluated by the resource co-ordinator, who is a CAS teacher, before the student is placed.

The various government created post-school training schemes which have borrowed from this model are devices to help the transition from school to work in a period of high unemployment. The New York experience has an altogether different principle – to learn about the world by learning in it, rather than about it at second hand within the confines of the classroom.

There are clearly resource implications for schools in attempting to redefine the boundaries of learning, but there is no reason in most places why fieldwork cannot be extended beyond the educational visit – often questionnaire and clipboard dominated. Most communities, rural or urban, are rich in resources – human, natural and manufactured – that can serve as live experiences for learners, and bring an increased power and relevance to the process of learning deliberately in and through experience.

FILOFAX LEARNING

The personal organizer as pioneered by Filofax has become the symbol of a society which has become so frenetic that the personal management of one's life cannot be left to chance. Detractors, perhaps with a deep fear of cultural labelling, see only the fashion factor, while exponents are pleased to take advantage of a device designed to bring structure and a more systematic approach to their daily living.

We have much to learn from the Filofax revolution. In secondary education, pupils are expected to be more organized than ever before with homework to schedule, complex timetables to negotiate, option schemes, work experience, GCSE coursework assignments, records of achievement and extra-curricular activities.

Very little attention seems to be given to developing the skills of personal management in school. From their earliest days pupils should be encouraged to value the potential of personal management tools: notebooks, diaries, planners and review forms. Many schools provide pupils with A4 ring folders in which to store their written work, but provide very little in the way of systematic training in note-taking, paper organization, data management, indexing and cross-referencing.

There is now a great deal of knowledge and understanding in the areas of time management and personal organization. Becoming a skilful and successful learner is increasingly dependent on acquiring and developing good study and work management skills. There is enormous potential in using the personal organizer concept to assist the development of good learning habits that will transfer into adult life.

Rather than providing a standard issue personal organizer, pupils should be encouraged, as part of a specific course in personal management, to design their own systems. These can incorporate personal interests and home needs as well as school requirements. Schools could produce their own custom-designed inserts for timetables, records of achievement and other specialist items.

FLIPCHARTS

The flipchart is an essential piece of equipment for effective group work. Used as a means of recording thinking, noting ideas, listing possibilities, defining tasks and registering decisions it is indispensable. All group members are able to see it and it provides a focal point for the management of group work. Its advantage over chalkboards and whiteboards is the permanency and flexibility of the record.

Charting the tasks and processes of group work is an important skill to develop for individuals as well as a vital part of systematic group process. The visual focus adds an important dimension to the process. Ideas are easily captured, connections made, thinking stimulated and creativity encouraged. Far too often in the exclusively verbal format of most group activities, ideas are lost, decisions confused and creativity inhibited.

Commercial flipchart stands are expensive and commercial pads tend to be made of high-quality paper. Cheaper alternatives can be made by stapling together sheets of A1-sized kitchen paper.

FLOWCHARTS

This is a generic term to describe activities which are *thinking on paper*. Far too much written work in schools is of a formal descriptive or narrative kind. For most writers, this is the final stage of the creative process rather than the first, and we need to provide more opportunities for pupils to experiment with ideas and possibilities and to develop a range of preparatory techniques – the planning stage of written work.

Flowcharts are essentially the working diagram of the creative process. Most people who use them develop flowchart styles of their own. A useful one to try out with pupils is the wheel chart. This is a circle in the middle of a sheet of paper with the key question or task written inside it. A number of spokes are drawn from the edge of the circle and pupils are encouraged to record ideas or responses at the end of the spokes. More sophisticated flowcharts can be developed according to requirements (see Conceptual maps, p.84).

Using a flowchart can be a useful preparation for almost any kind of school exercise – writing a story, planning some topic work, creating a drama, devising some research or solving a problem.

As pupils develop skill with flowcharts and become more creative in their applications, they may find they want to use them to deal with issues and activities in their personal lives.

FUTURES

One of the consequences of living at a time when the pace of change is rapid and accelerating is that the future seems to arrive increasingly early. As educators, we are faced with the challenge of preparing children for adult life in a future we cannot predict with the same assurance that was once possible. Therefore we cannot be sure that what we teach them will be valid and useful in twenty or thirty years' time. Placing an emphasis on knowledge, much of which is likely to be irrelevant in two decades' time, runs the risk of disabling learners who may have a lot of knowledge and information but are living in a world where it is of little use to them.

Alvin Toffler (1971), writing about the disorientating nature of rapid change, has suggested that the real beneficiaries of the educational system will be those who have acquired the skills of learning rather than those who know a lot. It is the difference between capability intelligence and knowledge intelligence: between those who can adapt and those who cannot.

One way to help learners acquire this capability intelligence is to place a concern for the future in the curriculum, in much the same way that we place the past. At any moment in the learning journey a pupil is poised between the past and the future. Looking back on past experience enables us to draw out lessons – to assess successes and achievements as well as to select areas for improvement. Looking forward to the future enables us to take account of changing circumstances, present trends and to make plans for the next time.

This use of a future dimension helps pupils to understand that the value of learning lies in its application at some future time. The experiential learning cycle is itself future-oriented as well as action-focused – it is concerned with change, development and growth.

In a wider, global sense a concern for futures is vital if the next generation are to be more successful in managing the planet than past and present ones have been.

The Global Futures Project, based at Bath College of Higher Education, is providing a positive focus on the role of the future in pupils' learning. The project is designed to help pupils and teachers to:

1   Develop a more future-oriented perspective on their own lives and events in the wider world.
2   Identify and envision alternative futures which are just and sustainable.
3   Exercise critical thinking skills and the creative imagination more effectively.
4   Participate in more thoughtful and informed decision-making in the present.
5   Engage in active and responsible citizenship, both in the local and global community, on behalf of present and future generations.

In *Education for the Future: A Practical Classroom Guide* (Hicks 1994), a rationale is set out listing pupil outcomes in relation to knowledge, attitudes and skills:

1   Pupil motivation
2   Anticipating change
3   Critical thinking
4   Clarifying values
5   Decision-making
6   Creative imagination
7   A better world
8   Responsible citizenship
9   Stewardship

In a fast changing world, the development of future perspectives becomes a vital prerequisite for successful living and learning.

GAMES

Games fulfil an important function in our lives. They are deliberate attempts to have fun. Yet even today, despite developments, games are often seen either as alternatives to work or as rewards for hard work. The traditional orthodoxy that if learning is to be effective it has to be painful still retains a strong grip in the schooling system. Very often it is when we engage in games that we are most alive, alert, intelligent, skilful, energetic and motivated. Games give us permission to enjoy ourselves and the opportunity to extend ourselves that other situations do not seem to allow.

Games are not necessarily competitive. In recent years we have seen deliberate attempts to create games which have a co-operative rather than an opposition focus and to invent games that bring people into social situations just for the fun of it. Participants in these new games report that these activities are also vibrant with learning and have a considerable contribution to make to the learning process in schools.

Writing in *Games for Social and Life Skills* (1986), Tim Bond says:

> Games are an exciting and rewarding method of social education
> because of the way they use social situation within groups. This
> means that the responsibility for the outcome of the game does not
> rest entirely on the facilitator's shoulders but is a responsibility
> shared with the participants and is in itself a valuable experience.
> Games build on the energy of informal interactions rather than
> repress them in ways more rigid methods of learning require.

Over countless generations, children have demonstrated a powerful creativity in their capacity to invent games from the most meagre of resources and situations. This capacity has been somewhat subdued by such passive activities as watching television, but schools can do much to reactivate and harness it in the pursuit of active learning.

GESTALT

The theory and processes of Gestalt therapy have much to teach us about our work with learners. Essentially, Gestalt therapy sets out to help individuals to increase self-awareness of the present existential reality of their lives. In other words, what we are really feeling at this moment rather than what we think we should be feeling or what we want other people to think we are feeling. Fritz Perls, the originator of Gestalt therapy, contended that growing up is a process of developing an alternative to the real self that we were born with. From earliest life we experience a need to present ourselves in ways that satisfy others' conditions for us. Consequently we build two personalities – a *real self* full of our basic feelings and thoughts, and a *presenting self* that we offer to others – designed more to satisfy their expectations than our own needs.

The presenting self does however fulfil a very important function. It enables us to adjust to the social world around us, to fit in with it and become socially competent. When we arrive at school we quickly learn that there is yet another set of conditions to satisfy: those of the school values system, and those of our individual teachers. We learn to suppress our real feelings and develop conforming behaviours that are often at odds with our real feelings and inclinations. The tendency to rationalize that we (our real selves) are wrong and they are right is the beginning of self-defeating patterns that may well plague our future lives in relationships and organizations.

The experiential learning cycle places great emphasis on the importance of reflecting on experience as a means to increase understanding and widen choice. For this process to be useful it needs to help us get in touch with our real selves rather than the presenting self we so often invoke in school.

Among the ideas of Gestalt therapy that are relevant to classroom life are the following:

Self-responsibility
Helping learners to take charge of themselves, their learning, behaviour and choices. An effective learning process encourages the increasing acceptance of self-responsibility and the gradual reduction of teacher dependence.

Focusing awareness
Helping learners to tune in to the experiences of the classroom – how they are feeling and what they are thinking – and to disclose to others their sensing of that experience.

Here and now
Helping learners to concentrate on what is happening in the present moment of their lives, rather than what is history or what others have said or done.

Direct communication
Learning to speak directly from our real self, using *I* statements rather than *they*, *one* or *people*.

GLOBAL LEARNING

One of the significant educational developments during the 1980s has been the move to encourage the introduction of a global perspective in the curriculum for schools. Those working in the areas of global education and world studies have argued that since children now become aware of world events at an early age through the medium of television the learning process in schools should be concerned to:

- Help them to make sense of the enormous range of phenomena they encounter.
- Appreciate that the last two or three decades have seen the world change to a complex system of interconnected parts with a growing web of global interdependence affecting the lives of all citizens.

- Recognize that the citizens of the world are facing a series of global crises which need urgent actions and responses if the planet is to provide an appropriate environment to sustain human life.

Global education and world studies are seen as dimensions across the curriculum, rather than as separate areas for study. The World Studies 8–13 Project (Fisher and Hicks 1985) has suggested the following objectives:

- *Knowledge* – describing, explaining, evaluating
    Ourselves and others
    Rich and poor
    Peace and conflict
    Our environment
    The world tomorrow
- *Skills*
    Enquiry
    Communication skills
    Grasping concepts
    Critical thinking
    Political skills
- *Attitudes*
    Human dignity
    Curiosity
    Appreciation of other cultures
    Empathy
    Justice and Fairness

Writing in *Global Teacher, Global Learner* (1988), Graham Pike and David Selby propose five aims 'which together constitute the irreducible global perspective':

- Systems consciousness
- Perspective consciousness
- Health of planet awareness
- Involvement consciousness and preparedness
- Process mindedness

Global learning can be seen as the third dimension in a map of learning which places the learner in three distinct but interrelated contexts:

1 *Personal learning* – learning about me;
2 *Social learning* – learning about the social networks of my life;
3 *Global learning* – learning about the world, the way it works and my role in it.

It is vital for pupils to have constant opportunities to link their learning in classrooms with daily events in the world outside. They need to develop a powerful sense of connection to the real world so that in due course they can assume a full and responsible participation in the management of its affairs.

GOAL-SETTING

Sadly, pupils are rarely given the opportunity in schools to identify and consider their own learning needs and hopes. The 1988 Education Reform Act has produced a seemingly endless flow of glossy brochures for parents and detailed folders of data for teachers but nothing at all for the pupils themselves, explaining how these new educational phenomena are designed to affect their lives. There is still the remnant of a belief that, given a chance, pupils would choose inappropriate material for study or seek to avoid *work*. But responding to pupils' needs and hopes is much more than merely offering choices. Deep down, most pupils want to succeed in those things that schools and society traditionally hold dear: the skills of literacy and numeracy. What the school needs to provide are chances for pupils to address the nature of their own learning, to take some responsibility for it, and to take risks in reaching out for what seems a bit beyond them without fear of failure.

As teachers, we can begin to do this by exercising more skill in sensing our own pupils' frustrations and unsatisfied learning needs. Person-centred teaching is really about being able to do this well. One positive and practical step is to help pupils develop skill in identifying and clarifying those particular areas of their learning where they would like to improve. The following exercise helps them to focus on such a need and to work out ways to satisfy it:

> The part of my work I would really like to improve is . . .
> If I could improve, things would be better because . . .
> If I don't improve then . . .
> I could help myself to improve by . . .
> The most difficult thing to do will be . . .
> I could get help in this by . . .
> The first step I need to take is . . .

Exercises such as this do help pupils to come to terms with their learning difficulties as well as to focus on the more positive aspects of their learning aspirations.

It is useful to photocopy sentence stem exercises like the one above and have a ready supply for pupils to use. Pupils can also be encouraged to suggest improvements and design their own lists of questions.

Another important aspect of goal-setting is preparation for a learning task. Far too often, pupils embark on learning activities without knowing why they are doing it, how they will benefit and in what form the final outcome will be assessed. We should always share the purposes and objectives of any learning activity we facilitate with our pupils. Pupils themselves should also be encouraged to be active in clarifying these aims for themselves. One way of doing this is to supply planning and preparation forms for pupils to use (see Figure 4.9). Not only will this help improve the quality of work, it will also instil good planning and management skills which will have a direct application in a wide variety of situations.

List the learning task(s).	
Specify the targets.	
Describe the learning activities that need to be undertaken.	
Do it!	Start on: [ ] Due to finish on: [ ]

Figure 4.9 Planning sheet.

GROUP WORK

This is a method of organizing learning in which the focus is on the group as a whole rather than on its individual members. It facilitates a shift from passive to active and experiential learning.

Group work has the potential to provide a number of conditions which other forms of classroom organization – whole class instruction or individual work – are unable to match:

1 It creates a climate in which pupils can work with a sense of security and self-confidence.
2 It facilitates the growth of understanding by offering the optimum opportunity for pupils to talk reflectively with each other.
3 It promotes a spirit of co-operation and mutual respect.

In her exploration of the role of group work in pupils' learning, Miriam Steiner (1993) makes the following propositions:

● Children need to go beyond the apprentice relationship and to talk purposefully with each other; to be challenged cognitively and socially by their peers; to explore their own conclusions, tentative hypotheses,

emerging opinions and values. They also need a purpose for this thinking and space to do it in.
- Children can gain deeper understanding of abstract concepts through structured group tasks which require them to talk through their ideas, listen to others and collectively arrive at some form of conclusion.

Since group work may involve a change in the way that learning is organized in the classroom, it is important to be clear about the relationship of the teacher to the pupils. The main emphasis in group work is on the group itself rather than on its individual members. Other modes of teaching tend to focus on the individual pupil, who is expected to work alone and who is assessed on an individual basis and in relation to performance levels of other pupils. What goes on in group work is often more important than the end-product or task in hand. It is the experience of interacting and co-operating which is so valuable and the incidental learning facilitated by the process can be particularly significant. It is important for the teacher to see groups as distinctive and cohesive entities rather than as collections of individuals.

Some of the specific characteristics of group-focused learning are:

1 It is an active process where pupils are learning by sharing their knowledge, ideas and experience.
2 The raw material for learning is within the group in the form of the group members' own knowledge, ideas and experiences.
3 Formal content and subject matter are of secondary importance in group work since the real subject matter is the pupils and what they learn about themselves and each other.
4 Success is not measured only by how well a piece of work is done by a group but by how far group members feel they have deepened self-awareness and developed their skills. In group work the emphasis is on self-assessment.

Group work can be of two kinds:

1 That which requires the group to achieve a set task in a set time, e.g. *Design and prepare an information leaflet. You have one hour.*
2 Open ended activity where the emphasis is on exploration of ideas and issues, e.g. *In your group use the situation of the family we have seen in the film to talk about similar experiences you have encountered.*

Both types of group work are important. The first is particularly good at developing skills of co-operation, planning, decision-making and executing joint tasks. The second provides opportunities for developing self-awareness and understanding and the interpersonal skills of disclosure and empathy.

To operate group work successfully, it is useful to bear in mind the following points:

1 Provide groups with clear information about their task and purpose. Groups need to know exactly what is expected of them.
2 Indicate a time limit. This generates a sense of purpose and facilitates group management.

3   Have adequate materials and equipment to hand – group
    instructions, discussion materials and equipment required for tasks.
4   Provide time for debriefing with each group. This is one of the most
    important features of group work, for it is the interactive reflecting on
    the group process which makes group-focused learning truly
    experiential. If it is not possible to debrief each group personally,
    encourage groups to do it for themselves by giving them time to reflect
    on the group process, drawing out through discussion how decisions
    were made, how ideas were formulated and how individuals
    contributed to the group task. For example, it is particularly
    important for a group which feels it has not succeeded in identifying
    the possible reasons and to consider how they could be overcome in a
    future task.

Effectively managed group work has the potential to transform the
learning process for many pupils in our schools. This will involve a
searching and critical examination of the type of group work which is
already going on. A number of recent observational studies of classrooms
have pinpointed the fact that a great deal of activity which is carried out
under the label of group work is in fact either pupils sitting in groups
undertaking different tasks, or work which still places emphasis on the
individual performance of the pupil and not the group as a whole.

We are now at a stage in social psychology when the power and
potential of the group is being rediscovered. As a social unit the tribe had
discovered something of this potential but our recent social and political
history reflects a tendency towards large institutions and social group-
ings. Even the idea of the family can be regarded as a flight from *the
group*. Our society no longer has the human infrastructure to create
conditions conducive to the satisfying of human needs and hopes or
indeed of developing our human potential much beyond the minimum. A
dependence on the state and large institutions has created what Freire
(1972) has called 'the culture of silence' – an incapacity of individuals to
control and transform their own lives.

Those involved in the transformational process are very aware of the
tremendous potential of the group. The key to more successful and
satisfying life-styles may well depend upon the way that this potential is
exploited. Those teachers who have organized learning through group
methods will be aware of a new and exciting dynamic among the
learners, some of whom for the first time begin to glimpse something of
their own skills and capacities for personal growth and development.

Combined with person-centred teaching, group work has enormous
possibilities. As with other forms of organization we need to be guided by
the pupils themselves, sensitive to what works well for them and ready to
change and modify our ideas. We need to engage our pupils in a
negotiation of the curriculum as well as in deciding the appropriate
methods to bring it to life in our classrooms. Exploring the possibilities of
group work in the interactive workshop is both an exciting and an urgent
challenge.

GROWTH

The relationship between learning and growth is central to the concept of reflective and experiential learning. While much of the learning that we do has practical and specific targets in mind, it is important that learners see beyond the utilitarian purposes of education and come to recognize and appreciate that learning is above all about making our way in the world, of bringing ourselves into a powerful relationship with reality so that we experience purpose, intention, action, achievement and understanding.

Many school brochures claim that a key aim of the curriculum is to help pupils to grow intellectually, emotionally, physically and spiritually, yet little time and opportunity is provided in their classroom experience to focus on the nature of this growth and to increase awareness of its processes. This involves giving attention to the inner life of the learner as well as to the learning activities and their outcomes. Each phase of our lives has its distinct and different challenges, and formal learning processes need to pay attention to them. Far too much of child education is given to anticipating adult life rather than to help children to be successful children with an appropriate balance of challenge and security in their lives. Above all, the education process needs to help children to make sense of the phases of childhood, to understand their growth concerns of self-image, identity, aspiration and experience.

Writers like Erik Erikson, Bruno Bettelheim, Frank Lake, Daniel Levinson and Gail Sheehy have emphasized the importance of helping children to manage the key tasks at each phase of their lives so that they enter the next one with confidence, and with much of the work of the previous phase reasonably completed.

Many of the teachers now working in classrooms were trained with Piaget's theory of pupil development in mind. Recent and current research is now showing that children are not confined within the intellectual boundaries defined by Piaget, but from their earliest moments are engaging in intellectual and rational pursuits of the most complex kind. As adults, we have the capacity and tendency vastly to underestimate the capacities of the young and make confining assumptions about the nature of their growth and development.

GUIDED VISUALIZATION

Since reflective and experiential learning attempts to create a holistic emphasis, it is necessary to pay attention to those parts of our experience that have tended to be neglected in schools. In our obsession with the cognitive domain of hard facts, rationality and logic we have marginalized that part of our thinking life which is most vibrant: the world of the active imagination.

One particular device has found particular benefits in classrooms: the use of guided visualization. This technique is both enjoyable and efficient. It can enhance intellectual growth and develop imaginative creativity at the same time that subject matter is dealt with. Unlike most other teaching methods, guided visualization provides an easy way to develop the ability to conceptualize.

The active imagination occupies a great deal of our time. Used as a technique in the classroom, it is consciously put to work in the learning process. By using the technique, the teacher is laying the groundwork for future cognitive growth, bringing the ability to visualize under control and improving the capacity for creative problem-solving.

It is useful to have had some experience of being led through a guided visualization before trying it with a class. What is important is believing in it, creating the right conditions in the classroom and being prepared to have a number of tries at it until self-consciousness is minimized.

Essentially the technique is quite simple. Pupils should be prepared for the experience by being encouraged to relax themselves and shut their eyes. The role of the teacher is to narrate the visual journey, making the necessary pauses when required. When the narration is complete it is important to bring the pupils back to reality by reminding them of their physical surroundings and then providing a brief opportunity for stretching and adjusting. The participants should then be encouraged to debrief the experience, first with a partner and perhaps then in a small group of two pairs. Written work or drawing can follow if required.

Almost any subject matter can form the basis of a visualization and the technique is suitable for participants of any age. The following is offered as an example and is a good one to try with learners who have not experienced the technique before.

In a moment or two, I am going to ask you to close your eyes while I take you on an imaginary journey. Make yourselves still and comfortable . . . and close your eyes . . . As I describe the journey to you try and picture it in your mind. Try to remember the sorts of feelings you have and what happens to you. When I have finished I shall ask you to draw some part of your journey.

I want you to imagine you are at home . . . Choose the room you want to be in . . . Look around you . . . what do you see . . . Go to the window and look out. There is a lot to see from the window, try and notice some of the different things . . . Now I want you to imagine a different view from this window . . . As you look out you can see in the distance a path that leads up a hillside towards some trees . . . imagine you are walking up this path . . . There are fields on either side of you . . . The sun is shining, the sky is blue. Wild flowers are growing beside the path and birds are singing in the trees . . . As you approach the trees you see the path leads into the wood . . . Follow the path . . . It is cooler in the wood and the leaves and branches make shadows on the ground . . . Not far in front of you there is a brick wall . . . It is a high wall and there is an old wooden door in it . . . When you open this door you are going to be in a place which is yours, a special place only for you . . . There can be anything there that you want, a house, a garden, people, animals . . . Now go through the door . . . What do you see? . . . Have a good look round at what is there . . . What is it like, this place? . . . What sort of feelings

do you have? . . . What is the most important thing in your place? . . .
Have a last look round now because soon we will be leaving . . .

In a few moments I want you to open your eyes, and when you do
you will be back here in the classroom . . . When you are ready open
your eyes and start to draw the place where you have been. You will
have about ten minutes to do the drawing and then you will have a
chance to talk to your partner about it . . . Start your drawing as soon
as you are ready.

The language needs to be appropriate to the age of the class or group. In
this particular case it was a class of 8 year olds. Pauses can be varied, but
it is important not to make them too long in the early stages or pupils will
lose their way and find it difficult to sustain the imagery.

HOPES

The National Curriculum for schools is sometimes referred to as an
entitlement curriculum, yet the entitlements have been conceived and
constructed with little or no involvement of receivers and consumers of
the curriculum. An important question to answer is: what do pupils
consider their entitlements in the schooling process are? Adults, both
within the teaching profession and outside it, often assert that children's
views about what is good for them are either naive or not to be trusted.
Prior to school admission, children have invested enormous energy and
enthusiasm in their learning. This commitment is not always sustained
within the formal context of schooling which may be due to the fact that
the ownership of direction and purpose in learning is taken from them
and placed in the hands of the state and its educational system.

In Chapter 2, a key question for educators from Theodore Roszak (1981)
was quoted: 'Everybody has an interest in education, but what is the
child's interest – independent of all adult intervention and influence?' A
key concern for experiential educators is how to keep children's hopes and
aspirations alive in a system that so often seems to deny their existence
or importance. In a piece of action research conducted with a family of
schools feeding into a neighbouring comprehensive, teachers were asked
to engage pupils in dialogue about their hopes and fears about school,
learning, teachers and their futures. From the vast range of data
collected in the exercise, the following list of pupil-defined entitlements
was extracted.

- to be interested and involved in the activities on offer;
- to evaluate and assess my own learning;
- to acquire the knowledge, skills and abilities necessary for my future;
- to be valued and respected for who I am, rather than for what I do;
- to learn how to be an effective learner;
- to have my experience of learning accepted as valid;
- to have time to reflect on what I learn and make sense of it;
- to know what is expected of me;
- to satisfy my curiosity and learn through my own interests and
  enthusiasms;

- to learn how interesting and complicated the world is;
- to know and understand the aims and purposes of the learning experiences offered me;
- to make mistakes and not to be punished for them;
- to share my learning with others;
- to learn at my own rate;
- to have a rich variety of first-hand experiences.

Only if pupils' hopes and aspirations are expressed, explored, developed, acted upon and reviewed can they truly be said to be safeguarded. The approaches and methodologies of experiential learning do attempt to vouchsafe the pupils' interests and hopes.

HUMANISTIC EDUCATION

This is an emphasis in education which places humanness at the centre of considerations and which sees learning and growth as a natural part of development. It recognizes that we are all born with an awesome potential for learning and that education is the process of optimizing this precious resource. Humanistic education emphasizes the importance of personal discovery as a key ingredient in the learning process. It also values the development of a sense of wonder and mystery while at the same time respecting traditional virtues of respect for discipline and competence.

By focusing on the learner rather than on the curriculum as the central foundation of structured learning, humanistic education advocates the creating of a suitable climate and environment to respond creatively to the needs of the learner, not the adaptation of the learner to an already existing environment.

By encouraging the development of self-responsibility for learning, humanistic education strives to reduce pupil dependence on the teacher for direction, control, motivation and evaluation. It sees learning as an act of creativity, a bringing to birth of human potential. Humanistic educators see their role as one of safeguarding that potential, of creating conditions in which it can flourish and grow.

Hall and Hall (1988) link the growth of humanistic education with the development of humanistic psychology and offer a number of defining factors:

- In humanistic education learners are seen as having choices and cannot be limited by their heredity or past experience.
- Humanistic education is concerned with the whole person and places equal emphasis on the intellect and the emotions.
- Humanistic education aims for the full development of the individual.

Our educational upbringing and training has tended to emphasize the knowing dimension at the expense of the being, so that we come into leadership roles incomplete and in many ways inadequately equipped to face the challenges and demands made upon us. What is required is a balancing of the two, an integrating of what we know and what we are as a result of experience. Both aspects are vital to the expression of the whole person that a leader undoubtedly needs to be. Leading others is predominantly about managing our own being, exercising the multiple intelligences referred to earlier. What is missing from much of formal education is a curriculum for being; it is also missing in many programmes of management and leadership training.

This is not to suggest that knowing is of no importance, but to point to the dangers of relentlessly pursuing it to the exclusion of other important aspects of living and being. Our success as teachers depends upon our ability to help learners to break through the boundaries of self-limitation. This involves encouraging them to take risks with their learning – to bring out what is sometimes hesitant, raw and unrefined.

IDEAS

Ideas are the very stuff of learning. In traditional structures, the ideas are fixed, predetermined and unquestionable. In the new paradigm of learning they are regarded as immanent – waiting to be brought into being at the appropriate time and place. It does not help the learning process always to be told that the only useful ideas are the ones that someone else has already had. Good teachers create a climate in which ideas can be brought out sometimes from deep within us, where they can mix with other ideas and flow backwards and forwards in an elaborate dance of creativity. Schools need to develop an *ideas culture*, where ideas that arise from pupils' own thinking and imagining are celebrated, explored, developed and recorded.

Children's ideas about their experience, their social reality and the world at large are often fragmentary, confused and incomplete. Helping them to grow in awareness and understanding involves building on their own ideas rather than replacing them with a correct or official set as laid down in the programmes of study. Most knowledge inputs should be preceded by an activity to establish what ideas are already held by pupils on an issue under consideration. Using techniques like Brainstorming (p.71) and Flowcharts (p.123) will help to bring out the current state of awareness which can then be used to explore new lines of enquiry and clarification.

IDEOLOGIES

Ideologies are sets of ideas which form the basis for systematic theories and belief patterns. Children are born into a world characterized by conflicting ideologies. Any good system of education should help pupils to come to terms with the ideological nature of human living and to develop the skills to operate well within it. Providing time for work on ideologies will serve a number of important purposes:

- To help pupils find their way through the complex maze of ideologies.
- To help pupils develop a capacity to examine ideologies through the framework of critical thinking.

- To help pupils develop a respect for the part that ideologies play in defining human reality and aspiration.
- To help pupils develop their own ideological frameworks through enquiry and exploration.

Reflective and experiential learning techniques provide an excellent framework for these purposes, allowing pupils to use first- and second-hand encounters with the world of ideas, ideologies and beliefs. Helping pupils to examine, change and develop their personal attitudes, values and beliefs is a vital part of good learning.

One of the most valuable things schools can do is to help pupils to develop capacities to engage in dialogue about ideologies, not only in order to understand the differing ideologies themselves, but to learn how to handle dispute, discord, prejudice, bigotry and zealotry. We are surrounded by failures and breakdowns in these capacities. The future may depend on placing the dialogue of tolerance very much higher on the school agenda.

IMAGINATION

Imagination is an essential and powerful part of holistic intelligence. It is the seat of human creativity and the foundation of achievement. Writing in *Left-handed Teaching* (1978), Gloria Castillo writes:

> Each of us has an imagination. Some of us are freer to use our imagination than others, and some of us find it more accessible under some conditions than others. It is an aspect of the learning process that is uniquely human and that most often goes uninstructed in our schools.

Imagination draws on experience, fantasy, emotion and thinking and the task of bringing it under appropriate management is essential if learning is to be successful. It is in our imaginations that we formulate the responses that learning demands of us. The formal educational process needs to help us to develop the capacity to use imagination deliberately and productively in the pursuit of knowledge and understanding. This will not happen unless imagination is afforded the same respect and reverence that is extended to thinking and remembering. This applies not only to the creative domain of the curriculum but especially to the cognitive. The great scientists, inventors and mathematicians have succeeded because they had lively and powerful imaginations, not despite them.

Castillo further observes:

> We can learn, and teach students to be intuitive and expressive, flexible and perceptive, and we can do it without giving up reason, communication, purpose, or emotional control. We can learn, and teach students to distinguish reality from fantasy and to discriminate the inner from the outer world without destroying either.

Reflective and experiential learning approaches positively enhance both the inner and outer worlds since they create the optimum conditions for both right and left brain functions to be activated in the learning process.

Imagination is an essential component of what is sometimes referred to as *crystallized intelligence* – that intelligence compounded through the integration of all human capacities. If intelligence, in its traditional sense, has brought us to our present state, then perhaps it is time to give imagination a chance.

INFORMATION

During the last half of the twentieth century we have witnessed in western industrial society a steady shift from a manufacturing economy to an information economy. More workers are now employed in information activity than in manufacturing, and knowledge has replaced minerals as the key raw material of the economy. New technologies have revolutionized the ways in which information can be stored, transferred and accessed. Although slow to impact on the educational system, information technology will also revolutionize the way we manage learning in schools and in homes.

Pupils now entering our schools will need to develop information skills of a high order if they are to lead successful lives in the twenty-first century. Experience within schools has shown that even without formal teaching the youngest children in the schooling system are capable of using computers and other forms of information technology with great skill and efficiency, often out-learning their own teachers.

In the future, the knowledge base that forms a central part of the curriculum will be in a constant state of flux with an increasing range of new ideas, theories, explanations, evidence and achievements in all fields of learning. The skill of being able to access new information will become far more important than remembering it and the successful learner will be the one who can work efficiently to replace old data with new.

The appropriate use of new technologies in the field of information management, problem-solving, planning and designing will form a whole new set of experiences for pupils to reflect upon. They will need help to decide when technology is appropriate and when more traditional techniques provide the best approach. Increasingly, learners will be building their own databases, writing their own learning management programmes and producing their projects through word processors. They will become what John Sculley (1987) has described as 'knowledge navigators', finding ever more inventive ways of using this tantalizingly attractive technology in the pursuit of learning.

One of the difficulties for teachers will be that of managing their own knowledge base. Those who trained before space travel, genetic engineering and artificial intelligence became part of the new intellectual culture need to find ways of updating their rapidly ageing ideas. One impact of the new technologies is likely to be an equalizing of the relationships between teacher and taught, since both partners in the educational enterprise will be seekers of information, managers of new ideas and appraisers of new theories. The experiential learning cycle will become more important than ever before as we strive to grapple with an increasing avalanche of new information and data.

INNER WORLDS

One of the key shifts in educational emphasis in recent years has been from a concern for the external world of the learner to a respect and concern for the inner world. An increasing number of educators are realizing that the capacity of pupils to cope with their lives in the future cannot be achieved unless they can enter adulthood with a secure sense of self, and an awareness of their own inner processes. Not only does reflective and experiential learning bring the pupil into closer touch with the inner world of experience, thinking and imagining, it also helps pupils to build an effective relationship between the inner and outer aspects of living.

This involves the careful building of a phenomenological framework for learning – one that recognizes and accepts the pupil's personal view of the world as their reality, and strives to relate that view to other views. This requires the creation of opportunities to frame, describe, explain and explore personal viewpoints in relation to others. It involves testing and comparing attitudes and perceptions, searching for mutuality as well as respecting difference. Above all it is about accepting flux rather than certainty as a key feature of human experience.

Rather than expecting pupils to receive an official and carefully designed world view, we should recognize that the task of teaching is one of helping pupils to build their own world view within a framework of critical development.

The best practical way to help pupils value the inner space is to engage them as often as possible in sharing their thinking and feeling with others. There are two key activities here:

1   Reflection on experience by reviewing first – or second-hand experiences.
2   Sharing these reflections, emerging theories and ideas in critical friendships, where the emphasis is on exploration, insight and discovery, rather than argument.

In enabling and supportive learning environments this will happen informally all the time, but it may be necessary to provide training in the process by providing regular structured exercises to encourage the development and familiarity of the two activities described above.

INSIGHT

Insights are the essential building blocks of learning and growth. The endless questions of the young child are attempts to acquire insights, to illuminate the darkness that lack of knowledge creates. As adults we have a tendency to think of childhood as a pre-real world where the child's access is controlled by adults. We do our best to protect children from its chilly realities. But too often this becomes a process of mis-information and disinformation – a way of closing the doors of under-standing; of constructing a temporary pretend world which we feel serves children better than the actual one.

Children are absorbed by television soap operas. Perhaps watching them is the only way they vicariously gain insights into the world of adult constructs. By watching them, they have the opportunity to test their own often confused theorizing and obtain glimpses of explanation.

Achieving insight is a complex process of unravelling constellations of facts, perceptions, ideas, experiences, and memories. Joseph Zinker (1977) conceives of this process in a very graphic way (see Figure 4.10). Our skill as teachers lies in resisting the temptation to steal the moment from the learner and stifle the insight at conception. What we should engage in is a sort of intellectual midwifery – helping birth on its natural course and then celebrating its arrival. This is what discovery learning

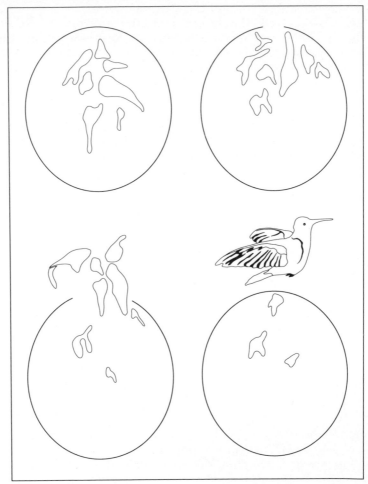

Figure 4.10 Birth of an insight.

means: *Once I have created this insight, I have it forever. If I have done it once I can do it again.*

Abraham Maslow (1976) coined the phrase 'peak experience' to describe those intense moments when the world seems to be at our fingertips, when we feel in command of our thinking and feeling in quite powerful ways. It is with the creation of an environment in which these peak experiences can flourish that we should be concerned. Perhaps peak experiences should replace attainment targets as the real measure of educational success.

INTELLIGENCE

In its basic sense intelligence is that property which provides the potential for fulfilment in all aspects of our lives. It provides the capacity for physical survival, emotional balance and intellectual enquiry. In the formal world of organized education, intelligence has acquired a very restricted meaning – the ability to perform in a narrow range of cognitive activities. In these terms our capacity to solve a number puzzle is regarded as a sign of intelligence, whereas a capacity to provide comfort and support a friend in need or cook a nutritious and tasty meal is not.

It is interesting to note that the full range of cognitive intelligence is represented among the patients in institutions of mental health.

An alternative, more human and more actualizing definition is desperately needed if we are to prevent future generations from falling into the intelligence trap.

In *The Empty Raincoat* (1994), Charles Handy offers a working list which contains several different types of intelligence:

- factual intelligence
- analytical intelligence
- linguistic intelligence
- spatial intelligence
- musical intelligence
- practical intelligence
- physical intelligence
- intuitive intelligence
- interpersonal intelligence

This offers an altogether new and richer view. As Handy observes:

> It is the tragedy of much of our schooling that we are led to think that logical intelligence is the only type that matters. Any observation of our friends and colleagues in later life will prove that the other intelligences are at least as important, if not more so.
>
> (Handy, 1990)

We should, he argues, train ourselves not to ask how intelligent people are, but which type of intelligence they have the most of.

The traditional view of intelligence emphasizes 'cleverness', mental agility and intellectual strength. Denis Postle (1989) describes four types of intelligence:

1   *Emotional intelligence*:
    ● radiating warmth
    ● awareness of own feelings
    ● sensitivity to feelings of others
    ● creating harmony and goodwill
    ● dealing with emotional issues openly
    ● empathizing with the experience of others.

2   *Intuitive intelligence*:
    ● gut feelings
    ● hunches
    ● speculating about the future
    ● using imagination
    ● willingness to take risks
    ● capacity for change.

3   *Physical intelligence*:
    ● concerned with fitness and health
    ● enjoyment of physical activities
    ● pride in manual skills and dexterity
    ● sensible and balanced diet
    ● love of the outdoors
    ● good at household tasks.

4   *Intellectual intelligence*:
    ● reasoning
    ● problem-solving
    ● analysis
    ● calculation
    ● handling information
    ● abstract ideas.

It is with the pursuit of this more comprehensive intelligence that this book is concerned. What we can do in our work with learners is to come to see in each of them a more rounded intelligence at work, to value their physical achievements as surely as we would once have praised their intellectual prowess, that we acknowledge their growing capacity to manage emotions sensitively and assertively. This does not mean reducing the value and importance of intellectual intelligence, but simply of placing it more equally alongside the others.

INTERACTIONS

It is very often in the process of relationship that the most important leaps in our learning are made. The role of the sensitive and caring teacher has always been seen as the fundamental key to the education of the young. Unfortunately, this wisdom was lost as learning began to be organized in institutions. Interaction with a learner was replaced by structured instruction, and rigid behavioural controls were introduced to manage the process. It was control rather than interaction which became to be seen as the key to effective teaching.

It is fortunate that the fundamental role of human relationship in schooling is being reclaimed. Increasingly, teachers are recognizing that schools provide a unique setting in which to help learners to become skilful in their interactions with others, and at the same time increase their opportunities to learn effectively in the wider context of the school curriculum.

Pioneering work in client-centred counselling has led to the recognition that a structured, helping relationship is one of the most powerful ways to assist learning that we have at our disposal. Essentially, this style of relationship is characterized by three essential assumptions about the learner by the helper:

1 That the learner is a capable learner.
2 That the learner wants to learn.
3 That the learner's unique experience is a key resource for learning.

Secondly, the helper is more likely to be effective if three particular behaviours are demonstrated:

1 A warm, caring respect for the learner.
2 A genuine relationship with the learner.
3 Empathy for the learner's experience.

One of the difficulties inherent in the schooling system is that, given current class sizes, teachers do not have the time to offer the sort of relationship described above on a consistent basis. Interactions with pupils tend to be short, probably averaging out at less than a minute.

What classroom life does offer is the opportunity to create a set of helping relationships between the pupils themselves. By the age of school entry most of us have developed a capacity to relate well in one-to-one situations. It is with the exploitation of this natural capacity that experiential learning is concerned. By building on natural and acquired behaviours the teacher is able to develop interactional skills to powerfully assist the learning process. Fortunately, the tyranny of *no talking* classrooms is quickly disappearing. What is needed is the recognition that structured rather than casual interactions between pupils holds the key to more powerful and effective modes of learning.

INTERDEPENDENCE

The continual building of pupil dependence on teachers, on the syllabus and on school rules inhibits healthy growth. Independence, so important in many areas of our life, can, if pursued too excessively, lead to an unhealthy individualism and the denial of the roles that others can play in the structuring and management of successful learning.

The concept of interdependence in the learning process can offer us a range of new assumptions:

1 Teachers are learners too, and indeed have the most to learn from any classroom experience.
2 Learners are teachers too, and have much to offer to other class members and to their teachers.

3   Learning is best seen as a process of human co-operation – a shared journey to understanding and competence.
4   Only when we release our skills and abilities in a climate of genuine enquiry and support can learning truly flourish.
5   We are all responsible in the school setting to work to create and build a learning enterprise where effort, endeavour and curiosity are regarded as more important than performance, conformity and dependence.

INTERPERSONAL EDUCATION

Perhaps the single most important capacity to achieve fulfilment in life is that of being able to relate successfully to others. This involves the ability to make relationships, build friendships, develop partnerships, to work effectively in teams and groups and to be a responsible citizen in society. Despite pioneering developments in personal and social education and the building of an important pastoral dimension in school life, the knowledge and skills to develop these capacities have never featured as part of the formal curriculum and were disregarded when the framework for the National Curriculum was drawn up. We tend to have acquired what skills we have through a process of disciplined correction:

- Don't answer back.
- Look at me when I'm talking to you.
- Don't forget to say, 'Thank you for having me'.
- I want you to be on your best behaviour.

Such messages can send shudders of pain through adults as they recall these parental messages, and cause them to relive the smouldering resentment such statements activated. Yet as children we saw adults behaving in exactly the ways they attempted to force us out of. We learned about interpersonal living painfully, through trial and error, and sometimes through trial and success if we were very lucky.

History tells us that most of the wars and conflicts in human history have been caused by breakdowns in human relationships, yet still we have continued to ignore the obvious necessity to focus on interpersonal living in the formal schooling process. As society becomes more complex, the models of interpersonal behaviour become increasingly limited in their capacity to offer creative and effective solutions to complex interpersonal situations. We are living in an age where we have had to create conciliation professions to help us unravel our interpersonal lives when they become so confused and damaging that we can no longer sustain healthy living. We have developed elaborate therapies to help us to sort out our own lives when the pain of unhealthy relationships has become unbearable. A telling paragraph by Palomares and Ball (1972) summarizes the situation:

> Most patients in psychotherapy are middle aged, middle class, married and educated; they function tolerably well as jobholders, parents and citizens. They are also men and women bitterly

disappointed with the quality of their lives, who have sought help from the professional therapist because their disappointment has become unbearable. These people have large, complex lives; they are a mass of habits, assumptions and responses gouged out by time and hardened by the pressures of social competition and adult respons-ibility. Therapy, for such people, is a painful, expensive, protracted experience. It is rarely wholly successful and it is often too late. This is a painful and frustrating experience for the therapist as well, and it was for these reasons that I turned, looking for a better approach, to the very young school child. I wanted to see if effective, large scale preventative measures could be taken that would assure normal, healthy emotional growth, much as a sound balanced diet can ensure the development of children who are physically normal and healthy.

It is to attempt to reverse this sad and appalling situation that we need to look to the educational process. Any effective and life-enhancing curriculum needs to include the art and practice of living.

An interpersonal curriculum will not only need to help pupils increase their awareness of the interpersonal nature of their lives but provide them with the constructs to understand and explain their various interpersonal experiences. It will also need to help in the development of effective communication behaviours:

- Listening
- Non-verbal communication
- Disclosing
- Empathizing
- Assertiveness
- Conciliation
- Negotiation
- Counselling
- Confronting

All these are skills which we need to begin developing early in our lives if we are to become effective in the interpersonal landscape described in Chapter 2.

INTRODUCTIONS

Within schools, learning is characterized by a sequence of reasonably short activities – either lessons or tasks within lessons. For most children this can involve as many as a hundred different learning tasks per week. Since time is the rare resource – a hundred activities gives an average of fifteen minutes per activity – it is vital that the quality of those fifteen minutes is as high as possible.

One way of improving quality is to look to the nature of our introductions. We need to be both effective and efficient. We can improve in both directions by adopting a systematic approach. This involves ensuring that the following components are covered in any introduction to a learning activity:

1 *Purpose*: what the activity is designed to achieve. Pupils should be able to complete the sentence which begins: 'I am doing this in order to . . .'
2 *Outcome*: what will need to have been done by the end of the activity. 'At the end of this activity I shall have . . .'
3 *Specification*: the detailed requirements – the specific criteria – Any end-product will need to satisfy.
4 *Queries*: how questions and queries will be dealt with.
5 *Role*: 'My role as teacher will be to . . .'.

The attraction of such a systematic approach lies in its capacity to get pupils started on tasks they are clear about, which have specific purposes and goals and where the criteria for success are established. The approach also offers a structure for reviewing progress when the task is finished.

INTUITION

Intuition is concerned with how we know things. It is a way of knowing that is controlled by the right hemisphere of the brain. Because intuition extends beyond the realms of logic and rationality into areas of inspiration and creativity, it has tended to be disregarded in our intellectual tradition and dismissed as feminine logic. In *The Second Centering Book*, Frances Clark (1977) writes:

> Intuitive experiences are usually associated with increased or new awareness. Often they are intense experiences which are felt to be total, involving the whole of one's being. Persons reporting such experience often refer to a sense of being guided or directed by something other than reason. Such experiences are frequently unexpected and yet marked by a sense of clarity and a feeling that the experience is 'right' or appropriate for the individual at that particular time.

At the reflective stage of the experiential learning cycle it is important to help learners to develop their intuitive intelligence. In prompting them to describe their learning experiences we should avoid using *why* questions which probe for explanation before awareness is sufficiently crystallized. Questions designed to encourage learners to describe *what* their experience was like, or *how* it felt, are more likely to develop the intuitive capacity. Denis Postle (1989) describes our preoccupation with *why* questions as the interpreter function of mind which constantly seeks for meaning in well-ordered and sequential steps:

> But intuition which provides direct access to the bodymind's non verbal processing that precedes the interpreter, gives a different quality of knowledge. It comes in the form of hunches, gut feelings and inspired guesses.

As teachers, we need both to acknowledge and to promote this type of intuitive functioning in learners as part of the journey to a more balanced intelligence and enhanced learning.

Philip Goldberg (1989) has noted the vital link between curiosity and intuition and stresses how important it is to keep curiosity alive: 'One thing we need to do, then, is convey the delight of discovery to students at an early age so that they leap after knowledge for the sheer exhilaration of it.' Goldberg observes that education tends to use external motivation almost exclusively and that learning seems to have more to do with avoiding punishments and seeking rewards: 'From the earliest grades we penalize errors severely and even reprimand pupils who offer up guesses, half formed feelings, and vague hunches – the very things that frequently lead to discovery.' Such an approach, argues Goldberg, tells children that it just does not pay to take risks, so they become mistrustful of their own thinking and feeling when it seems not to be what the teacher wants. In short, children learn to play safe and keep clear of intuition as a resource for learning and living.

INVENTING

In the literature of pedagogy it is almost impossible to find any reference to the development of inventiveness as a capability in learners. Yet the capacity to be inventive is often a key requirement in job recruitment. Inventors are often considered to be a somewhat eccentric group, lost in a world of ideas. This is almost certainly due to the fact that inventiveness stems more from the right than the more prized left hemisphere of the brain. What we actually find in the inventor is a successful blending of both brain hemispheres to produce effective solutions to human problems.

We are born inventive and well-equipped to satisfy an almost insatiable curiosity about the world. Unfortunately we learn to suspend our curiosity and wait to be told, and to eschew inventiveness because it does not always bring forth the correct answer at the first time of asking. When the prevailing educational culture is about getting it right first time, it is no wonder that we fail to build on and extend the glorious capacity for invention with which we are all born.

The early stages of primary education have attempted to rekindle inventiveness by immersing children in a world of enquiry and exploration. Teachers help children to become fascinated with possibility rather than certainty, with speculation rather than fact, leading them sensitively towards understanding and insight.

Some simple changes in the ways we phrase our instructions to pupils would encourage inventiveness. Rather than saying, 'Find the answer to . . .', why don't we say:

- Invent ways of . . .
- Design a method of . . .
- Create a . . .
- Discover three ways of . . .

The pursuit of the single correct answer in so many subject disciplines has resulted in a preoccupation with right and wrong. It is fortunate that real inventors and scientists have thrown away such damaging constraints to their creativity.

How wonderful it would be to read in a record of achievement or school report: 'Her many inventions include . . .'.

INVOLVEMENT

In the shift from passive to active participation in the learning process it is vital to find powerful ways of involving learners in the management of their own learning. Evidence suggests that assumptions about the presence and growth of intellectual ability in young children has been vastly underestimated and the traditional dependency model of teaching has severely inhibited this potential for growth.

Careful observation of the play of young children demonstrates this well. It is also curious to note that many of the skills that are selected as the basis for management training later in life – motivation, leadership, teamwork, planning and communication – are naturally present in young children and evident in their play. As the schooling system strengthens its grip of control, developing a competitive rather than co-operative and participative approach to learning, these skills fail to be built on and developed. Management training becomes a mid-life remedial exercise. By insisting that pupils learn individually and separately we are failing to take advantage of one of the key opportunities provided in schools: a collaborative setting.

Pupils are unlikely to take full responsibility for their learning if they are not involved in the management and organization of it. Traditionally, the system seems to have a deep-seated fear of this. Learning becomes something that is done to you, rather than something you both do for yourself within the helping and support structures of the school.

The following questions are offered as a way of assessing our capacity and desire for pupil participation in the learning process:

1   In what ways do I share with pupils the rationale behind my curriculum design?
2   In what ways do I help pupils to understand the purposes of the learning activities I organize for them?
3   What do I know about their individual learning aspirations?
4   What practical steps have I taken to raise my own awareness of their individual learning concerns and anxieties?
5   What specific opportunities have I provided for pupils to reflect on their own learning?
6   In what specific ways do I organize pupil feedback on learning activities I arrange?
7   What range of decisions about the management of learning have I delegated to pupils?
8   In what ways do pupils participate in the planning of programmes, projects, activities and tasks?
9   In what ways do I help pupils to develop self-management skills – co-operation, teamwork and leadership?

JOURNEY

If we regard the learning process as an end in itself, then we simply emphasize its utilitarian value. Once we recognize that learning *is* living and not just a preparation for life we begin to appreciate some of the intrinsic values in the long childhood of growth. Part of the problem lies in perceiving education as a function of childhood – a temporary preparation stage before adulthood is assumed. If instead we can conceive education as a process of travel and not the pursuit of a single destination, we see that learning and teaching is a shared journey to the future, a voyage where we accompany the traveller on part of his or her hazardous quest for happiness, fulfilment and meaning. When we do this, we gain a sense of what it really means to be a teacher.

JUDGEMENT

Through judgement, teachers come to make decisions about pupils and their educational lives. Pupils also need to develop discernment and judgement in order to make sensible decisions about themselves, their learning and their futures. But far from being seen as a process of arriving at conclusions and making decisions, judgement is used as a way of modifying, correcting and disciplining children. The long childhood for many of us has been a journey through judgements about our behaviour, appearance, manners, accents, school results, choice of friends and decisions about a career. Judgement has come to define a way of controlling behaviour.

In this sense judgements are merely opinions, passed as if they had a higher moral authority. Hence, as parents, we pass judgements on our children, and as teachers we do the same with our pupils. Yet the act of judgemental condemnation has been found to be one of the key barriers to effective communication (Bolton 1979). Particularly when associated with name-calling, criticizing, diagnosing and evaluative praise, passing judgement has the effect on the receiver of attacking self-esteem, confidence and self-belief. When we feel 'put down', we are likely to withdraw ourselves from full and active involvement in the educational tasks and challenges facing us.

In his description of the directional tendency in all human beings, Carl Rogers (1967) has pointed to the need for a safe psychological climate in which this directional force can be released, experimented with and developed. Central to this nourishing climate are the attitudes, skills and qualities of those responsible for growth and education. A key quality in teachers is what Rogers describes as a 'warm, non judgemental caring and respect for each pupil as a person' (Rogers 1983).

In the interests of effective learning and growth it is necessary to moderate the moral certitude implied in so many of the judgements applied to children, and to help the learners themselves to weigh and balance facts and evidence in the pursuit of good decisions.

JUSTICE

Children seem to develop a sense of justice very early in life. They feel outraged if they have been wrongly accused or falsely blamed for something they did not do. Life in the family, and perhaps more powerfully in school, becomes the context in which this sense of justice is sharpened and developed.

It is difficult to see how the young can acquire a sure sense of fairness and justice when as a group they are not regarded as worthy of many of the entitlements to justice expected by adults in our society. Corporal punishment for adults is widely rejected but quite happily advocated for children. Most adult bullies – both physical and psychological – boast about how they were beaten as children and were not harmed by it!

The sure way to help pupils to grow in increasing awareness of justice and its importance in the social structure is for them to experience its benefits. Good teachers have always taken pains to support pupils in resolving their conflicts and coming to terms with their transgressions and misdemeanours. One of A. S. Neill's (1968) concerns for the proper growth and development of his pupils was to engage them fully in the management of justice at Summerhill. Pupils need to be agents as well as subjects of the justice system if they are to grow to respect its importance and to benefit from its application.

KNOWLEDGE

Knowledge has long been regarded as the central pillar of education. The emphasis in the National Curriculum is very biased towards what needs to be known rather than how well multiple intelligence can be used in the pursuit of meaning and understanding.

Charles Dickens (1854/1961), writing in *Hard Times*, made the point very clearly in the words of Thomas Gradgrind:

> Now what I want is Facts. Teach these boys and girls nothing but Facts. Facts alone are wanted in life. Plant nothing else and root out everything else. You can only form the minds of reasoning animals upon Facts: nothing else will ever be of any service to them. This is the principle upon which I bring up my own children, and this is the principle upon which I bring up these children. Stick to Facts, sir!

Knowledge, accumulated for its own sake, does little to help in the development of intelligence, reasoning, creativity, intuition and imagination, all of which are the basic ingredients of human endeavour and achievement. The education system has been obsessed with testing knowledge, yet curiously has done very little to help children acquire the skills of using memory successfully.

On the other hand, knowledge is supremely important, too important to devote so much time to remembering it. Children have the highest respect for facts and are both fascinated and tantalized by information. Knowledge provides a sure foundation for learning, but it is not learning itself.

A refreshing view of knowledge and its applications is illustrated in the objectives contained in *World Studies 8–13, A Teacher's Handbook* (Fisher and Hicks 1985). Here, knowledge is regarded as the pupil's capacity:

- to explain
- to describe
- to evaluate

This places knowledge within a practical framework. A useful question for pupils to ask themselves is: 'In what specific ways will I be able to use this information?'

Alvin Toffler, writing in 1971 about the changed conditions of the future, pointed to a revolution in information: 'Tomorrow's schools must teach not merely data, but ways to manipulate it. Students must learn how to discard old ideas, how and when to replace them.' This idea of skilful forgetting is a novel concept in education, but a vital one if we are to succeed in managing an ever-increasing range of new facts, ideas and information.

LATERAL THINKING

Lateral thinking is a way of thinking that incorporates powerful cerebral resources that traditionally accepted patterns of thinking have tended to neglect.

A process as exciting and challenging as learning needs all the resources we can muster. These resources are not identical in each learner and they become organized and patterned in elaborate and sometimes idiosyncratic combinations in individual learners. The challenge for teachers is to appreciate the subtle characteristics in thinking style that distinguish one learner from another.

In 1967 Edward de Bono published *The Uses of Lateral Thinking*. In the Foreword he poses the question: 'Why do some people always seem to be having new ideas while others of equal intelligence never do?' The answer is that many of us allow our thinking to become limited to the rational and linear processes of the left brain – so celebrated in the western intellectual tradition – so that our capacities for intuitive insight and leaps of the imagination, so characterized by the great minds in history, are severely limited.

Since 1967 de Bono has written and lectured extensively on the processes of lateral thinking and has produced a programme for developing lateral thinking in schools.

It is difficult to understand, given the prominence afforded to rational and logical thinking in education, that it has never been taught. Most of us have had our inadequacies as thinkers pointed out to us and many have been exhorted to *think harder*.

It is also fascinating to speculate why it is that we judge pupils on their ability to think, yet do virtually nothing to help them learn to do it successfully.

LAUGHTER

Many pupils end up laughing *at* their teachers because they are never encouraged to laugh *with* them. The separation of fun from the learning process is one of the most damaging inheritances of Victorian education. In the struggle to identify useful performance indicators, let us not forget to find a place for laughter. Its absence in schools should always be a cause for concern.

In describing some of the characteristics of work in successful organizations, the distinguished American writer Rosabeth Moss Kanter (1989) refers to 'the five fs' – fast, focused, flexible, friendly and fun – a good recipe too for the effective classroom.

LEADERSHIP

There is a vast and growing literature on the theory and practice of leadership and hardly any of it is about schools and the work that teachers do within them.

Leadership is an essential element of good teaching – the motivation and facilitation of activity by others. John Heider (1985) observes:

As a rule, the leader feels more wholesome when the group process is flowing freely and unfolding naturally, when delicate facilitations far outnumber harsh interventions.

The best teachers are those who have discovered the art of leadership and apply it consistently well in classrooms. They know that leadership is about enabling and empowering others to be successful. They build on success more than they dwell on failure. They encourage self-respect in the learners they work with and they reward risk-taking in the pursuit of learning ambitions.

There has been a shift in our understanding of what leadership is. In modern organizational life, leadership is seen as a function that needs to emerge in working situations, rather than as the responsibility of a specified role-holder. In schools, leadership is exercised by all members of staff; it is not the prerequisite of head and senior staff. Teachers exercise it most powerfully of all in their management of the learning process. As the graffiti says: 'People don't want to be managed, they want to be led.'

We need to realize that leading and being led are interchangeable functions; they do not depend on title or status, but on location and need. Leadership is a shared function to be taken on by different individuals as appropriate and according to the nature of the task in hand.

Given this enhanced definition it is vital that leadership should be encouraged and developed in pupils, not merely in the captaining of sports teams but in a wide variety of learning situations. Pupils need to be helped to see that leadership is that quality which anyone can call forth to assist the direction of an activity. The reflective and experiential emphasis in education enables pupils to gain confidence and an ability to develop and practise their leadership capabilities.

LEARNING STYLES

Most teachers learn very early in their careers that children, as learners, bring to their work a wide range of skills and abilities, and that within any class of pupils the spread of those abilities will be wide and differentiated. Careful observation of learners at work will reveal that no two pupils conduct their learning in exactly the same way. The schooling system has not easily acknowledged this differentiation, and has developed the assumption that the only effective learning style is the one that responds best to the teacher's preferred style of teaching. What we have come to realize is that treating all pupils the same is a recipe for disaster.

One of the best things we can do in our classroom work is to help learners gain an acute awareness of their learning strengths and difficulties. This involves encouraging them to experiment with different methods and approaches in order to discover what works for them and what does not. If they learn best in one particular way then that is the way that should be encouraged. Many pupils discover personal ways of managing simple mathematical calculations, often involving some visualization in their minds. A great deal of mathematical failure has been caused by teachers attempting to correct these idiosyncratic techniques.

A key role of the teacher is to help learners to discover their unique repertoire of learning strengths, and to acknowledge and affirm their sometimes eccentric styles of gaining understanding. Studies of autistic children have shown that, free from *interference*, the human brain can discover amazingly powerful functions.

The beauty of the reflective and experiential approach is that it both provides opportunities to experiment with different attitudes to learning and enables learners, through the process of reflecting on their learning experiences, to come to terms with their own strengths and difficulties.

There is a wider discussion of particular learning styles in Chapter 2.

LIFE SKILLS

Life skills is a phrase coined by Barrie Hopson and Mike Scally to refer to those areas of personal growth and development that have largely been ignored by formal education. In the Preface to *Lifeskills Teaching* (1981) they declare their stance:

> We believe in education, because through learning we discover not only the world we live in, but ourselves. We can begin to see ourselves as instruments capable of being in tune with our environment or terribly discordant and at odds with it. The tuning comes not from outside us but from within. We are each our own drummer and we must find our own beat. Sadly, we are only too aware that much of what passes for education falls short of this. Education should be by the people, but all too often it is merely for

them; it should be expansive rather than restrictive; stimulating not boring; peaceful not aggressive; accenting strengths not highlighting weaknesses; fun not dour; uplifting not depressing; communal not solitary; about self discipline not punishment; about ideas not rituals; creative not conformist; focused on achievement not intentions.

The book sets out the skills which the writers believe should form an integral part of a curriculum for self-empowerment. They cover a broad range of human development including:

managing resources, problem solving, developing creative potential, managing time, discovering interests and values, setting goals, taking stock, making effective decisions, handling emotions, physical well being, communicating, making relationships, helping others, managing conflict, being assertive, influence, working in a group, expressing feelings, negotiating, how to study, discovering educational and job options.

From modest beginnings, Lifeskills Associates has developed into an international education service, helping wide ranges of people to develop their learning skills in pursuit of life goals and ambitions.

LISTENING

As one of the key dimensions of effective communication and successful learning, listening has been almost totally neglected by the schooling process. Even in the English document of the National Curriculum, listening is regarded as a rather subsidiary skill compared to reading and writing. Not only is it important for teachers – who probably spend more time talking to pupils than listening to them – to practise and develop active listening skills, but pupils themselves should have the opportunity to build on a listening facility that is naturally present in infancy.

Active listening can be defined as a dynamic process in which the listener attempts to gain insights into the perceptual, intellectual and emotional world of the speaker. It differs from passive listening in that the active listening stance is a deliberate one, concerned only with the agenda of the speaker. Any concerns of the listener are temporarily suspended. The whole stance is concerned to enable the talker to explore in as full and complete a way as possible their own ideas and concerns.

If we are to be successful in adopting this stance, there is an increased responsibility to display effective communication behaviour. While improved listening skills would benefit all human interactions, they are particularly important when a pupil has a problem and wants to talk it through with somebody they can trust.

The capacity to be an effective and active listener depends upon the appropriate use of a cluster of skills (see Figure 4.11).

Establishing rapport
This initial cluster of skills is concerned with establishing the right conditions for the active listening stance. Conveying a sense of active attention to the other person requires:

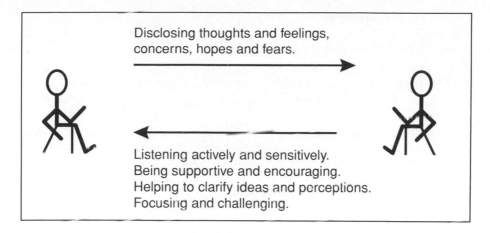

Disclosing thoughts and feelings, concerns, hopes and fears.

Listening actively and sensitively.
Being supportive and encouraging.
Helping to clarify ideas and perceptions.
Focusing and challenging.

Figure 4.11 Active listening.

- an environment as free from distraction as possible;
- sitting reasonably close to each other;
- chairs set at a slight angle to each other;
- leaning slightly forward in a posture of interest and involvement;
- the conscious use of appropriate gestures and facial expressions;
- good eye contact.

These actions and behaviours help to create an interpersonal climate conducive to effective interaction. They convey to the talker a sense of our commitment to the task, that we have time to listen and are interested and concerned in their experience.

Supporting the talker
Once a suitable climate has been created it is necessary to get the other person to talk, and to encourage ideas and feelings to be expressed. The cluster of skills required here include:

- inviting them to talk: 'Would you like to begin by telling me what the problem is?'
- encouraging them to keep talking: 'Could you say a little more about that?'
- using limited but focusing questions;
- keeping an attentive silence.

All these factors are to do with creating the sort of environment in which the talker feels safe to disclose their difficulties and problems. Once they have begun to talk it is important to keep communication going so that the real issues and concerns are brought out. This means good non-verbal communication and some minimal verbal responding. Active listening is different from conversation and it is important to resist the temptation to intervene and take the agenda away from the talker by focusing on our own experience. Maintaining an attentive and sensitive silence is the skill to cultivate if this is to be avoided.

Conveying understanding
The final cluster involves conveying to the talker a sense of being understood. This requires:

- reflecting the talker's feelings;
- reflecting the talker's thoughts and ideas;
- paraphrasing what has been said;
- summarizing from time to time.

It is facility with this cluster of skills that makes the difference between active, effective listening and merely hearing. When the talker truly gets the feeling that we are really interested, are prepared to stay with their agenda and not to intervene in a judgemental way, then effective communication can be said to have been achieved.

LOVE

Many school brochures declare an aim of helping pupils to acquire a love of learning which is lifelong. Fewer brochures declare the aim as helping pupils to love their learning. In his powerful analysis of the learning process, Seymour Papert (1980) suggests that education has little to do with explanation but everything to do with engagement, and that to be successful as a school learner the pupil needs to *fall in love with the material.*

Southgate and Randall (1978) observe that it is the unloved who tend to retreat and get away. Perhaps those learners who do disengage from the process are those who perceive themselves to be unloved, disapproved of and punished for not succeeding.

A. S. Neill (1968) has said, 'Love means approving of children, and that is essential in any school. You can't be on the side of children if you punish them and storm at them.'

MANAGEMENT

The word 'management' tends to be used to refer to a set of skills unique to people in high-status positions in organizations. During recent years a wider definition has been emerging which regards management as a set of skills that enable us to tackle the challenges which face us in various aspects of our lives. Society has tended to sort us into those who manage and those who are managed. We serve in both capacities throughout our lives. It is important for learners to acquire sufficient management skills to give them optimum capacity for self-management, self-direction and self-responsibility.

One way of looking at the skills of management is to consider the elements of managerial intelligence referred to earlier (see p. 141). In attempting to create an enhanced view of human potential it is necessary to proceed on the basis of a wider view of personal aptitude and capability. An integrated, holistic and systemic view of intelligence helps to change the concept of management from one of channelling limited capability to one of realizing and empowering unlimited potential.

Watching young children in their play, or at work in active classrooms, we see all of these functions in operation. Children are natural managers, and it is sad that the schooling system has failed to build on these emerging capacities. Management training is something that should continue when children start school, not something which is undertaken as remedial work when adults get into supervising roles very much later in life.

MARKET RESEARCH

In a fast changing world it is vital to keep up with new ideas and developments. In a complex world which demands ever-increasing awareness and information it is as necessary for learners to be tuned into the world and its ever-changing patterns.

Market research is the process undertaken to gain sufficient information in order to make intelligent decisions about the future. Learners are seldom concerned with *markets* in the business sense, but have much to gain from the concept and disciplines of market research.

Marketing can be defined as the process concerned with the creation of the optimum balance between the mission and resources of the organization, and the needs, aspirations and opportunities presented by the market. Market research is the process of gaining the information to proceed with this. Applying this to the learning situation, we can say that a vital part of success and achievement in school is creating the optimum balance between the resources of the school with the needs, aspirations and ambitions of the learner. Key questions for learners are:

1   What is the current state of my own learning and how does it relate to my needs, aspirations and ambitions?
2   What are my specific strengths and abilities and how can I extend and develop these?
3   What are my developing needs and aspirations and what new learning will I need to satisfy them?
4   What action is necessary to achieve a closer relationship between the resources of the school and my own aspirations and ambitions?

There appears to be a general acceptance that the pupil's own aspirations and ambitions have no place in the schooling process; that those with more experience and expertise have already decided what you need, what is good for you, and what you will be required to do with your compulsory attendance at school.

An increasing issue for pupils is that of recognizing the value that their learning experiences are likely to have in the future. They need to know what sort of dividends their investment in learning will have later in life.

As teachers, we need to recognize the importance of helping pupils to seek answers to such questions as:

What will be the value of this particular piece of learning –
(a)   in the short term;
(b)   in the medium term;
(c)   in the long term?

This is a process of helping learners to build a relationship between what they are learning and how it can profitably be applied in the everyday world of the present and the future. Pupils will be more motivated to learn when they can see powerful advantages and opportunities in the future: opportunities of their own identification and not only those linked to certification and higher education – opportunities which focus on the personal interests and enthusiasms of their lives.

MEDITATION

This is the term given to a range of activities designed to help learners focus on the inner self, the private perceptual world. It provides time to be alone with our thoughts in the inner space of our being.

Meditative techniques have long been associated with spiritual discipline, particularly with eastern religions and philosophies. In recent years many of these ideas and practices have begun to find favour in the West and have now become an accepted part of the reflective process. In the highly complex, demanding and stressful contexts of modern living, pauses for quietness and reflection are finding an increasingly important place in people's lives, both at work and at home.

John Hammond *et al.* (1990) outline a range of techniques designed to help pupils value quietness, stillness, reflection and contemplation and to practise specific techniques in their learning. Adopting quiet and reflective times in school would add a rich and valuable dimension to the learning process in all subjects.

MEMORY

Since the schooling process has traditionally placed so much emphasis on committing facts to memory and then testing the capacity for accurate, factual recall, it is surprising that the skills and techniques of memorizing have not been afforded a high-status place in the curriculum.

Many of us envy those who have a so-called photographic memory, believing them to have an unfair advantage in life. What these people have been fortunate enough to discover, probably by accident, are specific techniques of the mind that are, in fact, available to everyone.

Thanks to the pioneering work of Tony Buzan (1982, 1986, 1988a, 1988b), we now have the opportunity to give memory an altogether new deal in the schooling process. Most people have a fear of forgetting things. This is because they have never been helped to cultivate a natural capacity to remember things. The brain has an enormous capacity to remember and recall, provided that we acquire certain useful techniques and mind tools. Much of the memory work that children are asked to undertake could be achieved quite simply by using the techniques Buzan explains in his books.

MIND MAPPING

In the section on Conceptual maps (p. 84), the basic approach to the mind-mapping technique was outlined. As well as their obvious uses by pupils, they can also be used very profitably by teachers to assist various aspects of classroom management, e.g. planning classroom activities:

1   Place the aim or attainment target in the centre of the page and draw a frame around it.
2   Think of the attainment target in terms of pupils undertaking work connected with it. As ideas begin to form, draw out lines from the centre and jot down the idea.
3   Move out in all directions but do not worry about sequence – the aim is to register all the ideas that come.
4   Look at the pattern of ideas and see if any links or connections suggest themselves – draw lines and arrows for this. Use different colours to frame and connect up these ideas.
5   Try a second branching – listing resources, names of particular pupils, follow-up activities.
6   A second map can be drawn if necessary, structuring the ideas in a more organized way.

A similar approach can be used to monitor pupil progress:

1   Put the pupil's name in the centre of the page.
2   Imagine the pupil at work.
3   Jot down achievements, difficulties, interests, behaviours.
4   Use another colour and a second branching to record strategies to respond.

Mind mapping can also be used in a whole range of areas:

Specific events
● educational visits
● school concerts and performances
● sports activities
Management activities
● departmental meetings
● development plans
● curriculum guidelines
Critical incidents
● a difficult meeting with a parent
● a classroom incident
Professional development
● reflecting on an INSET experience
● preparing for a selection incident

Practice and experience will bring an individual style to mind maps. It is a good idea to share some of them with pupils, for example, photocopying project outlines and lesson plans. Pupils are more likely to value the technique if they see it used in real situations.

MOTIVATION

While issues of motivation have figured largely in the theory and practice of business management, it has generally been ignored as an issue in education. Yet the quality of learning for each pupil is mainly determined by motivation.

One of the most important yet challenging tasks of learning management is the creation of a high motivational climate. Motivation is the process of responding to pupils' inner needs and drives. While individuals will have needs that are particular and specific, they will also have needs in common with all other learners. Within the classroom setting, five sets of needs have especial importance. These are:

- A sense of belonging.
- A sense of achievement.
- A sense of appreciation.
- A sense of influence.
- A sense of involvement.

Herzberg (1966) has suggested that in organizations workers are also highly motivated when:

1 The work itself is intrinsically satisfying and challenging.
2 They have a decision-making role and are involved in the management of the organization.
3 Successful work leads to the possibility of promotion.

He also discovered that workers are badly motivated when:

1 They are over-supervised and there are too many rules and regulations governing personal as well as professional activity.
2 Workers have difficult relationships with senior staff and when 'bossy' attitudes cause frustration and anxiety.
3 There are poor relationships with co-workers, poor staff morale and divisive attitudes.
4 The working conditions are poor.

This emphasizes how important it is to be person-centred and to pay attention to the human factors of classroom life. It is also vital to balance this with a high sense of purpose through the identification of specific tasks and objectives and the clear definition of roles and responsibilities.

MOVEMENT

The phrase 'healthy body, healthy mind' has long been used by exponents of physical education as a key reason for PE in schools. Whilst this has tended to be scoffed at by those in the cognitive domain, research has reinforced the link. Brain power increases with brain use, and energetic physical activity helps to multiply the number of connections the brain is able to make.

The separation of physical education from intellectual education is emphasized in the National Curriculum. PE was later on stream than all the cognitive subjects. Even today, pupils in primary schools are sometimes threatened with 'No PE if you haven't finished your work'.

What is needed in schools is a less divisive curriculum design, one that recognizes and affirms the complementary nature of different aspects of learning. In an attempt to promote a more balanced view, Denis Postle (1989) has redefined intelligence in terms of:

- emotional intelligence
- intuitive intelligence
- physical intelligence
- intellectual intelligence

He comments:

> Another strand of intelligence that is frequently undervalued is body intelligence . . . This includes physical aptitudes displayed most dramatically by virtuoso pianists, jugglers, and champion pool and darts players, but which we all have to a considerable extent.

He suggests that the following qualities are all components of physical intelligence:

Strong	Poised	Vigorous	Facile
Tough	Relaxed	Virile	Handy
Energetic	Hardy	Dextrous	Quick
Agile	Rugged	Adroit	Co-ordinated
Nimble	Muscular	Deft	Sexual
Graceful	Athletic	A dab hand	Elegant

Evidence of the lack of physical intelligence is demonstrated in the vast energies expounded on slimming regimes and on various forms of physical therapy to correct poor posture. Babies are beautifully poised with straight backs and supple limbs. Perhaps it is the socialization and educative processes that have failed to help us recognize and develop a movement intelligence so vital to a healthy and balanced life.

MUSIC

Despite its overwhelming grip on popular culture, music tends to be among the least favoured aspects of the curriculum, particularly in secondary schools. Perhaps the distinction between the music of high culture and that of popular taste has done much to alienate pupils.

It is significant that many pupils like to do their homework to a background of music – and many adults also seem to work better if they can hear some of their favourite music. Some teachers have experimented with background music and report favourably on its capacity to create a more relaxed but purposeful atmosphere in the classroom.

Background music can be a very helpful accompaniment to the relaxation and visualization exercises outlined in the book.

What seems to be happening is that in left brain mode, which we tend to use when we are grappling with intellectual issues, the presence of music can stimulate right brain activity and bring a more integrated synthesis of the two distinct brain functions. Those of us firmly grooved in the left brain may experience confusion and discomfort – a sense of disturbance – whereas those used to a more integrated approach may be able to achieve a more powerful brain function with the added value of a musical presence.

The use of music as an accompaniment to learning needs a more imaginative investigation and trial.

NEGOTIATING

We tend to hear about negotiations in the context of industrial relations, and usually when the process of free collective bargaining has broken down. Perhaps one of the reasons negotiating seems to have become such a tortuous process is that developing skills and abilities in negotiation has not featured in the learning process in schools. Compliance of pupils has long been regarded as a requirement, and that even if they have a view about their rights and responsibilities in a given situation, they are supposed to suppress them.

'Because I say so' and 'Don't answer back' have become standard responses when children attempt to challenge decisions made on their behalf. As adults, we are inclined to take such challenges as attacks on us personally rather than recognize them as strongly felt attempts to seek understanding through explanation. We have much to learn about effective ways of responding to the attempts of the young to be involved in decisions affecting them, and not to be surprised when our insistence on arbitrary rulings is received so unsympathetically.

One positive way is for teachers to achieve good negotiating skills and to develop them in pupils. Roger Fisher and William Ury (1983) offer four principles for negotiation.

Separate the people from the problem
This involves negotiating on the issues, not on the personalities and histories of the participants.

Focus on interests and positions
This involves searching for underlying issues rather than the surface position:

> A father wanting his teenage daughter home no later than 10.30
> p.m. may be concealing the intensity of his worry and concern after
> this hour has passed. The daughter wanting to stay out later may not
> wish to lose self-esteem because her friends don't have to be home
> until 11 p.m. A solution to both interests could be that the daughter
> phones home at 10 p.m. to say where she is and how she is getting
> home.

Invent options for mutual gain
Far too often we enter negotiations with a win/lose outcome in mind. Such an attitude guarantees that neither participant will get what they really want. Creative outcomes involve searching for both mutual and separate interests and listing options to satisfy them. If participants look upon negotiation as an opportunity to satisfy both their own interests and

the interests of the other, the issues of winning and losing can be overcome.

Insist on objective criteria

When absolute positions are taken up, arbitrary criteria tend to be set: '10.30, not a minute later!' Far better to negotiate on objective criteria: 'The film ends at 10.15, half an hour for a coffee and ten minutes to get home, let's say 11.00.'

On another occasion it may depend on the time of the last bus. The vital factor is that each of the partners is committed to the criteria.

NETWORKING

One of the most significant communication revolutions of the late twentieth century has been the emergence of networking. Simply stated, networks are people talking to each other, sharing ideas, information and resources. The point is often made that networking is a verb, not a noun. The important part is not the network, the finished product, but the process of getting there – the communication that creates the linkages between people and clusters of people.

Schools need to build on the natural and informal networks that pupils become part of and find ways to harness these in the learning process. Self-directed study and examination revision networks are already well established among many of the exam-takers in our schools. As pupils are encouraged to take an increasing responsibility for the direction and management of their own learning they will find in networks of like-minded and like-focused colleagues the encouragement and support to enable them to extend their own learning aims and aspirations.

NON-VERBAL COMMUNICATION

In helping learners to develop their skills as interpersonal communicators it is important, in addition to work on listening and talking, to focus on the influence of non-verbal communication.

Drama provides a rich opportunity to explore the structure and nature of non-verbal communication. A useful technique to demonstrate its power is to record some television drama and play it back to pupils with the volume turned down and ask them to consider and discuss what is happening between the actors. Analysis of non-verbal communication will provide major clues to the states of minds of the participants, their feelings about themselves and each other and their attempts to influence others.

There are a number of purposes for focusing on non-verbal communication (NVC):

1 To raise awareness of the importance of NVC in conveying mood, emotions, intentions and feelings.
2 To develop awareness of how we project our own thoughts and feelings through our pattern of NVC.

3   To increase our capacity to use NVC sensitively and appropriately in a variety of interpersonal situations.

In human interactions the majority of information about the other person tends to be communicated non-verbally. Any consideration of personal and professional relationships must therefore give attention to this important phenomenon. Eight forms of non-verbal communication have been shown to be particularly significant (Argyle 1983).

1. Facial expression
The main function of facial expression is to communicate emotional states and to convey attitudes of like or dislike. Most of us can quickly recognize facial expressions which suggest happiness, surprise, fear, sadness, anger, disgust and interest. The mouth and eyebrows are particularly significant in creating specific expressions but each state also involves a configuration of the whole face. Facial expressions tend to be used as social signals as well as indicators of emotions. Most people are fairly aware of their expressions and can control them, although 'leakage' does occur when the emotions involved are particularly strong.

2. Gaze
This is the principal means of gathering non-verbal information but also functions as a social signal itself. Eye contact is a very important feature of interpersonal relationships and we tend to engage in more eye contact with those we like. It is also used as a device to synchronize speech.

3. Gestures
Movements of hand, body and head are closely co-ordinated with speech and are used to add emphasis to what is being said. They can also be indicative of emotional states.

4. Bodily posture
Each of us tends to have a characteristic repertoire of bodily movements, but postures do provide some information about how tense or relaxed a person is and may indicate something about self-image, self-confidence and emotional state.

5. Bodily contact
This is controlled by strict rules in our culture and is mainly focused in family relationships and between lovers. However, there are a range of socially acceptable touching rituals often to do with greeting and departing. Informal touching between friends and as a means of encouragement and reinforcement seems to be on the increase with a relaxation of some traditional taboos.

6. Spatial behaviour
Proximity is an indication of intimacy in most relationships and also relates to the degree of formality in interactions.

Orientation of chairs in relationships can also have an effect on the nature and quality of interactions. Generally speaking, chairs placed at an angle of about forty-five degrees make for the most conducive arrangement, facilitating sufficient eye contact to sustain effective interaction.

7. Clothes and appearance

Although social expectations about dress are more relaxed than they once were, what we wear is an important part of social behaviour. Our clothes and appearance can be manipulated to some extent and can be used to convey information about status, occupation and class; and also attitudes to other people like rebelliousness or conformity. This category is more susceptible to changing fashions than the others mentioned here.

8. Voice

This form of non-verbal behaviour refers to tone of voice, speed of talking, timing, accent and inclination to talk or to keep silent.

Non-verbal communication functions in four specific ways (Argyle 1975):

1 Communicating interpersonal attitudes and emotions.
2 Self-presentation.
3 Ritual.
4 Supporting verbal communication.

Each of these non-verbal behaviours can be seen at work in the classroom and it is important to be aware of just how powerful an effect they have on the psychological climate of the school as a whole and upon particular relationships. The vital point to remember is that it is not *what* we do that matters as much as the *way* that we do it. In other words, the particular combination of non-verbal behaviours that we exhibit is likely to have a more powerful effect on those we work with than any other aspect of ourselves.

OBSERVATION

Developing skills of observation is usually thought to be the concern of science in the curriculum. While it is of crucial importance in this and other areas of the curriculum, it is also of use in reflective and experiential learning. In the process of reflection it is vital to call upon the detailed aspects of experience – what actually happened and the effects it had. This requires high-level observational skills in the context of behaviour.

Observation will become of increasing importance in two key areas of professional activity: assessment and appraisal. As teachers, we base our judgements about the quality of pupil learning on what we perceive from the learning behaviour and the tangible products and outcome of their activities. The more precise requirements of formal assessment in the current changes require a shift from informal and incidental assessment to deliberate and specific assessment.

Observation is a key skill in acquiring information about the behaviour of others. No other activity has quite so much potential to produce the sorts of data and information necessary to help form judgements about achievement, attainment, quality and progress. For the appraiser, observation is the means by which a shared experience can be used profitably to highlight and illuminate professional activity.

It is useful to make a distinction between two levels of observation: incidental and deliberate. The first level is more in the nature of *noticing* and is observation that is applied incidentally in the course of normal professional activity. While teachers are engaged in the organization and management of classroom learning they will also be observing pupils at their work. Some of what they will see and hear will constitute evidence that learning has taken place. Vast quantities of information are collected incidentally in this way, some of which will help the teacher to build a developing understanding of pupils and their learning.

The second level is more deliberate and purposeful. It is employed when a teacher sets out to use observation as a precise technique to acquire information about pupils and their learning. One of the practical constraints of a complex and demanding teaching role is that of being able to operate in this second mode for any sustained period of time without the assistance of a colleague. The introduction of more formal methods of assessment and teacher appraisal has raised the importance of deliberate observation.

A further issue arising out of the use of observation lies in the important distinction between experience and behaviour. In the process of trying to understand human activity we observe behaviour – we see what people are doing and we hear what they say. What we cannot do is observe their experience, which is the individual's understanding and sensing of that behaviour. In the context of appraisal which involves observing the teacher at work, it is important to keep this distinction firmly in mind and to resist the temptation to create explanations and interpretations of that behaviour. Observation will produce the factual details of what has been observed. Dialogue will be necessary if insights and explanations about these behaviours are to be generated.

PAIRS

It is through talking in one-to-one situations that we bring meaning to our experience, share our ideas and get feedback on them. Talking with another person helps us to clarify our thinking and to test out our values. It is a vital learning experience which schools have traditionally tended to deny their pupils. Talking between pupils has for too long been regarded as an interference with the learning process.

Structured talk in pairs is not merely conversation, but an important learning experience. The best classrooms are always those where pupils work with and through their colleagues, sharing problems, testing out possibilities, seeking reassurance or offering help. Look at any group of adults engaged in a task. One thing is certain: they are most unlikely to complete it in silence. Adult working activity is dominated by groups, committees and working parties all based on the same belief – that many hearts and minds working in co-operation are better than one. So it is with learning. Even when we do have to work at a problem on our own, the talk continues in our own head if not aloud.

Working in pairs in the classroom can be used in countless situations. For example, after having spent ten minutes or so drafting out ideas for a piece of written work, pupils can be formed into pairs and asked to share their drafts with each other. The object is for one pupil to describe and explain the draft to the other who listens attentively and seeks clarification on points that are not clear. After five minutes the pupils change over. The role of the listener is not to criticize or appraise the other's work but to help by seeking clarification, following up interest points and trying to understand the ideas being expressed.

Breaking into pairs also provides variety in lesson format, providing opportunities for:

- clarifying thinking;
- talking through a problem;
- assessing the progress of a piece of work;
- debriefing from a television programme;
- responding to some formal teacher input;
- developing ideas;
- creating solutions.

Points to note in organizing pair work are:

- Be very clear about the task;
- Give a time limit and stick to it;
- Announce the change-over of talker and listener;
- Invite any general comments and feedback before proceeding to the next part of the lesson.

Splitting a class into pairs for a short period of talking and listening is one of the most effective ways of engaging in reflective and experiential learning. Working in pairs also optimizes the opportunity for each pupil to disclose and explore their own experiences and to listen with empathy to those of a colleague.

PERCEPTION

Reflective and experiential learning is a process designed to support the growth of understanding. Perception – the process of recognizing and identifying something – is an important element in this. Effective learners are those who have succeeded, through personal discovery, in identifying their own learning strengths and difficulties. Successful learning involves employing as many of these strategies as possible.

Deliberate and structured reflection of learning increases our opportunity to do this.

If we are to help learners to derive benefit from reflective and experiential learning we need to be able to help them manage their perceptive processes successfully. This requires attention to:

- *Selection* – how we focus on the things that matter.
  - (a) Stimuli: these attract our attention, particularly when it involves change or contrasts; unvaried and repetitious phenomena direct our attention inwards.
  - (b) Motivation: we tend to be stimulated by those phenomena which feature among our interests and concerns.
- *Organization* – how we sort out information, experiences and ideas. What we single out as significant and to which we attach priority or preference. It involves taking account of as much information as possible.
- *Interpretation* – how we bring meaning to experience.
  - (a) Being guided by past experience.
  - (b) Assumptions about human behaviour.
  - (c) Expectations: how we relate current incident to anticipation and expectation.
  - (d) Knowledge: knowing the context, background and detail.
  - (e) Self-concept.

It is through reflection and dialogue that these important issues can be attended to. Helping learners to gain an appreciation and understanding of their perceptual processes is a vital role of the teacher.

PERSONAL AND SOCIAL EDUCATION (PSE)

During the past twenty-five years or so there has been a concerted effort by many teachers to promote curriculum activity on the personal and social development of pupils. While PSE has not been recognized as a subject for inclusion in the National Curriculum, it is now seen by most schools as a vital cross-curriculum dimension. It is defined by HMI in *Personal and Social Education from 5 to 16* (DES 1989) as follows: 'personal and social education refers to those aspects of a school's thinking, planning, teaching and organisation explicitly designed to promote the personal and social development of pupils.'

Among the learning approaches recommended are:

1 Taking responsibility for learning and exercising choice within and between activities.
2 An emphasis on achievement.
3 Everyone's contributions deserve attention.
4 Working in groups and experiencing leadership.
5 Role play.
6 Use of the imagination.

The document gathers together a set of objectives for PSE:

1 The development of personal qualities.
2 Knowledge and understanding.
3 Personal and social abilities and skills.

For some years PSE was seen as a predominantly secondary school concern. In the last few years there have been concerted efforts to carry the importance of PSE to the primary phase of schooling as well.

One advantage of sustaining PSE as a cross-curricular dimension is that personal and social learning does not get relegated to occasional slots in the timetable. For too long the development of personal and social awareness has been separated from cognitive development in schools. Raising standards and achieving a more complete education require a deliberate synthesizing of emotional, intellectual, intuitive and physical aspects of learning and growing.

PERSONAL MANAGEMENT

In *The Personal Management Handbook* John Mulligan (1988) states:

> In today's complex world, just surviving requires skilful personal management. Realizing your own potential, and helping to realize that of others, demands highly sensitive and well developed personal management skills. Rounded development, including the ability to manage yourself and others, is not being formally recognized as a vital part of the manager's toolkit. And effective personal management is essential if you are to make the most of your life and potential, whether you are managing a large organization, your own life affairs or bringing up a family.

Personal management is increasingly featuring in programmes of adult education but should also have a prominent part in the PSE programmes of schools.

The following aspects of personal management should feature in the curriculum:

- Developing a sense of direction in life.
- Building self-esteem and self-confidence.
- Making life choices.
- Developing personal skills and abilities.
- Personal effectiveness.
- Managing stress and crisis points.

It is naive to think that the traditional and formal curriculum of schools will equip learners adequately with the life process skills so necessary to self-fulfilment and happiness.

PERSON-CENTRED TEACHING

This can be defined as an approach to teaching which attempts to relate formal learning in school to the wider process of personal growth and development. It emphasizes learning rather than teaching and places the relationship of the teacher to the pupil as the key factor in the process.

The key exponent of person-centred teaching has been the eminent American humanistic psychologist, Carl Rogers. In his book *Freedom to Learn for the 80s* (1983) he suggests that the system of schooling we follow today is built upon ten basic assumptions:

1 Pupils cannot be trusted to learn.

2 An ability to pass examinations is the best criterion for selection and judging potential.
3 Evaluation is education: education is evaluation.
4 What a teacher teaches is what a pupil learns.
5 Knowledge is the accumulation of content and information.
6 The truths of subjects are known.
7 The way a pupil has to learn to work is more important than what is being studied.
8 Creative people develop from passive learners.
9 The *weeding out* of the majority of pupils and students is the best way of producing the *well educated*.
10 Pupils are best regarded as manipulative objects, not as people.

Another way of looking at the basic assumptions about schooling is to refer again to the work undertaken by Douglas McGregor, who suggests that the quality of work in an organization is affected by the assumptions managers have of the workers. Applied to the schooling system, the theory he developed can be summarized as follows:

Theory X
Pupils dislike learning and try to avoid it. They have to be coerced and controlled and even threatened with punishment to do it adequately. Most pupils wish to avoid having to take responsibility for their own learning and prefer to be directed.

Theory Y
Pupils enjoy learning and find it as natural as any other part of their growing. If allowed to pursue learning which is relevant to their needs and interests they will work with energy and enthusiasm. They will willingly and ably take responsibility for their own learning and prefer to work this way.

In the organizations which McGregor studied he found that when managers held Theory Y assumptions the work rate was higher and the quality of the product better than in those organizations where Theory X assumptions were held. Person-centred education believes that Theory Y assumptions are essential if pupils are to learn successfully in schools.

We need to question whether a bureaucratic professionalism will increase or decrease our disability to affect the lives of the pupils with whom we are concerned. We have to address ourselves, person by person, to the evidence about the relationship between teacher values and attitudes to pupil learning. We need to accept that we ourselves have as much to learn from classroom experience as the pupils who share it with us. We need to develop a sensitive but honest appreciation of our own personal skills, particularly those of listening, talking and relating to others. Are we able to understand the meanings that classroom learning is having for each pupil? Are we able to accept in a non-judgemental way these meanings, and above all, to have genuine respect for each pupil?

In all phases of education we need to find ways of increasing our personal contacts with pupils through more profound consultations, and to look particularly to small group activities to provide opportunities to bring the reality of pupils' own lives into the classroom. We need to reduce the intellectual monopoly in schools and give a new deal to creativity. We need to build an acceptance that the pursuit of happiness is the real purpose of education.

PERSPECTIVES

In helping learners to develop their own personal world of meaning and understanding it is important to help them relate their own world view to that of others, and to appreciate and value the diversity of viewpoints that exist.

Pike and Selby (1988) see *perspectives consciousness* as one of the key aims for the global learner:

> Students should recognise that they have a worldview that is not universally shared. Students are helped to realise that they have their own particular perspective, that they interpret reality from within a particular framework of thought and perception and that there are difficulties and dangers attached to using that framework of reference as a yardstick for interpreting and judging the lifestyles, patterns of behaviour and values and worldview of others. They are also encouraged to see how perspective is shaped by factors such as age, class, creed, culture, ethnicity, ideology, language, nationality and race.

In the classroom this requires us to focus on:

1 The capacity to develop, describe and explain personal objectives.
2 The capacity to summarize the perspectives of others.
3 The capacity to empathize with others whose circumstances and experiences have led them to a different view from our own.

In the section on Behaviour (p. 66), R. D. Laing's distinction between experience and behaviour was noted. In the context of perspectives, this is worth restating:

- I can observe your behaviour. This behaviour then becomes an experience of mine.
- You can observe my behaviour which then becomes an experience of yours.
- I cannot observe your experience which is inside you, but I can try and understand your experience if you disclose it to me.
- You cannot observe my experience which is inside me, but you can try and understand it if I disclose it to you.

(Laing 1967)

This emphasizes the vital importance of feedback and especially disclosure through dialogue, and the dangers of leaping to conclusions, relying automatically on assumptions and failing to seek the understanding behind the words and the non-verbal behaviour.

PHOTOGRAPHY

An increasing number of pupils are having opportunities to use photography as a key tool in their learning. Not only is photography a useful way to develop the skills of observation and perception, it is an excellent aid to the making of high-quality presentations of project work. Many schools have dark-rooms, and good-quality photographs can now be produced quite cheaply.

Pupils equipped with cameras and small tape-recorders have excellent opportunities to produce visual and oral evidence to support investigative and project work.

With the rapidly increasing power of technology, schools will have easy access to a wide range of high-quality and sophisticated reprographic facilities which should be made full use of in the learning process.

A good deal more use could be made of photographs in most subject areas, not only those in textbooks and teaching materials, but particularly those in published collections of eminent photographers.

PLANNING

Planning is a key ingredient in getting things done effectively. This applies to personal management as much as to the activity of large organizations. The quality of learning can be improved considerably if learners are encouraged and helped to develop skills in planning the management of their own learning. Unfortunately this is seldom regarded as necessary in the schooling process.

If pupils are to become self-disciplined in their learning, and to demonstrate good work habits, they need to be given time and training in the skills of planning work. Practise in a systematic approach will pay enormous dividends. One such approach entails tackling new projects in a planning sequence (see Figure 4.12). Planning forms can be produced which help learners acquire the skill and discipline of systematic planning.

Many organizations have laboured under the false belief that getting into action quickly is the key to efficiency and effectiveness. Wiser and more successful organizations are realizing that it is futile to go into action before sufficient planning and preparation has been undertaken. So too with learning tasks. We need to help pupils to become skilful and effective planners, enabling them to lay strong foundations for any learning task they engage in.

PLAY

In the very early stages of formal education, play is seen as a vital activity in the all-round development of the learner. Through play, children are able to explore the world of ideas and feelings as well as to bring meaning to their concrete experience. Unfortunately, schools tend to abandon play too early in the learning journey, and by the beginning of Year 3 it has largely disappeared from the curriculum.

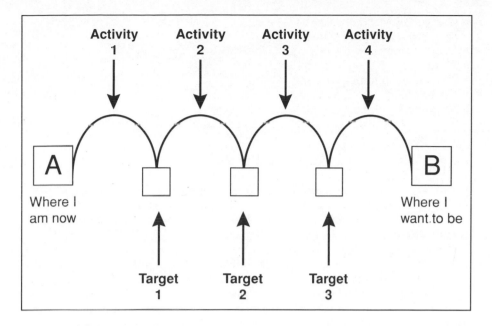

Figure 4.12 Action planning.

One of the reasons for this discarding is the assumption that play is easy, that it is less rigorous or focused than the other subjects children are expected to grapple with. Also, of course, play is associated with pleasure and enjoyment, and the traditional view that learning should be painful if it is to be effective clings on in some quarters. Yet it is often in their play that we see children at their most absorbed, applying remarkable levels of intellectual energy and involvement. Play brings into the learning process all the powerful attributes of learning: physical activity, intellectual enquiry and problem-solving, intuitive application and emotional engagement.

One of the great dangers of cutting the play approach to learning too soon is that children lose one of the few truly holistic activities in their schooling.

POWER

In a compulsory and highly-structured system of education it is important to consider the part that power and authority plays in the learning process. A number of factors combine to create a sometimes alienating power relationship between the teachers and the taught:

- The compulsory nature of schooling.
- Coercive models of upbringing.
- The long journey to adulthood.
- The deep traditions of schooling.

- The tendency to see schools as corrective institutions, concerned with discipline and punishment.
- Patterns of regimentation and conformity.
- Emphasis on preparation for life.
- The encouragement of competition.
- Categorization of knowledge and experience.
- Exclusively didactic models of teaching.
- The emphasis on examinations and certification as gateways to the future.

Excessive power struggles can inhibit the learning process and in recent years there has been a concern to minimize some of the more damaging traditions of schooling – corporal punishment, school uniforms, regimentation, arbitrary rules and didactic teaching – although the damaging and disputatious debate between *traditionalists* and *progressives* continues unresolved.

Organizational life will always create power issues, but there is a distinction between *power over* – the coercive use of authority to limit the rights and opportunities of learners; and *power to* – the liberating use of power and authority to create opportunity and to empower initiative.

When power and authority are used in creative rather than limiting and inhibiting ways, then the learning process will be facilitated. One way of examining the part that power plays in the life of the school is to consider its presence in the following framework:

Intentions – the use of power and authority to:
- create a clear sense of direction;
- present a compelling vision of the future;
- articulate purposes and aims.

Structures – the use of power and authority to:
- enable and promote self-responsibility for learning;
- support enquiry and endeavour;
- optimize opportunity.

Climate – the use of power and authority to:
- create a sense of a learning community;
- a sense of shared endeavour towards learning;
- develop person-centred teaching.

Outcomes – the use of power to focus on achievement:
- learning through successes as well as through failure;
- ensuring that achievements are celebrated.

One of the crucial elements frequently referred to in the analysis of organizations is the presence or absence of trust, which is central to the debate about power in relation to leadership. This was dealt with in the earlier section on Control (p. 88). A good way to gauge the effects of power dynamics in an organization is to ask those in lower-status positions about the extent to which they feel trusted by their higher-placed colleagues.

One of the great challenges for the future is how those with power and authority in schools can move away from the power/coercive models of the past to more all embracing, liberating and life-enhancing approaches to the development of those for whom they have responsibility.

PRESENTATIONS

Many of the attainment targets of the National Curriculum give a new emphasis to the end-products of pupil learning. We are gradually replacing the reliance on the exercise book with an altogether more imaginative set of product targets for pupils. As we increasingly appreciate the added value to learning of pupils sharing the outcomes with a wider audience than the teacher, we will be able to form a closer relationship between living and learning. With an important emphasis on coursework in the GCSE examination we are gradually replacing a total emphasis on the end of course tests with a more balanced approach to assessment. It is to be hoped that the current dispute about assessment procedures will soon be resolved and a greater value placed on high-quality pupil presentations.

It is useful in the planning stage of a learning experience for pupils to envisage clearly and then define the tangible end-product of a learning task. This will help pupils to create a sense of precisely what completion and achievement will look like right from the start.

A variety of presentations are possible.

- Pupils work in twos, describing to their partner a completed piece of work, drawing attention to its aims, processes, content and conclusions.
- Presentation groups – pupils work as a group to devise and present the end-products of each other's work to another group.
- Group presentations – in which the group working together devises a team presentation for the whole class.

Occasionally, wider audiences can be involved:

- Assembly presentation to part or whole school.
- Displays and exhibitions in local shops or library.
- Presentations to governors.
- Exhibitions, displays and presentations to parents.

Dealing with presentations in this way helps to build the vital relationship between the acquisition of learning and its effective application in real situations. When pupils know they will be involved in managing a presentation on the completion of a piece of work they are often motivated from the start, more determined to do well and more committed to the learning process.

PROBLEM-SOLVING

Problem-solving is a vital skill in a fast-changing society. Rapid change increases the range of problems to which solutions need to be found, and we have to learn to resolve problems faster than ever before.

Creative problem-solvers tend to be divergent thinkers who are not satisfied with the idea of a single, hopefully correct solution. They are concerned to view the problem from a variety of perspectives in order to collect a range of possibilities before selecting one solution to try. Developing divergent thinking involves the freeing up of ideas of right and wrong in the context of problem-solving. The simple technique of brainstorming (see p.71) is one of the best ways to increase our imaginative and lateral thinking capacities.

Another way involves pupils in tackling some of the real organizational and management problems that arise day by day inside the school:

- more productive use of wet breaktimes
- timetable issues
- resource management
- care of school premises
- school rules and sanctions
- themes for assembly
- out-of-school activities
- inter-school co-operation

The more pupils can become engaged in the management of the school, the greater is their likely sense of belonging, participation and involvement. A school full of lively minds is a wonderful resource to have access to, and we need to find ways to harness this enormous potential for creative problem-solving. Pupils need to join school think tanks – small task groups set up to investigate and report on current issues being faced in the school.

PROJECTS

These are the stock in trade of many schools, and teachers are highly imaginative in their capacity to devise interesting themes for students to study. The National Curriculum will pose new challenges to cross-curricular ingenuity and teachers will have endless opportunities to bring varied attainment targets together in interesting and exciting combinations.

There are four key purposes to project work:

1   To help pupils to gain knowledge, skills and understanding in specific areas of the curriculum.
2   To develop skills of enquiry, research, organization, presentation and evaluation of material and ideas.
3   To create a vehicle for learners to apply the knowledge, skills and understanding they have acquired.
4   To engage in collaborative learning, developing the skills of group co-operation, teamwork, leadership and shared responsibility.

The following ideas offer ways in which project work can be extended and developed so that there is a balance between the four purposes given above.

- Using information technology more creatively to provide high-quality documentation, presentation of data, word processing, desk-top publishing and databases.

- More varied documentary end products:
  - hand-outs
  - posters
  - pamphlets and brochures
  - newspaper and journal articles.
- Media technology:
  - overhead transparencies
  - tape/slide presentations
  - video recordings
  - photography
  - multi-media presentations
  - computer assisted design.
- Building up a bank of pupil-produced material as a resource for other pupils. Pupil material should be referenced and acknowledged in the same ways that other sources traditionally are.
- Exhibitions, conferences and seminars organized by pupils as the final stage of a project.

Inspectors' reports have often been very critical of project work, noting that much of it amounts to little more than copying from textbooks. Project work needs to be managed as any other task needs managing, and it is important that pupils learn to approach their projects in a systematic and business-like way, giving careful attention to the planning as well as the execution. More help in these vital management processes would ensure a significant increase in the quality of end results.

PROMOTIONS

Promotions are organized attempts to bring issues to the attention of others. Schools are becoming places in which learning can be presented in ways which are of interest and benefit to other pupils. A whole-school approach to effective learning will place the promotion of learning among its highest and most important intentions.

What it will be vital to see in the schools of the future is much more emphasis on the skills, methods and technologies of learning. One way to begin this process is to create opportunities for learners and teachers to share their own experiences of learning. Occasional learning fairs could be organized where pupils could set up their stalls:

- How I learned speed reading.
- Short cuts in word processing.
- Getting started on the guitar.
- Organizing homework projects.
- Roller-skating techniques.
- How to ask for what you want.
- Using the telephone effectively.

Pupils who become noted for their special expertise in particular areas are a vital school resource and may well have value to the wider community.

Teachers need to encourage pupils to describe the techniques they have discovered and help them in their promotion. The skills of inventiveness and ingenuity have tended to be marginalized in the pursuit of strictly cognitive objectives. They need to be given a prominent part in the learning lives of pupils in schools.

QUESTIONS

A fundamental problem about the role of questions in education was raised by Postman and Weingartner (1971) in *Teaching as a Subversive Activity*:

> What students are restricted to (solely and vengefully) is the process of memorising (partially and temporarily) somebody else's answers to somebody else's questions. It is strange to consider the implications of this fact. The most important and intellectual ability man has yet developed – the art and science of asking questions – is not taught in schools!

In the twenty-four years since that observation was made, not a great deal has happened to remedy that absence. Postman and Weingartner give clear reasons for their own concern:

> Knowledge is produced in answer to questions. And new knowledge results from the asking of new questions; quite often new questions about old questions. Here is the point: once you have learned how to ask questions – relevant and appropriate and substantial questions – you have learned how to learn and no one can keep you from learning whatever you want or need to know.

If we are to create powerful and lifelong learners it is vital that we help them to acquire the varied art of questioning. There are two aspects of our learning where questioning is crucially important.

1. Increasing knowledge and understanding

There is much that we need to do in classrooms to improve the use of questioning. The majority of questions are asked by teachers to assess if previous teaching has been remembered. This is a limited use of a very valuable learning tool.

Some ways to utilize questions are:

1 Try and avoid too many closed questions, those that have a single, perhaps correct answer.
2 Increase the number of open-ended questions, particularly those which begin 'How . . .?' and 'What . . .?'
3 Help pupils to develop their skill at formulating questions by using such devices as:
   • 'If you could ask the Prime Minister only one question, what would it be?'
   • 'How could you get all the following information using only three questions?'

4   Show television interviews to compare styles of questioning. Which sort of questions seem to get the fullest answers? Which the shortest? Which are the most informative?
5   Encourage pupils to devise questionnaires to test attitudes, seek information and gain insights.
6   Help pupils to use questions to satisfy their own curiosity and learning needs. Instead of the rather peremptory 'OK, any questions?' try, 'What are some of the questions we really need to ask about this?'

In a good interactive classroom it is the pupils who will do the majority of the questioning, not always of the teacher but sometimes of their colleagues, themselves and the class as a whole.

2. Interpersonal relationships

In everyday conversation questions can be used as a poor substitute for more direct communication. They enable us to place the responsibility for talking on to the other person and can serve to help us avoid disclosing information about ourselves. Used in this way questions are rarely simple requests for information, but an indirect means of manipulating the other person.

The most important use of questions in interpersonal situations is to facilitate the listening process. Here questions are used to seek deeper understanding and insights into the perceptions, ideas and feelings of the talker. It is better to seek clarification through open-ended questions such as: 'What happened then?', and 'How did you feel about that?'.

There is sometimes a tendency to seek explanations for behaviours through *why* questions. These often inhibit the talker rather than help release the information needed:

1   *Why* questions can sound aggressive and accusatory.
2   They move the talker into abstraction and speculation.
3   In grappling with the meaning of experience, interpretation is not usually very helpful.

What and *how* questions are usually more helpful in getting the other person in touch with their experience, for example, 'How did you deal with that?', and 'What did you really want to say?'.

Another important issue about the use of questions as a teaching technique is to do with the time provided for pupils to formulate their answers and responses. We have become so used to the testing of factual memory in the regular quiz programmes on radio and television that we apply the same quick-fire technique to all situations. It is important to deter pupils from developing a belief that questions are only a means of catching them out being wrong.

A more useful and effective way is to provide some thinking time – varied according to the nature of the question being asked – and then to go round the class or group sharing responses in order to discover what range of information and ideas can be brought to bear on the subject. This creates the realization that questions serve the purpose of discovery rather than that of assessing competence.

RACISM

Racism is one of the oppressive social forces that has denied equality of opportunity in the education system. During the 1980s there was a concerted effort among racial minorities to raise social awareness of racism and to encourage society to tackle the many injustices it created. Much of this work has focused on the education system. Many local education authorities have developed specialist services to promote anti-racist and non-racist practices in schools. While an increasing number of schools have produced anti-racist education policy documents it is essential to recognize that good intentions are rarely sufficient to root out deep-seated prejudices and oppressive behaviours.

Writing on race and education, June Henfrey (1988) makes the following points:

1   There are two main perspectives:
    (a) The effect on black children of a system permeated by racist attitudes, criteria and procedures.
    (b) The need to inform all children about the realities of race and racism in both the global and local context.
2   Addressing racism involves confronting the issue of where power lies, as between black and white communities, and introducing mechanisms which allow for a more equitable spread of control.
3   The task for education is to show how racial inequality has been constructed, how it continues to be exemplified and to point to ways in which equality might be achieved.
4   An anti-racist school is one which recognizes that race is not a marginal or peripheral issue but one which is central to young people's understanding of their society and of the modern world.
5   Schools need to develop structures which challenge the expression of racism. Schools with black pupils must ask themselves the simple question: 'Is this a safe and compatible environment for all our children including those who are black?'
6   A curriculum needs to be developed which avoids content and approaches which are unidimensional and ethnocentric.

Progress towards these aims is unlikely to be achieved if the learning process is itself oppressive, where pupils are expected to be passive receivers of prescribed knowledge. Active, participatory and reflective experiences are essential if pupils are to develop attitudes and values which are firmly based on justice and equality.

READING

In the early stages of the learning process, reading tends to be seen as an end in itself. The pressures on pupils and teachers to reach prescribed reading goals is enormous. This preoccupation with the mechanics of reading can sometimes result in the purposes of learning to read being neglected, and pupils failing to develop the wider skills that are so essential to successful learning.

The move towards *real reading* in which reading schemes are wholly or partially replaced by a varied collection of fiction and non-fiction books is one attempt to focus on the content rather than the form of the reading.

As children's reading skills develop, they need to be encouraged to acquire the techniques that will help them to manage information in documentary form.

This will require us to:

1 Reduce the insistence on reading aloud so that a pupil's silent reading speed is not held back to the speed at which the words are mouthed.
2 Encourage pupils to communicate with real audiences, through letters, memos, reports and surveys.
3 Give pupils access to as wide a variety of reading matter as possible. Some pupils, through their personal interests and enthusiasms, are attracted to non-fiction material. These should be modified as reading primers where appropriate. Not all children are motivated by stories of everyday life or exotic adventures, which are the content of most reading schemes.
4 Introduce pupils to some of the higher reading skills early, e.g. the structure of books:
   * title pages;
   * roles of authors, publishers, editors and printers;
   * the information on the back of the title page;
   * the use and function of preface, foreword, contents, index, bibliographies, references, footnotes;
   * skimming and scanning; and
   * the value of photocopied extracts and the use of highlight pens.

In a world where written information is one of the key raw materials for successful living, it is vital that pupils learn early in their lives how to handle and manage it successfully.

RECORDS OF ACHIEVEMENT

Records of achievement are one of the positive ways of involving pupils in the management of their own learning. Firstly, they encourage pupils to become skilful assessors of their own learning, and secondly, the emphasis is placed on success rather than failure.

Through records of achievement, pupils enter into an evaluation partnership with teachers. It is important that this relationship is as equal as possible if tokenism is to be avoided. Good records are the documentary evidence of critical friendship between pupil and teacher. Each has a unique and crucial perspective to bring to the process of assessment and evaluation.

For the pupil this will involve:

* stating learning needs and aspirations;
* detailing experiences of learning activities;
* identifying difficulties and concerns;
* expressing satisfaction, achievement and appreciation;
* relating outcomes to planned intentions.

What the teacher will bring to the process is:

- expertise in key areas of learning;
- experience of assessment and evaluation;
- a broad view of pupil achievements and levels of attainment;
- interest and concern for the pupil's current and long-term learning needs.

There is much debate about what records of achievement should include. While there are some obvious requirements within the National Curriculum that should be reflected in records of achievement, it is also vital that pupils are enabled to identify some sections themselves. If pupils are to take records of achievement seriously, they deserve to feel a sense of ownership of their own records.

A major danger of records of achievement is that where documentation becomes very fussy and prescribed the whole exercise can be reduced to a bureaucratic exercise. It is essential to build an understanding that records of achievement are about the future; they should help pupils to make decisions about what to do next in the light of past experience.

Developing good records of achievement is an ongoing process, and a high level of flexibility needs to be built into their use. Uniformity of design and use will do nothing to help pupils develop a powerful sense of their own learning skills and abilities, nor to build the capacity for rigorous self-assessment in their lives.

RELATIONSHIPS

One of the most significant educational developments of the last ten years has been the steady realization that it is in and through relationships that much of our best learning occurs. When we undertake learning activities in partnership with others (pairs or small groups) we have the opportunity to enact the experiential learning cycle in a far more powerful way than when we undertake learning on our own.

Through reflective dialogue, a number of important processes are activated:

- testing out theories and ideas
- building on ideas
- considering alternative views
- being encouraged to try out the idea
- motivation
- creating structure
- formulating goals
- planning
- reviewing

This is not to say that all learning should be conducted collaboratively or in partnership with other learners. What is desirable is to create a learning environment which optimizes opportunity – that respects the need to be private and alone with our work, that encourages the sharing of ideas, tasks and activities, and which builds on the assumption that all pupils are learning supporters for each other. Talking our learning work through with another is a powerful way to clarify our own understanding, to explore possibilities and to increase choice.

An interactive class need not be noisy or disorganized, and can, like a well-designed open plan office, produce an atmosphere which is calm, purposeful and highly productive.

Simply creating opportunities for reflective interaction is not enough – pupils need to be taught the skills of participative learning. These include:

- listening
- reflecting
- presenting ideas
- brainstorming
- systematic planning
- critical friendship
- co-counselling

RESEARCH

Research is generally regarded as a highly specialized form of enquiry. There are now clear reasons why the skills and techniques of research need to be more effectively utilized by learners in schools.

- The National Curriculum identifies very precisely the lines of enquiry that pupils will be required to undertake.
- The structure of attainment targets and levels of achievement will demand a more research-based approach with individuals and small groups working at their specific level and programme of targets.
- Rapid change will require us increasingly to adapt to new systems, structures and technologies. We will need to manage our own learning in even more efficient and effective ways.

The results of research are temporary – the data is ephemeral and effective for only a finite period of time. The same applies to the desirable learning of pupils – what they learn today is only a stepping-stone on the whole learning journey.

RISK

Very few accomplishments in our lives are achieved without risk. The first tottering steps as we teach ourselves to walk are perilous, but the outstretched arms of parents provide some reassurance and support. The child's achievements become the parent's triumph. How different it would be if, as parents, we punished our children who stumble in that major act of endeavour. Yet highlighting failure and difficulty becomes the dominant tendency in the management of children. Endless strictures about what to do, what not to do, and remorseless recriminations when things do not go totally according to plan, can crush the creative spirit and diminish the capacity to reach out in anticipation and hope.

In *Lake Wobegon Days*, Garrison Keillor (1987) describes a manifesto written by a former Wobegon resident as a dramatic complaint against his upbringing. One of the statements refers to the issue of risk. He writes of his parents:

> You have taught me the fear of becoming lost, which has killed the pleasure of curiosity and discovery. In strange cities, I memorize streets and always know exactly where I am. Amid scenes of great splendour, I review the route back to the hotel.

The manifesto is a very powerful insight into the terrible psychological costs of upbringing and should be a set text in all programmes of professional teacher training.

If our schools are to become places where learning is truly celebrated, we need to eschew the paranoid obsession with caution – 'Be careful you don't . . .' – and the thrall of mistake avoidance. Very little is achieved without risk, and we need to help learners to calculate it intelligently. As we gradually replace grading and unsolicited criticism with purposeful and systematic review we will enable pupils to experience risk as a prerequisite to successful learning, and help them to activate a capacity for experimenting and trying things out to see what happens.

Quality learning is often a leap into the unknown, a journey of optimism. If we play it too safe we inhibit our potential and settle for personal mediocrity and the apparent safety of the average. Somerset Maugham was once reputed to have remarked, 'Only the mediocre are at their best all the time'. When the average look enviously at the successful, what they perhaps realize is that if they too had been prepared to take the risk then they too could have been an actor, a global traveller, a successful entrepreneur, an effective parent.

The art of the teacher is to encourage pupils to calculate the risks they take. We need to help them replace the question 'What if I fail?' with 'What if I succeed?'.

ROLE PLAY

Role play – taking the part of others – is a powerful way of gaining insights into human behaviour. It also helps us to increase our understanding of social issues and challenges.

In essence it is a formal and structured extension of empathy – sensing what it is like to be in the shoes of another person. In role play the difference is that instead of conveying our sensing back to another person we try out behaviours which we sense they would display.

Young children do this quite naturally in their play and use it to explore the strange world of relationships where people behave inconsistently in a social world full of paradoxes and ambiguities.

In the classroom we can use role play to explore a whole range of human situations:

Technology – what is it like to operate a computer?
English – what would you do if you were Lady Macbeth?

Geography – what would be the reaction of the street trader in Buenos Aires in that situation?
History – how would the Aborigines have felt?

Role play is not the same as drama. In drama we interact in role. In role play we have many options:

- to think
- to write
- to talk
- to listen
- to solve problems
- to predict

Role play is not about performance and does not require acting skills. Its purpose is to increase insight and understanding. The benefits it brings are to help us appreciate the diversity and richness of human experience and behaviour, and to accept the uniqueness of the individual. Essentially, role play involves getting inside the experience of others in order to learn why and how things are as they are.

In terms of organization, preparation need not be elaborate. Within a lesson framework, role play can be activated for short periods of time as well as for longer ones. Basically there are three stages:

1 *Developing information* – getting as much detail about the role to be considered.
2 *Imagining* – getting inside the thoughts and feelings and experiences of the person involved.
3 *Responding* – disclosing through the methods described above the responses we imagine and sense such a person would make.

ROTE LEARNING

Many of us are where we are today because of rote learning. In *The Concise Oxford Dictionary* 'rote' is defined as 'Mere habituation, knowledge got by repetition, unintelligent memory'. It was from recognizing the limitations of rote learning that major attempts were made to replace it with more intelligent and effective approaches. But in throwing away memorizing we may have discarded a vital tool.

Research into the functioning of the brain has now given us information that will enable us to replace rote learning with more effective and successful ways to commit important information and knowledge to memory.

One of the joys of being a person is knowing things and being able to demonstrate that knowingness. Although we have traditionally placed great reliance on rote learning, we have underestimated the capacity of the brain to store and retrieve data. The work of Tony Buzan has helped us to appreciate that it helps to know the mechanisms and techniques of memorizing – mere habituation and repetition is a somewhat half-hearted attempt to get the mind working.

SELF-CONCEPT

The self-concept refers to the collection of ideas, attitudes and beliefs about ourselves that inhabit self-awareness at any moment. In other words it is about the kind of person we see ourselves as being. In addition to ideas and thoughts about who we are, we also have feelings about our perceived identity. This is sometimes referred to as self-esteem – the extent to which we like, value and respect ourselves as people.

Within any organization there will be considerable differences, as well as some similarities of self-concept. These will depend upon each individual:

- level of self-awareness
- intellectual response to that awareness
- emotional response to that awareness

A strong and positive self-concept is conducive to healthy growth and development, and necessary if effective relationships are to be established. A poor or negative self-concept can generate feelings of insecurity and a general sense of unworthiness. Attention to the self-concept is a very important part in the learning process and some aspects of the self-concept are particularly important in the collective setting of the classroom (Elliott-Kemp 1982):

1 *Self-awareness* – the extent to which we are aware of our own attitudes and values and of the effect our own behaviour has on others.
2 *Will to achieve* – the extent to which we respond to and seek new challenges in our learning and personal lives.
3 *Optimism* – the extent to which we feel positive about learning and our capacity to develop effectively.
4 *Positive regard* – the extent to which we respond to others with warmth, caring and respect.
5 *Trust* – the extent to which we are prepared to place trust in those with whom we work, i.e. teachers and other pupils.
6 *Congruence* – the extent to which we are secure enough to be ourselves with others.
7 *Empathy* – the extent to which we are able to understand the circumstances of our colleagues' lives from their point of view.
8 *Courage* – the extent to which we are prepared to take risks in our learning and the extent to which we are prepared to admit to a need for help from teachers and others.

When these qualities are well-developed in pupils then learning is likely to be of a high order. The person-centred school is one which not only focuses on developing the self-concept of pupils, but one which attaches high importance to the self-concepts of staff. Such a school works towards creating conditions in which these particular considerations are given space and time to develop. When the self-concept of a particular teacher is low it is in the interests of all other colleagues to be concerned.

Since pupils with a strong and positive self-concept learn more effectively, teacher behaviour should be geared to developing that self-concept. The following pointers can be helpful in building a climate which is conducive to this purpose.

1 The self-concept can be changed for good and bad. It tends to grow well when teachers are warm and caring, encouraging about pupils' hopes and aspirations and take time to listen to what pupils have to say. It tends to diminish when teachers make learning a negative experience, employ ridicule and sarcasm and use harsh methods of control.
2 The self-concept develops relatively slowly, so consistency of teacher attitude and behaviour is crucial.
3 Society places a heavy emphasis on academic success, and less intellectually able pupils can develop a sense of failure when they compare their achievements with apparently more able colleagues. Effective teachers have the ability to help all pupils see themselves as capable learners with high potential for success and achievement.
4 Virtually all pupils respond to compliments which are offered with care and courtesy, especially when they are accompanied by reference to their first name. Such attention by the teacher should reflect an awareness of the whole person, not only academic ability.
5 Creating a learning environment of mutual support is perhaps the most important contribution a teacher can make to the healthy development of the self-concept. Pupils need the opportunity to express their feelings openly without fear of ridicule. They need to know that they are valued and will receive affection and support.
6 When pupils encounter difficulty with their learning, particularly over a period of time, it is likely that the problem has some connection with self-esteem and self-confidence. Attention to self-concept elements is just as important as trying to tease out specifically cognitive difficulties.

SEXISM

Many schools have formal policies to develop and sustain equal opportunities between boys and girls and there is a growing amount of literature on the subject.

One of the key challenges to the experiential educator is that of helping both girls and boys to identify the extent to which their own learning capacity is affected by sexist assumptions that have accrued through socialization, and the extent to which internalized messages about gender have conditioned and affected their learning behaviour.

As teachers, we need to be alert to disclosures from pupils which suggest that limitation or inadequacy in learning is gender-related, for example, 'Boys don't need to know about that stuff', or, 'Girls are no good at that sort of thing'. Once pupils have rationalized that lack of learning success is gender-related, it is very difficult to replace disbelief.

We also need to seek examples of successful learning behaviour which contradict the established and deep-seated stereotypes. In *Making Global Connections* (1989), Steiner and Hicks emphasize five ways we can help:

1   Using language carefully and creatively to model a non-sexist approach to living.
2   Helping learners to examine critically the resources that are used, detecting bias and sexist assumptions.
3   Using active and experiential learning methods so as to value everyone's experience and to model a more equal environment.
4   Developing global awareness so that pupils are able to understand the injustices experienced by girls and women worldwide in respect of their limited access to education.
5   Looking to our own behaviour and practices with a view to making changes in personal habits and practices.

SPIRITUALITY

During the past few years a great deal of attention has been paid to the ways religious education should be taught in schools. All this concentration on the religious aspect can result in a failure to take account of the important issue of spirituality. Schools have traditionally demonstrated their concern for both body and mind, but they have shown less concern for spirit. It is also important to make a distinction between religious education and spiritual education.

We can encourage pupils to explore this important area of their experience by:

1   Accepting and acknowledging that inner experiences do not always have rational explanations.
2   Accepting that intense inner feelings in response to experience are a valid and vital part of being.
3   Finding effective ways for pupils to explore and share these experiences with each other.
4   Expressing something of our own spirituality by disclosing our own sense of awe and wonder at phenomena and our particular ways of celebrating it.

Effective and successful learning may well depend on our capacity to activate this aspect of learners and to help them fully integrate it into the whole learning experience.

SPONTANEITY

Spontaneity is a natural behavioural trait in young children. Childhood has become a long process of bringing this tendency under control so that all our social behaviours are brought within an acceptable threshold of conventions and rituals. Social life certainly needs to be a happy balance between spontaneity and control. To achieve this we need to give spontaneity a better deal in schools.

In *The Mind Gymnasium* (1989), Denis Postle describes the cultivation of spontaneity as one of the greatest gifts parents can give their children:

Confidence, self esteem, energy and spontaneity are qualities many adults yearn for and long to develop. Children who are actively encouraged to be themselves, to be angry, sad, disappointed, excited, enthusiastic, tearful, hurt, delighted or bored when they feel like it, have little trouble with these qualities.

Part of good reflective and experiential learning is the determination to create spontaneity and genuineness in the learning lives of pupils. But we cannot encourage this in our pupils if we are not able or prepared to exercise it in our teaching. The capacity to seize the moment, to latch on to an incident or a comment in the daily life of the classroom and take a valuable detour has long been one of the classic hallmarks of the quality teacher.

STEREOTYPING

Stereotyping is an attitudinal behaviour which results when generalizations are drawn from limited evidence or experience. In a world of complexity, making generalizations is one way in which we attempt to make sense of the world, and much of the information that needs to be conveyed to pupils is of necessity simplified and generalized.

Helping pupils to develop critical thinking will do much to instil in them a capacity to look for wider perspectives and to seek evidence to support assertions. Much can be done to combat stereotyping by encouraging in pupils an appreciation that the world is complex and defies simplistic explanations.

STRESS

In a society where we face unprecedented demands and pressures created by constant and accelerating change, it is important to consider how stress in pupils contributes to learning difficulties and failure to cope. Among the stress factors that can exert a harmful effect on pupils are:

Overtight supervision
- structures and rules that inhibit rather than encourage;
- being treated the same as everyone else;
- not being allowed to pursue grievances;
- having learning difficulties ignored;
- being over-controlled;
- automatically being mistrusted.

Absence of support
- not having sensitive and sympathetic adults to turn to;
- not being given the opportunity to share learning experiences with colleagues in pairs or small groups;
- not being encouraged to reflect on learning so as to understand it more.

Time pressures
- not being allowed to learn at your own pace;
- being expected to do more than time allows;

- not being given time for planning and review;
- not being helped to develop time management skills.

The main strategy to avoid the harmful and inhibiting effects of stress will be in knowing individual pupils well, how they see themselves, and their perceptions of their own learning successes and difficulties.

SUPPORT

Only in recent years has the concept of pastoral care entered the schooling system and provided a focus for pupil welfare and support. Organizations such as the National Association for Pastoral Care in Education and the Counselling in Education division of the British Association for Counselling have provided a focus for activity in developing precise approaches to care, support and welfare.

One of the difficulties is the belief that if you are to succeed in life, you have to stand on your own two feet. This has created a tendency to the view that anyone who needs support in their work or learning is somehow lacking in energy, commitment or ability. Support is acceptable in extreme crises in our lives such as bereavement, but here too we are expected to quickly pull ourselves together and get back to normal.

What is needed for us all to be more effective and fully functioning is a new set of assumptions about the process of support:

- We are social beings and rely on others to manage our lives effectively.
- We have responsibilities to help and support friends and colleagues in the pursuit of their needs and aspirations.
- Life is a journey of challenges which we need help, encouragement and support to meet.
- Having a sense of being well supported brings the best out in people and tends to increase effectiveness.
- While we have a right to expect support from others we also have a responsibility to provide it.
- Seeking support is highly intelligent behaviour.

One of the secrets of the successful classroom is how the participants succeed in facilitating the countless needs/support exchanges that arise as part of the daily round of activity and work. In this sense we are all helpers of each other. The notion of the needs/support exchange is useful. Every time help or support is offered and received it has the potential to satisfy both personal and learning needs. It also provides opportunities for those offering help to exercise their skills and qualities in well-directed and appropriate ways. Successful organizations, and indeed healthy relationships, thrive on such exchanges.

We all have the capacity to respond to the needs of others and in so doing optimize the likelihood of achievement. In low-achieving organizations people tend to ignore the needs of others and avoid seeking help themselves. Over-competitiveness and a disregard for the shortcomings of others creates a low threshold of tolerance about mistakes, the separation of responsibility, and a defensiveness that can be self-defeating. In these situations compliance rather than commitment becomes the characteristic work ethic.

To be an effective helper we need to be skilful at:

- noticing needs and responding to them;
- clarifying the needs;
- identifying the nature of the help required;
- making the help available.

This means that we should:

- be aware of these needs and the other person's capacity to disclose them in the search for help and support;
- be attentive to the person with the need;
- be sensitive to their feelings about needing help and their difficulty in admitting it;
- make help available so that the person in need feels supported but not excluded from the activity.

If an organization is to be successful in establishing effective needs/support exchanges then it will be vital to build development on positive assumptions such as:

- Feeling the need for help does not imply incompetence. Some tasks we are faced with require more resources than any of us has currently available.
- It is not a sign of weakness to seek or accept help. It is an indication of commitment and strength that we are able to recognize our own limitations in any situation.
- Successful organizations thrive on interdependence, by building and developing dynamic patterns of mutual support.
- We are usually better at solving complex problems together than struggling with them alone.
- There will be some situations that will be beyond anyone's competence to resolve.
- We all find some aspects of our learning difficult and we all make mistakes. It is better to admit to these early on rather than try to cover up later.

The capacity to create a genuine helpful and supportive classroom climate depends on the quality of the relationships and on the levels of communication skill that we exercise within them.

Support structures and networks are essential in any classroom and are far too important to be left to chance. They have the capacity to enormously enhance the effectiveness of an organization and create the capacity to bring the best out in all the participants.

SYSTEMS

At the heart of the holistic principle is an understanding of systems. General systems theory advocates that we take a total rather than a partial look at the issues and challenges that confront us in life. The theory suggests that each variable in any system interacts so thoroughly with the other variables as to make a simple cause and effect analysis hazardous. Rather than look at each aspect of the world in isolation, we need to look at them in terms of their interrelatedness.

In the world of learning this means, for example, that to isolate reading failure and concentrate on that variable alone is to miss the opportunity to discover from a much wider context of factors some of the elements that are combining to create difficulty. The experience of encountering a problem in learning to read is best understood by considering it in the context of the pupil's wider learning experience.

By increasing our capacity to understand what the reality of each pupil's learning experience is, we are more able to appreciate the interconnectedness of all aspects of the learning experience to the wholeness of their being. Within the context of the whole school we have an elaborate and complex web of systems and subsystems at work:

Whole school
- management
- curriculum
- pedagogy
- assessment
- power and authority

Pupil organization
- year groups
- classes
- pastoral care
- timetables

Personal systems
- learning
- relationships
- aims and aspirations
- successes and difficulties

As we become more systems-conscious, we learn to relate individual learning incidents to the wider context of a pupil's experience.

Part of the purpose of the experiential learning cycle is to provide structured opportunities for pupils to appreciate and understand the systemic nature of their own learning. This involves helping them to make connections between the different aspects of their learning, and to place specific elements within a framework of connections and relationships.

TALKING

Talking, the most powerful means that we have of communicating our ideas to others, was once banned in schools. Yet it is by talking things through that we activate and enliven our learning faculties. This capacity to learn through verbal exploration and explanation is a vital part of the reflective and experiential learning process. Rather than inhibiting inter-pupil talk because it wastes time or is disruptive, what we need to do is to bring classroom talk more deliberately into our repertoire of classroom teaching strategies.

In any class of thirty pupils there are potentially fifteen talkers and fifteen listeners. Splitting the class into pairs of pupils at strategic points in a lesson creates the optimum opportunity for them to talk through, explore and explain key aspects of their learning.

An important development in talk education has been the Oracy Project, initiated by the Schools Curriculum Development Committee. This project has facilitated the development of verbal communication through a wide variety of interesting and exciting classroom activities.

The English documents of the National Curriculum now give equal status to the four modes of language and throughout the National Curriculum a great deal of emphasis is attached to the pupils' ability to provide verbal accounts of work undertaken and to use verbal communication as the key method of transacting their learning.

TASK-DRIVEN LEARNING

This is a way of organizing learning where pupils, working in small groups or project teams, are asked to undertake specific tasks. It derives from the approach to management training and development employed by the Coverdale Organization, a management consultancy company.

The approach, which was tried in classrooms, was the subject of an article in the *Times Educational Supplement* (15 December 1989). It describes how pupils in a small village school in Oxfordshire worked on tasks provided by the teacher and approached them in a systematic way and with a focus on the quality of the teamwork.

> The 10 and 11 year olds in Carol Bevan's classroom have been learning this systematic approach for the past year. Given a task and a deadline, groups of four or five children swing impressively into action. When I was there they were devising ways of demonstrating magnetism and simple circuits to younger children.
>
> They had just under one hour. At the end, two groups had planned and made games to investigate magnetism. One was a fishing game, another a remarkably well finished Monopoly-type board-game. The third group had made a doll's house from a cardboard box, with a lighting system with two kinds of switch to show how completing the circuit lit the bulb. They had even got around to making furniture.
>
> The children worked hard, with a constant eye on the clock. Later, they would review not only what they had achieved, but the way they had tackled the work – what had gone well, what had gone less well, who had been dissatisfied or felt left out, what they should look out for next. Carol Bevan said they would also spend their free time improving their products.

The elements of the approach are:

1   Providing groups with a specified task and a time limit, e.g.
    - Make a poster to show three ways of . . .
    - Make a working model of some traffic lights.

2   Encouraging the pupils to adopt a systematic approach to their
    teamwork:
    ● Defining purposes and aims
    ● Setting standards for the product
    ● Collecting information
    ● Deciding what has to be done
    ● Agreeing a plan of action to involve the whole team
3   At the end of the task the team review their work in two ways:
    ● Review of task and the end result against the standards set.
    ● Review of process – drawing out aspects of teamwork that helped
      progress and aspects that hindered development.
4   Making plans for the next task incorporating the learnings identified
    in the process review.

TELEVISION

It is sometimes a cause of concern to teachers that some children spend
more time in front of a television screen each day than they do in
classrooms. Rather than seeking ways to control the amount of time
children spend viewing, we should be concerned to help them develop the
skills to use television appropriately and well.

Part of the role of media education is a concern to help pupils to develop
a more critical and discerning relationship with television. There is much
that teachers in all subject areas can do to assist this process:

● Share their own television interests and experiences with pupils and
  through discussion attempt to draw out critical issues.
● Search television programming schedules for programmes that are
  subject- or topic-related and ask pupils to watch them. Provide them
  with checklists and questions to help them focus on key issues and
  interest points.
● Acknowledge and accept that for many pupils watching soap operas is
  their only access to how others live their lives. Soap operas fulfil an
  important psychological function in providing access to the inner and
  outer lives of ordinary people. We can help pupils by taking this
  viewing habit seriously rather than scoffing at it.
● Occasionally setting TV programmes for homework.

The daily events of the world, as witnessed so graphically through
television, need to be seized on in classroom work and connected to
subject content.

THINKING

Despite its central importance in the educational process, thinking has
never been a skill that has been deliberately taught and is curiously
absent from the curriculum. We acquire our thinking patterns haphazardly
by experience. Yet frequently pupils are urged to think harder, assuming
a set of procedures that can be activated when we want to switch into a
higher mental gear.

How we organize and use our minds is one of the keys to effective learning and successful living. Since we are all different and have come to learning through a variety of experiential routes it is not a subject that can be taught simply. What we can do however, is to provide learners with a range of resources with which to cultivate and develop their own learning strategies. Among these are:

1 Some understanding of how the brain works, in particular the different functioning of the left and right hemispheres.
2 A framework for learning that draws attention to the relationship between the emotional, intellectual, intuitive and physical aspects of being.
3 The reflective and experiential learning cycle.
4 Specific strategies and techniques:
   - brainstorming
   - critical thinking
   - lateral thinking
   - mind maps
   - visualization
   - intuitive and emotional intelligence

Pupils need to be provided with opportunities to examine and explore their own ways of thinking and to share these insights and experiences with others. It is often useful to ask pupils to describe the mental process they operate in their thinking and learning.

THIRD WAVE

This is a theory advanced by Alvin Toffler (1981), who suggests that in this final decade of the twentieth century we are witnessing the emergence of a third great wave of change. The first wave took us from the dawn of civilization to the renaissance and was characterized by social patterns based on agricultural economics. In the second wave we saw these social and economic patterns change as industrialization created new structures. Now as we see the decline in industry and manufacturing we witness the beginning of the third great wave of change that is infinitely more complex and characterized by communication revolutions, rapid political change, ecological disasters and technological developments.

Those of us straddling the transition from the second to the third wave are experiencing a rate of change unimagined even fifty years ago, and the emergence of novel circumstances and conditions for which our second-wave socialization has ill-prepared us. The challenge for educationalists is to recognize the changed and changing circumstances of the third wave that pupils will now experience and to develop teaching strategies that will equip them for situations which we can no longer predict and make assumptions about.

Business organizations have already appreciated that survival depends upon a capacity to adapt to new situations, to break from the stranglehold of tradition and move into the future with leaner and more flexible structures.

Three particular sets of ideas create important agendas for the 1990s:

- *Thriving on Chaos* (Peters 1987)
  Success in organizations will depend upon a capacity to respond creatively to increasing turbulence, ambiguity and accelerating change. Those who will succeed in these conditions will be those who feel comfortable with complexity, uncertainty and chaos.
- *The Age of Unreason* (Handy 1989)
  The traditional foundations of rational argument and linear thinking will be inadequate to rise to the challenges of third-wave living.
- *The Renewal Factor* (Waterman 1988)
  Constant and organic change through renewal and development will need to replace ideas of permanence and long-term thinking.

Third-wave schools will be those that can adapt quickly to these conditions. They will have rethought traditional second-wave assumptions and conducted bold experiments with a range of learning structures.

TIME

One of the emerging needs in adult learning during the 1980s was that of time management. As the pace of change has accelerated, and the amount and flow of information increased, greater demands are being made on everyone's time. Our metabolism is geared for a gentler and less frenetic rhythm of life, and as we experience the pain of moving to more complex situations we struggle to find ways of coping.

Courses on time management are now a regular feature of management training and many teachers have found the Filofax approach to life management one of the ways to make their time management more deliberate. Systems abound, and now there are portable computers, pocket telephones and fax machines to help organize our increasingly complicated lives.

Pupils in schools are also part of this revolution. They are under more pressure than ever before to cram more learning into the same time span; to meet more targets and satisfy wider examination criteria.

Work planning and time management are two key life skills that need to feature in the school curriculum, not only to help pupils organize their learning more effectively but because the future pattern of adult life will not be properly managed without these new basic skills.

The reflective and experiential learning cycle provides opportunities for acquiring these skills deliberately through experience. Pupils need to experiment with time management structures and planning methods until they find ones which work for them. They need to review their experiments to discover in detail what works and what does not.

TRANSACTIONAL ANALYSIS (TA)

Among the attempts to bring practical psychology into the public domain, perhaps the most successful has been Transactional Analysis.

It is defined by the International Transactional Analysis Association as 'a theory of personality and a systematic psychotherapy for personal growth and personal change'. Its theory of personality offers three basic ego states which are the key dimensions of our psychological make-up:

P Parent: when my behaviours tend towards those adopted by my parents and other authority figures.
A Adult: when my behaviours are determined by responses to the situation.
C Child: when my feelings and behaviour correspond with those I used when I was a child.

TA is essentially a practical tool. Although it is free from the technical language that gives much of traditional clinical psychology a somewhat medical flavour, it does have a jargon of its own. Once this is acquired and understood, the theory can serve to illuminate the nature of interpersonal transactions and offer ways in which we can improve the quality of communication in classrooms.

TA is particularly helpful in:

- Increasing awareness of the ways that adults tend to behave towards children.
- Helping us to understand how our own experience of adult behaviours when we were young has affected our present communication behaviour.
- Providing tools to analyse and change our own transactional behaviour, particularly in relation to the children we teach.

TRANSPERSONAL EDUCATION

Over the past twenty years or so transpersonal psychology has attempted to structure a way of dealing with the unknown area of the Jo-Hari window. In a desire to build as fully integrated adults as possible it is vital that in schools we attend to this aspect of our being (see spirituality, p.188).

In *The Mind Gymnasium*, Denis Postle (1989) offers a useful checklist for transpersonal education:

- The development of a sense of wonder.
- Holding life sacred.
- Rituals that respect the passage of life.
- Acknowledging love as a more potent evolutionary quality than force.
- Political action that eradicates oppression is central to a fully formed spirituality.
- Spirituality and politics can practically co-exist.

In terms of how we tackle these issues in our learning he suggests:

- The value of self-directed exploration.
- Studying current ideas about how the mind works.
- Emphasizing scepticism about those who claim to have found 'the way'.
- Appreciating the interconnectedness of all things.

TRUST

Many of the harsh and oppressive attitudes and practices in education have developed because of an underlying belief that children cannot be trusted to learn. This repressive tendency has expressed itself in two ways:

1 *Generalized mistrust* – children cannot and will not learn unless cajoled to do so.
2 *Specific mistrust* – individual learners have to gain trust by performing to teacher demands rather than to their own aspirations.

Trust in schools is not created by pupils performing to regulations but when teachers begin their work with a deep belief in the interests and capacities of the learner, however modest those pupil capacities seem to be.

Trusting pupils is not about giving them *carte blanche* to do as they like. Rather, it is about believing in the inherent power of human growth and development, and of the processes involved in invoking that power within children in classrooms.

We need to be on the lookout for this process at work within our schools and to identify the contributory factors. Much depends upon our capacity to challenge traditional assumptions about trust. The question is generally taken to be, 'To what extent can I trust the pupils?' How much better it would be to raise an alternative question: 'To what extent can I expect pupils to trust me to safeguard their learning needs and aspirations and to seek the most effective ways to satisfy them?'

VALUES

Increasing attention is being paid to the issue of values in education. As the curriculum develops to reflect the complex and changing world that pupils inhabit, so it is necessary to find effective ways to help them acquire conceptual tools so that they can make sense of their daily living.

Values education is now seen as a legitimate thrust in the curriculum. Concerned with the process of *valuing* rather than with any particular set of values, it sets out to provide a framework in which values can be examined and analysed.

Woodhouse and Cross (1987) state:

In a very real sense we are what we value. We express our priorities through our values. The choices we make, and our attitudes in general, are shaped by our values. But personal and social ideals, goals and beliefs are too often ignored; perhaps that is because they are complex. They are also of crucial importance. Since values underpin our attitudes and find expression in our behaviour, we should be as clear as we can about the things that are important to us, and the positive and negative actions we take. Inevitably, what we choose to do influences the way that we are seen by others.

The National Association for Values in Education and Training has the following aims:

- To improve the quality of organizations by fostering the development of value-conscious individuals and value-effective programmes.
- To develop understanding and communication of the nature of values and their application within education and training.
- To encourage the recognition of the diversity of values and opinions within society and individuals.
- To enhance awareness of the powerful influence of value systems upon the climate of organizations by providing opportunities to challenge, discuss and reflect upon values, especially in the areas where conflict arises.
- To increase the ability of teachers and trainers to deal sensitively and critically with value issues that arise from attempts to understand themselves in relation to others and the environment.

A key responsibility of educators is to help learners to acquire and develop the means to apply a whole range of conceptual skills to the issues and dilemmas that face them in their day-to-day living.

WORD PROCESSING

During the 1980s we saw the gradual introduction of computers into schools. During the 1990s we shall see the steady increase in the use of information technology in the form of databases, faxing, electronic mail, desk-top publishing and word processing.

Word processing offers huge opportunities to the learning process from the very simple packages that early learners can use to the complex and powerful programmes of desk-top publishing. The steady spread of personal computers will change the environment in which formal education is transacted, from an essentially instruction-centred one to a learner-centred one. With home-based terminals, some of the needs provided by institutions will be obviated.

A major adjustment for teachers will be in the way that pupils' work is prepared and presented. Word processing will become the main method of preparing documentation and it is vital that skill in this facility is developed as early as possible in the schooling process. In the past, far too much written work has been undertaken by pupils as one-and-only final drafts.

To gain the benefits of the word-processing facility a number of prerequisite skills are essential:

- Generating ideas – brainstorming, etc.
- Systematic planning
- Collecting information and data
- Initial drafts and flowcharts
- Amendments and modifications
- Final draft and printout

The benefits of the word-processing capacity are:

- It encourages careful planning and preparation
- It develops a systematic approach
- It facilitates:
  - storage
  - change and modification
  - additions and deletions
  - electronic cutting and pasting
  - reorganization.

XENOPHOBIA

This is defined in *The Concise Oxford Dictionary* as 'a morbid dislike of foreigners'. The history of warfare will show that fear and dislike is justified, for within the global context genocide and invasion seem set to continue into the twenty-first century. But a wider definition – the fear of difference – is a challenge which needs to be accepted by schools. Over recent years there have been concerted efforts to raise consciousness about the oppression and injustice experienced by various groups in society: females, racial minorities and those with visible handicaps. Much excellent work has been done in schools to help pupils to grow in awareness and sensitivity about these social divisions, and to develop attitudes and behaviours appropriate in a world struggling for peace and well-being.

One of the paradoxes of human living is the need to pursue two apparently contradictory purposes simultaneously: international aspirations and national interests. Government ministers, when interviewed, will refer to other members of the European Union as either 'our European partners' or 'our European competitors'. It is this, and similar ambiguities, which we need to help pupils in school to come to understand and appreciate. The goal is how to pursue apparently contradictory aims simultaneously, without destroying and attacking the integrity of either.

Social, psychological and political awareness involves developing the capacity to appreciate and work with the 'vexatious factor'. This has been defined by Kumar (1991) as situations in society in which frustrations and conflicts are inherent and endemic. It is not only tolerance and respect for other cultures, groups and individuals which is important, but understanding the psychology of our own nationalism and pride. Xenophobia will not be reduced simply by condemning it; it needs to be understood. This involves paying more attention than we have been prepared to in the past to the emotional and psychological aspects of human living. Despite our supposed intellectual sophistication, our emotional and psychological naivety is frequently bewildering.

YOUTH CULTURE

One of the most complex and difficult features of social living is the gap that develops between parents and their children, and between pupils and their teachers. Legally, the long childhood is set at 18 years, and children have to wait out that time before their capacity to make judgements and decisions about the directions of their lives is wholly supported by law and they are entitled to take their place as full participants in the social structure.

Over this century, and certainly in the years since the end of the Second World War, the experience of this long childhood has changed drastically. Children in the West now live in a fast changing, high-tech global village, characterized by sexual permissiveness, out of control drug cultures, high unemployment, confused patterns of family life and rapidly increasing crime rate. This is the world they have inherited; they did not design it. While economic and technological change has obsessed government policy-making, the role of children as active participants in society and the role of adults in their upbringing and education has received far less attention. Few families escape the tussle for power and freedom as teenagers struggle to gain a sense of their discrete identity, separate from their parents. What many parents seem to experience fifteen or so years into parenthood is a sort of grieving for the children they feel they have lost – the helpless and dependent babies to whom they gave birth. What parents seem to want is acknowledgement and recognition by their children of the love, dedication and commitment they have made. Such gratitude is rarely given, and the more we seek it the more it seems to get thrown back in our faces. The poet Kahlil Gibran (1980) captures the dilemma well:

Your children are not your children.
They are the sons and daughters of Life's longing for itself.
They come through you but not from you,
And though they are with you yet they belong not to you.
You may give them your love but not your thoughts,
For they have their own thoughts.
You may house their bodies but not their souls,
For their souls dwell in the house of tomorrow,
    which you cannot visit, not even in your
    dreams.
You may strive to be like them, but seek not to make them like you.
For life goes not backward nor tarries with yesterday.
You are bows from which your children as living arrows set forth.

As educators, we are an inextricable part of this generational struggle. We can experience a deep dislike of the values, behaviours, musical tastes, dress sense and language of our children and pupils, but we need to appreciate that their values have to be different from ours, or they are not theirs. We also need to avoid the danger of becoming surrogate teenagers ourselves, adopting dress and musical preferences in a vain attempt to bridge a widening gap of communication. Perhaps teenagers have the most respect for those adults who combine a sturdy adherence to their own values, while respecting the attitudes, values, preferences and decisions of others.

Perhaps the best strategy is to help our children and young adults search for their distinct identity, separate from their parents, teachers, business leaders and politicians. We have to accept this struggle as the fundamental learning experience of the long childhood.

ZEN

In recent years there has been a spate of books about the Zen approach to life and living. Perhaps the most famous of these was Robert Pirsig's *Zen and the Art of Motorcycle Maintenance* (1976). Deriving from Buddhism, the Zen approach is more concerned with human potential and less with divine inspiration.

Essentially, Zen takes a view of life which is different from the ones we have traditionally been taught at home and in schools. In addition to a deep respect for rationality, intellect and logic, Zen also incorporates a significant concern for intuition. Perhaps more than anything it has come to espouse simultaneity, the need to hold together sometimes apparently confusing and contradictory elements. The essence of Zen is ambiguity and paradox. This is well captured by M. Scott Peck, who begins his book *The Road Less Travelled* (1987) with the almost heretical assertion: 'Life is difficult.'

This counters so much of the world view we have been taught – that life will be easy if we say 'please' and 'thank you', keep our bedrooms tidy and work hard at school. Part of the betrayal of upbringing is the realization, perhaps much later in life as we struggle with our marriages, our careers and our bank balances, that despite our doing all those things life has continued to be difficult.

Scott Peck continues thus:

> This is a great truth, one of the greatest truths. It is a great truth because once we truly see this truth, we transcend it. Once we truly know that life is difficult – once we truly understand and accept it – then life is no longer difficult. Because once it is accepted, the fact that life is difficult no longer matters.

What Robert Pirsig deals with in *Zen and the Art of Motorcycle Maintenance* is the struggle between two contrasting world views: the objective, with its concern for reason, evidence, measurement and agreed criteria and the subjective, with its attention to intuition, the felt experience, belief and pastoral criteria. What he struggles for in his 2000-mile journey is a synthesizing of subjectivity and objectivity into a crystallizing whole, creating an elegant integration and connection of the traditionally opposing perspectives.

What we have traditionally concerned ourselves with in the schooling system is serving the requirements of objective reality at the expense of the subjective dimension. Perhaps before a truly integrated approach can be achieved it will be necessary to introduce more elements of the subjective dimension into the learning process in order to create a more satisfactory balance of the two.

Zen in the art of teaching is about moving beyond an either/or approach to life. It is about helping learners to appreciate the awesome complexity of life and living, to have no fear of uncertainty and confusion and to accept the inevitability of the struggle. Happiness is not a state to embark on once you have your A levels, but a sensation to be captured in moments, often when least expected. Such moments occur constantly in classrooms. Current requirements are forcing us to pass them unremarked upon and unnoticed. Just occasionally, we might pause to realize that education is also about moments, lots of them piled together in a rich constellation of experience and possibility.

ZEST

Zest is that essential spark that activates the human will and transforms possibility into action. It is a vital component in the directional tendency of all human beings. The challenge for teachers is to activate this quality in the interests of learners. Education has as much to do with zest and energy and ambition as it does with information and knowledge and skill.

Zest is one of the most distinctive characteristics of the very young child. As we get older it becomes moderated as we learn to put away childish things such as playfulness, exuberance and spontaneity. Freud noted a glaring difference between children and adults: 'What a distressing contrast there is between the radiant intelligence of the child and the feeble mentality of the average adult.'

Perhaps what he alludes to is the lack of zest in the adult population. We are trained to take things seriously, to show little emotion and to suppress joy and excitement as we learn about the wonder of living. Zest is that quality we bring to an activity when we honour our yearnings and passions. It was perhaps captured best by Bill Shankly, one-time manager of Liverpool Football Club, who, when asked if football was really a matter of life and death to him, is reputed to have replied, 'Certainly not, it's much more important than that!' For too many pupils, learning falls very short of this compelling idea. If it is there when children begin their learning lives, we have to do all that we can to keep it alive much, much longer.

5

Conclusion

As we approach the millennium, we find the formally organized education of our country in a state of unprecedented upheaval and confusion. Facing the complex challenges of rapid, discontinuous and accelerating change, the government seems deeply confused about how best to manage education. Their response has been to look to the past, when simpler situations and circumstances seemed to prevail, and to attempt to retrieve concepts and ideas and apply them in the altogether different conditions of the present.

Those who survive the pressures of rapid change certainly draw lessons from the past, but they also recognize that to rely on traditional assumptions and former glories is a highly dangerous activity. Before the intervention of central government into the classrooms of the land, schools had already been engaged in a process of steady development and change. Many were challenging the taken-for-granted assumptions from the past, and striving to design processes of learning and teaching that reflected a world in flux. In many respects, the 1988 Education Reform Act interrupted this evolutionary process, setting in train changes designed to transform the structures of the schooling system and the curriculum for pupils. Absent from the reforms was any acknowledgement that the most powerful factors in the whole process of education in schools are how learning is managed in classrooms and the nature of the relationships between teachers and the taught. It was naively believed that abandoning 'trendy teaching methods' and restoring an essentially instructional mode of teaching would revive the system and redeem its failures.

This book is offered as a contribution to the difficult and often frustrating struggle to discover how formal education in schools can best be managed in a world characterized by constant change, confusion and uncertainty. Four assumptions underpin the ideas about teaching and learning that are expressed in the book. Firstly, that there can be no simple solutions to the complex challenges of providing effective education in a fast changing world. Secondly, that successful pathways into the future will only be arrived at through a process of creative and imaginative planning, rather than through a rancorous competition between opposed ideologies. Thirdly, that schools themselves, their pupils, teachers, parents and governors are the best agents of successful development and change. Fourthly, that successful education is more about vision, ambition and hope than it is about requirement, accountability and retribution.

What we need to take with us into this uncertain educational future is the recognition of our tendency to underestimate the enormous potential of people, and the realization that repeated patterns of coercion and control have acted to crush and limit human aspiration and achievement. Narrow definitions of competence and achievement have helped to create an intelligentsia characterized by only one of many attributions of capability, bringing about a dangerous and tragic separation of people and possibility.

Educational experience demonstrates that learning seems to work best where the learners themselves achieve a happy balance of clear vision, self-direction, high-quality support and a real sense of achievement and development. We need to appreciate that providing these important nutrients within schools and classrooms is extremely difficult. Rather than complain that schools are doing so badly, the government should be amazed that they are doing so well. If we were really concerned to reinvent education for the future, we might not choose schools as the solution to the problem. If we are to keep them, then they will certainly need to develop and change. Recent educational reforms have impeded these changes, requiring schools to focus on structure and content rather than on process and practice. The fundamental question is how we educate, not what we educate about and where we do it.

Teaching, like learning, is an infinitely intricate, complex and precarious activity. There are no simple solutions, no quick fixes and no easy remedies. There are only ideas and opportunities and efforts. Good education is the process through which ideas can be empowered, insights gained, possibilities explored, understandings reached and breakthroughs made. Change will not be accomplished by spectacular reforms, although we are always likely to be seduced by their glamorous promises, nor will it be achieved by a uniformly concerted effort. Change and development will be achieved through the often small but painstaking and dedicated steps of those, who as educators, have a passion for their craft, who love the learning process with all its confusions and messiness and who are committed to the causes of the pupils they teach.

Bibliography

Argyle, M. (1975) *Bodily Communication*. London: Methuen.

Argyle, M. (1983) *The Psychology of Interpersonal Behaviour*. London: Penguin.

Ashton-Warner, S. (1980) *Teacher*. London: Virago.

Aspy, D. and Roebuck, F. (1976) *A Lever Long Enough*. Washington, DC: National Consortium for Humanizing Education.

Ballard, J. (1982) *Circlebook – A Leader Handbook for Conducting Circletime, A Curriculum of Affect*. New York: Irvington.

Bennett, N. (1976) *Teaching Styles and Pupil Progress*. Shepton Mallet: Open Books.

Bennis, W. (1989) *On Becoming a Leader*. London: Hutchinson.

Bohm, D. (1980) *Wholeness and the Implicate Order*. London: Routledge & Kegan Paul.

Bolton, R. (1979) *People Skills*. New York: Prentice-Hall.

Bond, T. (1986) *Games for Social and Life Skills*. London: Hutchinson.

Boud, D., Cohen, R. and Walker, D. (1993) *Using Experience for Learning*. Buckingham: Open University Press.

Brandes, D. and Ginnis, P. (1986) *A Guide to Student-centred Learning*. Oxford: Blackwell.

Brookfield, S. (1987) *Developing Critical Thinkers*. Buckingham: Open University Press.

Buzan, T. (1982) *Use Your Head*. London: BBC Books.

Buzan, T. (1986) *Use Your Memory*. London: BBC Publications.

Buzan, T. (1988a) *Make the Most of Your Mind*. London: Pan.

Buzan, T. (1988b) *Master Your Memory*. Newton Abbot: David & Charles.

Canfield, J. and Wells, H. (1976) *100 Ways to Enhance Self-concept in the Classroom*. Englewood Cliffs: Prentice-Hall.

Capra, F. (1983) *The Turning Point*. London: Flamingo.

Castillo, G. (1978) *Left-Handed Teaching*. New York: Holt, Rinehart & Winston.

Clark, F. (1977) 'Building intuition' in Hendricks, G. and Roberts, T. *The Second Centering Book*. Englewood Cliffs: Prentice-Hall.

Day, C. and Baskett, H. K. (1982) 'Discrepancies between intentions and practice: Re-examining some basic assumptions about adult and continuing professional education.' *International Journal of Lifelong Education*, **1** (2).

de Bono, E. (1967) *The Uses of Lateral Thinking*. London: Penguin.

Department of Education and Science (DES) (1989) *Personal and Social Education from 5 to 16*. Curriculum Matters 14. London: HMSO.

Dickens, C. (1854/1961) *Hard Times*. London: Collins.

Donaldson, M. (1978) *Children's Minds*. London: Fontana.

Elliott-Kemp, J. (1982) *The Effective Teacher*. Sheffield: Pavic Publications.

Ferguson, M. (1982) *The Aquarian Conspiracy*. London: Granada.

Fisher, S. and Hicks, D. (1985) *World Studies 8–13, A Teacher's Handbook*. Edinburgh: Oliver & Boyd.

Fisher, R. and Ury, W. (1983) *Getting to Yes*. London: Hutchinson.

Fontana, D. (1987) 'A way of being.' *Changes*, **5**(2).

Freire, P. (1972) *Pedagogy of the Oppressed*. London: Penguin.

Galton, M. and Simon, B. (1980) *Progress and Performance in the Primary Classroom*. London: Routledge & Kegan Paul.

Gibran, K. (1980) *The Prophet*. London: Pan.

Goldberg, P. (1989) *The Intuitive Edge*. Wellingborough: Turnstone Press.

Hall, E. and Hall, C. (1988) *Human Relations in Education*. London: Routledge.

Hammond, J., Hay, D., Moxon, J., Netto, B., Raban, K., Straughier, G. and Williams, C. (1990) *New Methods in RE Teaching: An Experiential Approach*. Harlow: Oliver & Boyd.

Handy, C. (1976) *Understanding Organizations*. London: Penguin.

Handy, C. (1985) *The Future of Work*. Oxford: Blackwell.

Handy, C. (1989) *The Age of Unreason*. London: Business Books.

Handy, C. (1990) *Inside Organizations*. London: BBC Books.

Handy, C. (1994) *The Empty Raincoat – Making Sense of the Future*. London: Hutchinson.

Heider, J. (1985) *The Tao of Leadership*. Aldershot: Wildwood House.

Henfrey, J. (1988) 'Race' in Hicks, D. (ed.) *Education for Peace*. London: Routledge.

Herzberg, F. (1966) *Work and the Nature of Man*. New York: Staple Press.

Hicks, D. (1994) *Education for the Future: A Practical Classroom Guide*. Godalming: World Wide Fund for Nature.

Hoffer, E. (1985) in O'Toole, J. *Vanguard Management*. New York: Doubleday.

Holt, J. (1969) *How Children Fail*. London: Penguin.

Holt, J. (1971) *The Underachieving School*. London: Penguin.

Honey, P. and Mumford, A. (1986) *Manual of Learning Styles*. Maidenhead: Peter Honey.

Hopson, B. and Scally, M. (1981) *Lifeskills Teaching*. London: McGraw-Hill.

Jourard, S. M. (1971) *The Transparent Self*, revised edition. New York: Van Nostrand Reinhold.

Jung, C. (1971) *Psychological Types*. Princeton: Princeton University Press.

Kanter, R. M. (1989) *When Giants Learn to Dance*. London: Simon & Schuster.

Keillor, G. (1987) *Lake Wobegon Days*. London: Faber & Faber.

Kinsman, F. (1991) *Millennium: Towards Tomorrow's Society*. London: W. H. Allen.

Knowles, M. (1983) 'Andragogy: An emerging technology for adult learning' in Tight, M. (ed.) *Adult Learning in Education*. London: Croom Helm.

Kolb, D., Rubin, I. and McIntyre, J. (1971) *Organizational Psychology: An Experiential Approach*. Hemel Hempstead: Prentice-Hall.

Kumar, K. (1991) *Utopianism*. Buckingham: Open University Press.

Laing, R. (1967) *The Politics of Experience*. London: Penguin.

Lieberman, M. and Hardie, M. (1981) *Resolving Family and Other Conflicts*. Santa Cruz: Unity Press.

McGregor, D. (1960) *The Human Side of Enterprise*. New York: McGraw-Hill.

Marland, M. (1980) 'The pastoral curriculum' in Best, R., Jarvis, C. and Ribbins, P. (eds) *Perspectives on Pastoral Care*. London: Heinemann.

Maslow, A. (1976) *Religions, Values, and Peak Experiences*. London: Penguin.

Melamed, L. (1987) 'The role of play in adult learning' in Boud, D. and Griffin, V. (eds) *Appreciating Adults Learning: From the Learner's Perspective*. London: Kogan Page.

Mezzirow, J. (1983) 'A critical theory of adult learning and education' in Tight, M. (ed.) *Adult Learning in Education*. London: Croom Helm.

Miles, R. and Snow, C. (1978) *Organization Strategy, Structure and Process*. New York: McGraw-Hill.

Miller, A. (1987a) *For Your Own Good*. London: Virago.

Miller, A. (1987b) *The Drama of Being a Child*. London: Virago.

Minzberg, H. (1973) *The Nature of Managerial Work*. New York: Harper & Row.

Mulligan, J. (1988) *The Personal Management Handbook*. London: Sphere.

Mulligan, J. (1993) 'Activating internal processes in experiential learning' in Boud, D., Cohen, R. and Walker, D. (eds) *Using Experience for Learning*. Buckingham: Open University Press.

Murgatroyd, S. (1985) *Counselling and Helping*. London: British Psychological Society and Methuen.

Murgatroyd, S. (1988) 'Consulting as counselling: the theory and practice of structural consulting' in Gray, H. (ed.) *Management Consultancy in Schools*. London: Cassell.

Naisbitt, J. (1984) *Megatrends – Ten Directions Transforming Our Lives*. London: Macdonald.

Neill, A. S. (1968) *Summerhill*. London: Penguin.

Oaklander, V. (1978) *Windows to Our Children*. Moab: Real People Press.

Palomares, U. and Ball, G. (1972) *Methods in Human Development*. La Mesa, California: Human Development Training Institute Inc.

Papert, S. (1980) *Mindstorms – Children, Computers and Powerful Ideas*. London: Harvester Press.

Pascale, R. (1991) *Managing on the Edge*. London: Penguin.

Peck, M. Scott (1987) *The Road Less Travelled*. London: Rider.

Peters, T. (1987) *Thriving on Chaos*. London: Macmillan.

Peters, T. and Waterman, R. H. (1982) *In Search of Excellence*. New York: Harper & Row.

Phares, J. (1976) *Locus of Control in Personality*. New Jersey: General Learning Press.

Pike, G. and Selby, D. (1988) *Global Teacher, Global Learner*. London: Hodder & Stoughton.

Pirsig, R. (1976) *Zen and the Art of Motorcycle Maintenance*. London: Corgi.

Postle, D. (1989) *The Mind Gymnasium*. London: Macmillan.

Postle, D. (1993) 'Putting the heart back into learning' in Boud, D., Cohen, R. and Walter, D. (eds) *Using Experience for Learning*. Buckingham: Open University Press.

Postman, N. and Weingartner, C. (1971) *Teaching as a Subversive Activity*. London: Penguin.

Richardson, R. (1982) 'Talking about equality: The use and importance of discussion in multicultural education.' *Cambridge Journal of Education*, **12** (2).

Richardson, R. (1990) *Daring to Be a Teacher*. Stoke-on-Trent: Trentham Books.

Rico, G. (1983) *Writing the Natural Way*. Los Angeles: J.P. Tarcher Inc.

Rogers, C. (1967) *On Becoming a Person*. London: Constable.

Rogers, C. (1980) *A Way of Being*. Boston: Houghton Mifflin.

Rogers, C. (1983) *Freedom to Learn for the 80s*. Columbus: Charles E. Merrill.

Rosenblatt, D. (1975) *Opening Doors*. New York: Harper & Row.

Roszak, T. (1981) *Person/Planet*. London: Granada.

Rotter, J. R. (1966) 'Generalized expectancies for internal versus external control of reinforcement', *Psychological Monographs* **80** (1) (whole issue).

Rowan, J. (1983) *The Reality Game*. London: Routledge & Kegan Paul.

Rowan, J. (1988) *Ordinary Ecstasy*. London: Routledge.

Rubin, T. (1969) *The Angry Book*. New York: Macmillan.

Russell, P. (1980) *The Brain Book*. London: Routledge & Kegan Paul.

Schein, E. (1985) *Organizational Culture and Leadership*. San Francisco: Jossey-Bass.

Schmid, K. A. (ed.) (1887) *Enzyklopädie desgesamten Erziehungs- und Unterrichtswesens* (A comprehensive encyclopaedia of education and instruction) quoted in Rutschky, K. *Schwarze Pädagogik* (Black pedagogy). Berlin: 1977.

Sculley, J. (1987) *Odyssey: Pepsi to Apple*. London: Collins.

Southgate, J. and Randall, R. (1978) *The Barefoot Psychoanalyst*. London: Association of Karen Horney Psychoanalytic Counsellors.

Steiner, M. (1993) *Learning from Experience: Cooperative Learning and Global Education*. Stoke-on-Trent: Trentham Books.

Steiner, M. and Hicks, D. (1989) *Making Global Connections*. Edinburgh: Oliver & Boyd.

Tausch, R. (1978) 'Facilitative dimension in interpersonal relationships.' *College Student Journal*, **12** (Spring).

Toffler, A. (1971) *Future Shock*. London: Pan.

Toffler, A. (1981) *The Third Wave*. London: Pan.

Walford, R. (1981) 'Language, ideologies and teaching geography' in Walford, R. (ed.) *Signposts in Teaching Geography*. London: Longman.

Walker, D. (1993) *Using Experience for Learning*. Buckingham: Open University Press.

Waterman, R. (1988) *The Renewal Factor*. London: Bantam Press.

Whitaker, P. (1983) *The Primary Head*. London: Heinemann Educational Books.

Whitaker, P. (1993a) *Managing Change in Schools*. Buckingham: Open University Press.

Whitaker, P. (1993b) *Practical Communication Skills in Schools*. Harlow: Longman.

Whitehead, A. N. (1931) Introduction in Wallace, B. *Business Adrift*. New York: McGraw-Hill.

Whitmore, D. (1986) *Psychosynthesis in Education*. Wellingborough: Turnstone Press.

Woodhouse, D. and Cross, M. (1987) *Values in Education* 1(1).

Zinker, J. (1977) *Creative Processes in Gestalt Therapy*. New York: Vintage Books.

Index